The Art of Stealing Fire

CPA Seminar Series

The Art of Stealing Fire

Uranus in the Horoscope

Liz Greene

CPA

Centre for Psychological Astrology Press
London

First published 1996 by The Centre for Psychological Astrology Press, BCM Box 1815, London WC1N 3XX, United Kingdom, Tel/Fax +44 (0)20 8749 2330, www.cpalondon.com.

Second printing 1998.

First paperback edition 2004.

THE ART OF STEALING FIRE: *Uranus in the Horoscope*

Copyright © 1996 by Liz Greene.

Liz Greene asserts the moral right to be identified as the author of this work.

ISBN 1 900869 29 2

British Library Cataloguing-in-Publication Data. A catalogue record for this book is available from the British Library.

Printed in Great Britain by Antony Rowe Ltd, Chippenham, Wiltshire, SN14 6LH.

To Ian Gordon-Brown,

a truly individual Uranian spirit,

in loving memory

Table of Contents

Part One: Uranus in the natal chart

Part Two: The Transits of Saturn and Uranus

Part One: Uranus in the Natal Chart

This seminar was given on 20 January, 1996 at Regents College, London, as part of the Spring Term of the seminar programme of the Centre for Psychological Astrology.

Unconventionality and individuality

We have quite an exciting, or, shall we say, an electrifying theme to deal with today. Any outer planet presents us with a great challenge in interpretation, because we have no ancient astrological tradition to support our investigations. So I will begin by describing what, in my understanding, Uranus does *not* mean. When we interpret astrological symbols, we need to be extremely careful about the words we use. Precision matters enormously in the communication of astrological concepts, amongst ourselves as well as with clients, and sloppiness or vagueness can lead to misunderstandings. I have heard many astrologers describe Uranus as the "planet of individuality". But individuality refers to an individual, which means you or I as a separate, distinct personality – unique, not the same as anyone else, and developing according to an internal blueprint of unfoldment which is different from everyone else's.

Uranus is an outer planet. Because the outer planets reflect movements within the collective psyche, in which we all share, Uranus is not concerned with individual development. It may even prove inimical to individual values and individual emotional needs. We should realise the collective nature of Uranus by the simple fact that this planet is the co-ruler of the sign opposite the one which the Sun rules – in company with Saturn, it governs Aquarius, which is opposite Leo. This alone informs us that it symbolises the antithesis of individual expression (which is solar), because the individual is submerged in the group.

So a person whom we might describe as very Uranian may not be at all individual in the solar sense. There is often little awareness of personal values and personal identity. Uranus tends to view the world through a wide-angle lens, and matters of everyday life can easily be ignored or deemed unimportant. Such a person may be rebelling against existing structures or attitudes, or might reject a world-view that seems past its sell-by date. He or she may be in touch with progressive ideas and inspirations which are a long way ahead of their time. The Uranian person may be highly unconventional because of this; but unconventional does not mean individual.

How many of you have seen *Monty Python's Life of Brian*? Perhaps you remember the scene in which hundreds of eager, New Age-ish, redemption-minded people are gathered outside the chosen Messiah's door, chanting in unison, "We are all individuals!" Unconventionality can be so incredibly unindividual. It sometimes beggars belief how unindividual such behaviour can be, although this is rarely recognised by the person in the grip of the Uranian vision, because the very act of rebelling against something means that one is in some way deeply bound up with, and subtly dominated by, the very thing one is fighting. This is not an expression of individuality, because that comes from within, and is not dictated by attempting to be the opposite of something one perceives in the outer world. So please try to rid yourselves of the association of Uranus with individuality, because if you use this term when you read a chart, you may go badly wrong with it.

Very often, the special brand of suffering that Uranus can reflect springs from the fact that the person cannot express a sense of individuality. He or she may be dominated or driven by a revelation or world-view which is collective. It may be a revolutionary or transformative perspective on life, but it is collective nevertheless, which is why Uranian ideas usually arrive full-blown in the person's consciousness, without having been distilled from, or tested against, personal experience. If someone is trapped in such receptivity to the collective, without any individual sense of self to monitor, sift, and shape the revelation, he or she may lose touch with what is nourishing and creative on an inner level, and many important aspects of personal life may be unwittingly crushed.

One needs to be able to say, "Hang on a minute. This is a wonderful and inspiring vision of the future, but does it apply to the world in which I am presently living? Is it viable in terms of my experience of life and human nature? Do I believe in it with my heart and gut, as well as my head? Does this idea actually make sense in real terms? What is the time-scale? Can I contribute anything truly individual to making it work?" Without this kind of perspective, Uranus may wipe out individual values and individual authenticity, and what we have left is polemics. In its most negative form, these are the polemics of the terrorist, or the polemics of any mass movement which is aimed at destroying institutions or structures which are deemed in need of radical change. Recognising the need for change may be right and appropriate – although sometimes, like beauty, it may be in the eyes of the beholder.

But Uranus doesn't recognise the value and nature of time, or the importance of slow growth and compromise. Nor does it recognise the reality of individual human feeling. The vision of the future must happen *now,* and anything standing in the way must be annihilated or, at best, reformed. This can result in enormous suffering, for individuals as well as for the collective. The basic philosophy of Uranus is that, to make an omelette, one has to break eggs. The problem is that the eggs are the emotional and instinctual needs of individual human beings. Revolutions always have a way of going out of control.

Now, if this upsets any of you who belong to the Uranian Liberation Front, that's perfectly all right. You are entitled to be upset, and also to voice your feelings about it during the course of the seminar. But I am not suggesting that Uranus is "malefic". I believe we glamorise it in astrology, because we assume that change is always good. Often it is; but change for the sake of change may not open any creative doors. Also, the manner in which change is accomplished is critical, and Uranus is not very graceful about respecting the individual when change is required. The word "rights" is often on Uranian lips, but the deeper, inner rights of each individual may mean little in the face of Uranus' abstract ideals. Hopefully, as I go on, you will see why I am taking this perspective on the planet.

One of the most Uranian people that I have ever encountered came to me for a chart a few years ago. She had the Sun in Aquarius, trine Uranus in Gemini. She began describing her situation, her family life, and so on. Every time she referred to any event, feeling, or opinion, she always said, "We." "We" wanted to move to the country; "we" were very interested in astrology; "we" had had a difficult time in the last year or two; "we" didn't approve of the government's policy on health care. On inquiring who "we" were, I was told that this meant her husband, her three dogs, her two children, and her mother, who lived with her. I kept trying to elicit some personal response – some hint of an "I" in the midst of all this group concensus. "But what about you, what do you think?" I kept saying. She answered, "Well, we feel..." She simply could not say, "I". It was rather terrifying. She seemed to have no sense of herself as an independent entity. Eccentric and unconventional, yes. But individual? No.

The mythology of Uranus

What I am going to do now is put a rather simple diagram – actually, it's really a kind of list – on the overhead projector, to show some of the various connections which can help us to understand Uranus better. I am sure there are many more images and associations which you might think of as we go along, and it would be useful if you could offer your contributions, if you feel I have forgotten or overlooked something relevant. It is important for each of you to develop your own associations, with other planets as well as with Uranus, because your experiences and areas of study may be different from mine, but equally relevant. Each of these associations could require a seminar in itself, if we wanted to explore it thoroughly – for example, I have included the Kabalistic Chokmah, and in order to really grasp this, you would need to study the Kabala in some depth – so my comments will necessarily be incomplete. These Uranian associations are meant to be springboards for the imagination as well as the intellect, and I would like to try to get through them during the first part of the morning, so

----

that we can have as complete a picture as possible when we look at
Uranus in the natal chart.

Uranian Associations

Prometheus   Ouranos

The Hebrew Yahveh

Alice Bailey's "Group Soul" and "Plan in the Mind of God"

Mary Shelley's Frankenstein

The Enlightenment

The Pythagorean Numbers   Plato's Ideal Forms

Ritual magic   Bailey's Seventh Ray

The Muse Urania

The Egyptian goddess Nut   The Hindu Brahma

Kabalistic Chokmah   Tarot card "The Tower"

American, French, and Bolshevik Revolutions

I think these associations can help to give us deeper insight
into the core meaning of this planet, because we really need to
understand the core, emotionally and intuitively as well as with the

rational mind. We can't interpret Uranus by house, aspect, or sign without having a broader and more rounded sense of what it means. Keywords don't really help, because they don't connect us with the living energy of the planet; and keywords like "individuality" are a hindrance, rather than a help. We might do well to remember that the planets are indeed gods, in the psychological sense. They are living energies, with intent and volition, exactly like a person, but very much bigger. Each planet has a particular nature, a particular set of needs and desires, and a particular world-view. Planets are moving somewhere; they have intention and intelligence. Within us, they represent aspects of the psyche. You don't have to be pagan to appreciate this perspective on the planets. I am using the term "god" as a symbol of life-energy, an archetypal pattern at work in the whole of life. Because the planets are inside as well as outside us, and have life and a distinctive identity, we need to get a sense of what this identity really is. If we wish to know a person, we need to have to have a sense of what lies at the core – what constitutes reality for that person.

Prometheus the Titan

What lies at the core of Uranian intent, and what is the nature of the god? We will start with Prometheus, because amongst more discerning astrologers he is the figure that is most often associated with Uranus. You should all read Rick Tarnas' excellent little book, *Prometheus the Awakener*.[1] It is very useful to approach Uranus through exploring this figure. Although in myth there is no story involving a direct connection between the heaven-god Ouranos and Prometheus the Titan, all the Titans, including Prometheus, are the descendants of Ouranos.

I think you probably all know the general outline of the main Prometheus myth. Is there anyone who doesn't know it? Good, that saves me having to go through the entire story. But we might fruitfully focus on certain important features. First of all, we should

---

[1]Richard Tarnas, *Prometheus the Awakener,* Auriel Press, Oxford, 1993.

consider his Titanic nature, and what that implies. The Titans are not "gods" in the same sense as the Olympians, such as Zeus-Jupiter or Aphrodite-Venus. Myths, like dreams, are extremely precise when they describe something. They are not woolly or sloppy or loose, even though they evolve over time and change as they are adapted by the needs of different cultures throughout history. Myths are very specific in the way they put things, so if a divine figure in myth is a Titan and not an Olympian, then this is telling us something very important. The Titans are the children of heaven, but they are earth spirits and are embodied, because their mother is Gaia, the earth.

So Prometheus is not really a denizen of the celestial realm. He has a Uranian spirit, but his body is made of earth, and it can suffer pain, as it eventually does. We could say that he is somehow connected with the heavenly or divine spirit in incarnation – in other words, with the aspirational or visionary side of human nature, contained in the world of form. In fact Prometheus, whose name means "foresight", is credited with the creation of human beings, whom he forms out of clay, after which Athene breathes life into them to animate them.

Prometheus is a magician, an artist, and a culture-bringer. He teaches human beings astrology, architecture, and navigation – everything, in fact, that involves knowledge of how the cosmic or holistic system operates. In this respect he is different from other culture-bringers, who offer very specific arts or crafts, such as weaving (which is Athene's gift). Prometheus' knowledge always involves something heavenly or cosmic, translated into earthly form. Architecture requires an understanding of geometry, which, as any Platonist knows, is ultimately cosmic in nature; astrology and astronomy are obviously aspects of cosmic knowledge. One must have a broad understanding of the entire system to make these arts and sciences work. So Prometheus is a kind of inspirational *daimon*. He is a force within the psyche that has access to knowledge of how the cosmic system works, and how to apply it to the everyday affairs of human beings.

Most importantly, Prometheus steals cosmic fire, and gives it to human beings against the wishes of Zeus. This is a theme that has fascinated artists and writers over the centuries. What does this mean, the stealing of fire? If we can grasp it, we have got hold of what Uranus is really about. Rick Tarnas associates Prometheus' fire with "the creative spark, cultural and technological breakthrough, the enhancement of human autonomy, the liberating gift from the heavens, sudden enlightment, intellectual and spiritual awakening".[2] I would add another interpretation to this list: Prometheus steals the potential of consciousness from the gods. The fire he appropriates is solar; it is the divine spark of immortality, of awareness of the Self, which exists within each human being. It is also the fire of imagination and vision, through which solar divinity and individual creativity make themselves known.

Fire in the world's mythologies is always associated with divinity and with the eternal spirit, and we still preserve this symbolism in such expressions as the "eternal flame" at the Tomb of the Unknown Soldier or the Holocaust Memorial in Jerusalem. These flames, because they burn perpetually, remind us that, although the individuals have died, they have eternal life. In the Prometheus story, when human beings were created, they were not given the gift of fire, because if they had fire, they would be godlike. They would possess the power to create like the gods. Zeus prohibited this, and as a result humans were like the beasts, collective in nature and utterly subject to the forces of nature. In other words, they had no consciousness of themselves and their creative power.

Prometheus, with his gift of foresight, saw the *potential* of human consciousness. That is another extremely important feature of this Titanic figure. He had a vision of what human beings *could be,* if they were allowed to fulfill the potential they were given. So he went against the dictates of Zeus and stole a tiny spark of solar fire. He hid it in a hollow fennel stalk and brought it down to earth, and gave it to human beings as a collective. He didn't give it to one special or chosen person; he gave it to all. As a result, he was punished terribly for the sin of his theft, and so were human beings, through Pandora with her famous box of woes – although, once humanity had the fire, it couldn't be taken away again.

---

[2]*Ibid.,* p. 12.

There are a lot of powerful interconnected themes in this myth. The theft of solar fire, divine retribution, and a vision of human potential are fundamental archetypal images. From them we can begin to get a sense of what Uranus' core might be about. Uranus can see what is possible, because there is knowledge of how the cosmic system works. This is not "psychic" foreknowledge. Prometheus' "foresight" is exactly that – the ability to "see ahead". It is visionary, rather than psychic or instinctual.

Uranus sees things clearly, and recognises patterns and potentials that can be defined. Prometheus, who is a Uranian spirit, can see ahead, based on his knowledge of how the cosmic evolutionary process works. He knows that if fire is given to human beings, certain things will happen; certain potentials can be fulfilled. He has full knowledge of what those potentials are because he created human beings in the first place. Because he has brought fire to them, they are able to learn the sciences and arts that he teaches, and apply them with intelligence and creativity, rather than merely parroting by rote. They can grasp what he teaches, with all the implications and possibilities, because they have the spark of solar fire. The knowledge and the fire go together. On the deepest level, they are the same thing.

What Prometheus teaches *is* the solar fire. In Aeschylos' play, *Prometheus Bound,* the Titan soliloquises while chained to his high mountain. First he speaks of the sorry state in which humanity found itself before his intervention:

> For first, though seeing, all in vain they saw,
> And hearing, heard not rightly. But, like forms
> Of phantom dreams, throughout their life's whole length
> They muddled all at random; did not know
> Houses of brick that catch the sunlight's warmth,
> Nor yet the work of carpentry.[3]

Then he speaks of all the things he has given to human beings:

---

[3]Aeschylos, *Prometheus Bound,* trans. E. H. Plumptre, David McKay, London, 1931, p. 109.

> ...I showed the risings of the stars,
> And settings hard to recognise. And I
> Found Number for them, chief device of all,
> Groupings of letters, Memory's handmaid that,
> And mother of the Muses.[4]

He has, in effect, given men and women the means of mastering nature, through the power of vision and the knowledge of higher patterns and laws. This allows humans to free themselves from bondage to the instinctual cycles of the earth, and take mastery of the planet on which they live. They can create what we euphemistically call civilisation. That is the result of the fire he steals. Or, as Aeschylos puts it, offering us the real Uranian punchline:

> I made men cease from contemplating death.[5]

If we look at Prometheus as a psychological image, and understand him as something inside all human beings, then we can begin to recognise how this Uranian spirit has operated since the dawn of human history. It has, of course, existed despite the fact that the planet was only discovered in 1784. But since 1784 we have been aware, as a collective, of possessing it – however dimly and clumsily – and the discovery of Uranus coincides with the dawn of what we are pleased to call the Enlightenment. I will talk more about that later on. George Bernard Shaw once said that the balanced man accepts the world as it is, the unbalanced man is forever seeking to change it, and therefore all progress depends on the unbalanced man. It may be that we have to be a bit mad to receive what Prometheus is trying to teach.

If we think about the way in which animals and plants evolve, we can see that they do not move forward in the same way that we do. They are not driven to master nature because of a vision of potential perfection. They evolve out of necessity. Changes in the kingdoms of nature take place very slowly, and in accord with the pressures of climate, available food, and danger from predators; they

---

[4]*Ibid.*
[5]*Ibid.*, p. 102.

---

are part of a vast, interconnected, slowly developing life-web, which the ancients were fully aware of but which we are only recently beginning to recognise as part of our modern world-view. But human beings, the recipients of the gift of solar fire, have the irrepressible idea that they can, in one way or another, conquer nature's powers and patterns.

We can see Uranus' workings in history very clearly, if we understand the Promethean vision. At various junctures, an individual, or a group of individuals, is suddenly seized by a revelation that something could be improved, bettered, transformed, freed, or changed. Previously unrecognised potentials suddenly become obvious. Uranus always seems to carry a vision of human potential – the potential to be godlike, the potential to create a universe. Here is the human being wanting to be god. The Titan Prometheus himself doesn't want to be a god; although he isn't an Olympian, he doesn't appropriate the solar fire for himself, although he might easily have done so. What he does is give human beings the desire to be god, through providing them with the vision to recognise godlike potentials.

Uranian suffering and the punishment of Prometheus

The Titan's punishment is brutal. Zeus, the king of heaven, has absolutely no sympathy for what he has done, because human beings now have a little bit of what makes Zeus a god. In characteristic Jupiterian fashion, he is infuriated because now he has to share the stage with ordinary riff-raff. So Prometheus is chained to a mountaintop, and an eagle comes every day and eats away his liver. And every night the liver regenerates itself, and the next day the eagle comes back and has breakfast again. This is a terrible, savage mythic image – the noble Titan chained to the highest mountain, isolated and deprived of any contact with god or human, suffering perpetual physical and psychological torment, which doesn't kill him, but keeps him in a state of constant agony.

I think we need to explore this part of the myth, because it tells us the price we must pay for Uranian knowledge. We cannot dismiss it by saying, "Oh well, maybe we can avoid this unfortunate business of the liver if we do enough therapy or meditation or astrological charts, or if we have enough scientific knowledge." If we are going to profit from stolen fire, which every one of us has done, we must understand this image, because the bill will always be due at the end of the month. No one is exempt, because as a collective we have accepted Prometheus' gift. Those who develop the Uranian spirit very powerfully may get an extra-large bill. However, we can reassure ourselves a little by remembering that, in the myth, Prometheus is not chained to his rock forever. He is freed in the end. But what is his suffering really about? What might it mean on an inner level?

Audience: Isolation.

Liz: Yes, I think isolation is a very important part of it, both individually and as a collective. In recent times there has been a lot of discussion about "alienation", and about the heavy price we have paid, as a society, for our scientific and technological advances. The loneliness and sense of being odd, abnormal, or socially "unacceptable", which are so often experienced by anyone involved in "deeper" or "higher" explorations such as astrology, are probably well known to most, if not all, of you here today, and that is also Prometheus' isolation, on a more personal level.

Audience: The thing about Prometheus is that he destroyed the established order of the world, and it seems to me he is linked with the figure of the rebel, the outlaw who opposes law and order. He changes the world and is punished.

Liz: Yes, that is precisely how Nietzsche saw him – as a divine rebel who had the audacity and courage to challenge the natural order. The natural order is the order set by the gods, or, if you like, by the dictates of the instincts, or the powers of nature. Prometheus disobeys nature's laws, which are the same as the gods' laws, and as a result he is the rebel, the outlaw, the outcast, the prophet who is despised. The order that he disrupts is an order dictated by natural processes. If we

----

apply that to human nature, what Uranus does within us is to look at our own human nature and say, "Human nature in its instinctual form isn't good enough. Something could be changed. We could be different. We could be better."

We might also view the gods as the archetypal dominants within the collective unconscious. These inherent patterns are really what we mean by "fate" – they govern the unfolding of life according to certain fundamental designs or lines of energy. Consciousness, and knowledge of how the system works, can change our relationship with these archetypal dominants, although it cannot give us an escape from our essential natures; and it is possible that, as we become more conscious, we are less "fated" in the simplistic sense. This is really a process of internalising the godhead, which results in a lessening of projections of power onto the cosmos, and a strengthening of rational awareness and human potency. There are, of course, great dangers in this process – introjecting the godhead can inflate us and make us arrogant and incredibly destructive. And there are great creative benefits, because we become co-creators in the cosmic process.

Uranus is associated with revolutions that are based on an ideology of one kind or another. Uranian rebellions are not based on simple practical issues, which generally require adjustment and compromise rather than an all-out conflagration. They are based on an ideal of some sort which sets the collective alight, and there are plenty of examples of this historically. Don't make the mistake of thinking that Uranus is politically always on the left, because the Uranian spirit can also pursue extremely right-wing political ideals. Dictators usually take power through a revolution. Hitler, of course, had Uranus conjunct the Ascendant.

But whether Uranus swings to the right or the left (and sometimes it's hard to distinguish between the two), it always carries an ideology, a vision of social perfection that declares, "We will get rid of all the inferior, dark, barbaric elements in human nature, and create a perfect society in which human beings are godlike and without flaw." Uranus takes its stand against human nature, which is why Uranian revolutions usually go appallingly wrong, and spill a great deal of unnecessary blood. Human nature, without individual consciousness and reflection, cannot contain the Uranian vision, which tends to break loose and overwhelm the powers of individual reason and individual feeling.

This is another element involved in the suffering of Prometheus. We are not only isolated or alienated by Uranian vision. We may also have to suffer the heartbreaking realisation that the ideal world, the grand vision of perfection, is not possible at any given moment of time. As soon as we think we have fulfilled our potential, something else pops up to remind us that we are still a long way behind. The vision of human potential two hundred years ago, for example, included the conquering of certain diseases, such as syphilis, which we now have under control. But AIDS has come to take its place, and even tuberculosis, which we thought we had dealt with, is now returning in a more virulent, antibiotic-resistant form. Also, we are sometimes shocked by the realisation that our methods of mastering nature have created worse problems than before, because the natural order of the planet has been violated. Holes in the ozone layer, for example, which are a direct result of our meddling, may herald many future climatic difficulties, not to mention a marked increase in skin cancers, and we must swallow the fruits of our Uranian arrogance. Prometheus' fire carries many consequences – not because it is evil, but because human nature is slow in learning how to handle it responsibly.

At any point in time, whenever the Uranian vision arises, it is not possible to make it work in totality, because it flies in the face of nature. Uranus always goes wrong on one level or another, or it must be compromised in some way, and I think this is also part of Prometheus' suffering. It is as though Zeus is saying to his rebellious Titan, "Great, old chap, you gave human beings fire, very nice, very noble of you, and now look at what they have done with it. And it's all your fault."

The man who created the atomic bomb had a complete breakdown after it was dropped on Hiroshima and Nagasaki. He couldn't live with himself. He didn't really understand what he was unleashing, and when he saw the consequences, he couldn't bear it. In the sciences, this kind of suffering is not uncommon. I would not like to be the person who invented Thalidomide, or any one of a hundred

----

other medicines which were meant to heal and turned out to damage and destroy. There is a kind of blindness with which the Uranian scientist moves into spheres like genetic engineering, or the creation of new weapons.

In the grip of the Uranian vision, nothing else seems to matter, and individual consequences are not considered. The exhilaration of discovery obscures everything else, and usually – if not always – the motivating spirit is altruistic and progressive. One is so busy making the ultimate omelette that one doesn't notice that the broken eggs are screaming. Then the ways in which the new discoveries are used are revealed as a horror, and the creator must live with his or her creation. Insofar as we are all human, and share in the spirit of the age, we are all implicated, both in the creations and in the ways in which they are used. And we are all subject to Promethean suffering as a consequence.

Promethean suffering in the individual

On a smaller scale, we can see echoes of Prometheus' fate in any increase in consciousness through which suffering results. I might even go so far as to say that all increases in individual consciousness result in suffering, because they constitute a kind of "theft" from the collective unconscious. I will read you what Jung has to say about it: "The stronger and more independent our consciousness becomes, and with it the conscious will, the more the unconscious is thrust into the background, and the easier it is for evolving consciousness to emancipate itself from the unconscious, archetypal pattern. Gaining in freedom, it bursts the bonds of mere instinctuality and finally reaches a condition of instinctual atrophy. This uprooted consciousness can no longer appeal to the authority of the primordial images; it has Promethean freedom, but it also suffers from godless hubris. It soars above the earth and above mankind, but the danger of its sudden collapse is there..."[6] He was probably in a good position to know,

----

[6] C. G. Jung, *Alchemical Studies,* Vol. 13, *Collected Works,* Routledge & Kegan Paul, London, 1973, para. 13.

because Uranus was one of his chart rulers, opposing Saturn, the other chart ruler. Freud was probably also in a good position to know, since he had the Sun conjunct Uranus.

The great failing of Uranus in personal terms is that we don't foresee the backlash, the consequences which the theft of fire brings. Although the mythic Prometheus has foresight, as human individuals we often lack it, and we forget or fail to recognise what price will have to be paid. The results of this theft of fire are incalculable, because the moral qualities which we possess when we receive it may or may not be equipped to handle it in a creative rather than a destructive way. Consequently, there is often a dreadful shock for the Uranian person, not only at discovering what others might do with solar fire, but at realising what one has done with it oneself.

Audience: Could you say a bit more about the suffering caused by increased consciousness?

Liz: I think that consciousness, which is, in theory, such a desirable thing to the psychologically minded, often creates greater suffering than there was before, although it is of a different kind. Many counsellors and therapists discover this only after they have been in their own therapy for a long time and have worked with clients for a few years. Many astrologers discover it as well, after sufficient experience. At first, we believe we are going to enlighten people. We have a wonderful vision of an orderly cosmos and a deep faith in human evolution, and if we give this solar fire to people, we assume their lives will be better for it. Many people train as therapists with this reformer's vision in mind. One assumes one can heal anything, cure anything, change anything. This vision swept collective consciousness in the 1960's, when Uranus and Pluto were conjuncting and large numbers of people thought all one had to do was turn on, tune in, and drop out.

The Uranian reforming spirit has also had a powerful collective influence more recently, and in more obviously political spheres, under the Uranus-Neptune conjunction in Capricorn. Everyone thought *glasnost* would totally transform Eastern Europe, and now

----

there is the inevitable human mess which results when old structures have broken down and people don't know what to replace them with. When any individual becomes more conscious, he or she loses the luxury of blaming everyone else. It is extremely painful because there isn't any convenient outer tip into which one can dump one's psychic rubbish. Consciousness means internalising projections, and that means containing apparently insoluble inner conflicts. The degree of suffering which this causes can be very great, and some people feel it's a poor exchange.

I suspect that real suffering of the Promethean kind is not possible when one hasn't looked at one's internal conflicts. One can, of course, steal the fire and avoid getting caught. Then, to put it crudely, if the Promethean spirit within us isn't willing to take the consequences of the theft of fire, and go through this rite of passage symbolised by the Titan's suffering, then somebody else gets to suffer the pain – one's partner, children, or neighbours, or perhaps a social or racial group, or another nation. One can whinge and bleat and moan. But suffering of the kind imaged in the Prometheus myth, which is a necessary creative adjunct to the advantages of possessing fire, only comes when one confronts what one is and has done. Jung believed that the only resolution of the suffering lies in giving something back to the collective – an individual creation, to replace what has been stolen. This is perhaps the most profound way of viewing the meaning of Uranus for the individual.

Audience: What about the way Uranus blames nature for human suffering? If Uranus wants an ideal world, then nature is the source of all the evil.

Liz: Uranus is not inclined to perceive nature as evil; it perceives nature as unfinished. It's a bit like the declaration of the alchemists in the Middle Ages: "Our art perfects what Nature has left imperfect." I doubt that the scientist trying to discover an antibiotic that would cure tuberculosis said to himself, "These bloody bacteria, it's all their fault, the rotten buggers." He is more likely to have thought, "These bacteria are an unnecessarily destructive aspect of nature, and human knowledge is capable of improving on it."

Audience: You mean, "It shouldn't have to be like this"?

Liz: Yes and no. Uranus does say "It shouldn't have to be like this," but the implication is not moral in the ordinary human right-and-wrong sense. Perhaps a clearer way of putting it might be, "It doesn't have to be like this." This planet doesn't have the kind of morality that we adopt as individuals. This is another reason why the term "individual" is so inappropriate for Uranus. Morality is a highly individual business. Morality in the deepest sense comes from one's instinctive, heartfelt conviction of something not being in harmony with one's ideals, or what one perceives as the greatest good.

Audience: Is that more Neptunian?

Liz: Not in my experience. Neptune is also an outer planet, equally connected with collective movements and currents. If you want to find something in the chart which might tell you about individual morality, I think you must look at the Sun and Venus, as well as Jupiter, the Ascendant, and the 9th house. The outer planets won't help you.

Uranus is not concerned with morality; it is concerned with an efficiently working system, a furthering of the cosmic "plan". That is a kind of morality, I suppose, but it is vastly impersonal and bears little relationship to our human fears, needs and aspirations. Even Prometheus, who is sometimes perceived as a kind of cosmic social worker, is not moral; he is a thief, and is disloyal to Zeus. He has a vision of human potential and he wants to see whether it will work or not. Morality of the personal kind, the kind that is linked with individual feeling, is often strangely absent in the Uranus-dominated person.

He or she may claim the high moral ground on the basis of an ideal. But when one actually looks closely at how this ideal is applied, the apparent high moral ground often seems to vanish. We are back to the broken eggs. Uranus' vision is of a system which functions beautifully and efficiently, and this vision is born out of a perception of potential, rather than out of compassion. Uranus does not relate through compassion. It relates through vision, foresight, and revelation, not from the heart, which I think is the basis of morality. This is why it is so extremely important for the individual to have an inner sense of value and identity, so that Uranian vision can be processed through personal morality and actual life experience.

Ouranus the sky-god and the Pythagorean numbers

The Promethean myth is a replaying of the original Ouranos myth on a more intimate level. We now need to look at the actual god after whom the planet is named. He is the progenitor of Prometheus, because he begets the race of Titans on Gaia, his sister-wife. In Greek, the name *ouranos* means the sky spangled with stars, the starry heavens. I know of two mythic versions of his birth. One of them is that Ouranus and Gaia emerged out of chaos together. The other is that Gaia existed first, gave birth to him, and then mated with him. But even if he emerged out of the womb of the Great Mother, he is an archetypal creator-god. That is why I have included the Hebrew Yahweh in the diagram. Ouranus has a lot in common with the God of Genesis, who puts the stars in the firmament and creates the Sun and Moon, and whose spirit hovers over the face of the waters. The abode of Ouranus is the highest and most inaccessible region of the starry heavens, the "crystalline sphere" in which the fixed stars are set like jewels.

There were no cult shrines to Uranus in the ancient world. Because he is All and First, he is impossible to envisage; he precedes physical creation, and therefore has no form. What is there before there is any manifest cosmos? It is impossible to visualise, because it has no shape. All the potentials of creation exist within Uranus, but until they are made manifest, they are "ideas in the mind of God". They are Plato's Ideal Forms, the blueprint on which manifestation is based.

I bought a wonderful print at the British Museum some years ago, a medieval illuminated manuscript in which God is portrayed creating the manifest universe – earth, Sun, Moon, stars, and the four elements – with a pair of compasses. In medieval times there was a willingness to portray God, sometimes in quite startling ways. One wonders what was going on in the artist's mind, or perhaps more to the point, what the artist's father looked like. In the print I was just describing, God looks like a cross between Rasputin and Jeremy Irons on a bad day. But the Greeks were more circumspect. To portray the spirit of the starry heavens, they used geometry.

The closest that the Greeks come to expressing Uranus, and what it means, is in the sphere of Greek mathematics. Greek mathematics and science were not like our mathematics and science. The Greeks had an *a priori* assumption that the cosmos was interconnected. Science now does not have that *a priori* assumption; there is no overview, no real Promethean vision of the whole. Individual scientists who espouse this vision are usually considered "fringe". At present, orthodox science is more Saturnian than Uranian. It is slowly being dragged into the realisation of a unified cosmos, kicking and screaming all the way. Greek science perceived every aspect of life as part of a huge living system. Consequently, the development of Greek geometry is based on the idea that the inner structure of the cosmos is number.

If we consider the Pythagorean concept of the cosmos, we can get profound insight into Uranus. Anything that exists in manifestation starts with an abstract idea, and the purest form of that abstract idea is number. First there is one, or One; and this One can be expressed by both a point and a circle, never beginning and never ending. This is the famous analogy of St Augustine, who said that God was a circle whose centre was nowhere but whose circumference was everywhere. One gives birth to two; two generate three; and then a plane figure can be formed. Number is the most essential quality in the universe. Number eventually results in the plane figures, of which the triangle is the first, followed by the square; and the plane figures then become solid figures, of which the pyramid is the first, followed by the cube. These solid forms, which Plato wrote about so extensively,[7] lie behind the structure of what we perceive as manifest reality.

Any of you who might have done geometry at school will perhaps remember how magical the creation of the plane and solid figures can be, with only a pair of compasses to work with. Without calculators, computers, or other devices which we now depend on, the Greeks could conjure perfect forms, perfect harmony and symmetry, out of nothing. It is not surprising that they understood geometry as the essential shape of the divine. With a pair of compasses one can begin with a circle, create a triangle and a hexagon, and eventually construct those elaborate dodecahedrons or icosahedrons which can be cut out, stuck together at the edges, and hung like a magic lantern from a thread. Plato insisted that the study of geometry, like the study of astrology to which he related it, was guaranteed to lift the mind to the "eternal realities". If we had time today, I would love to give you all compasses and large pieces of heavy paper, so that you could play god and create the manifest universe. Then you would experience Uranus on a very different level.

This is another way of understanding the fire which Prometheus steals. The cosmological system, be it astrology, kabala, "sacred" geometry, higher mathematics, the structure of music, or anything else that teaches us the essential pattern and functioning of the universe, is the quintessential stuff which Uranus reveals to us. We traditionally associate astrology with Uranus, partly because in Greek myth there was a muse called Urania who presided over astrology. But the relationship is much deeper.

God the cosmocrator, the architect of manifestation, is most vividly embodied in the numerical and geometric structure of the universe, and nowhere is this better expressed than in the numerical and geometric structure of astrology. The actual practise of reading horoscopes is not, in itself, Uranian. Uranus reveals itself very powerfully in the study of astrological harmonics, which are a modern version of the Pythagorean cosmic vision. Harmonics are difficult for many astrologers to approach, because the theory all seems so abstract

---

[7]Plato, *Timaeus*, in *The Collected Dialogues of Plato*, ed. Edith Hamilton and Huntington Cairns, Princeton University Press, 1961, 32-58.

and impersonal, and how do we apply it to the unhappy client who is in the throes of a marriage breakup? But the more Uranian-inclined astrologer will insist that, without this broader understanding of the structure of astrology, we have no perspective from which to view the fragmented bits of individual human experience.

In order to get a better grasp of this dimension of Uranian vision, you should all read John Addey's book, *Harmonics in Astrology*, as well as *Working with Astrology* by Charles Harvey and Mike Harding. It is also worth remembering that Jung, who was steeped in astrology as well as Platonic philosophy, and who had an Aquarian Ascendant with Saturn rising closely opposite Uranus, used number and geometry as the basis of his mapping of the psyche. The trinity, the quaternity, and the circle are fundamental to Jung's understanding of the personality. A major part of his three alchemical volumes, *Psychology and Alchemy*, *Alchemical Studies*, and *Mysterium Coniunctionis*, is devoted to an exploration of the geometric structure of the psyche. Although this intensely Uranian approach is not necessarily useful in practise for every astrologer, it is important to have at least a basic sense of what it is about and what it is telling us – if for no other reason than that, as astrologers, we cannot really understand the Uranian vision without it.

The dimension of astrology which is suggested by Uranus is its fundamental design. This conveys to us the workings of the "mind of God", the cosmos as a unified whole. Every student of astrology has to start with the fact that everything in astrology is geometrically based, and functions through orderly numerical sequences. There are twelve signs, which are derived from the division of the ecliptic into four (by the two equinoxes and two solstices), and then into twelve. There are three signs in each of the four elements, four signs in each quality, and three qualities. Everything is rooted in the magic of the compasses. The major aspects are measured in derivatives of three and four. When one steps back and views the astrological system as a geometric design, its beauty and symmetry are breathtaking. It is Pythagorean in nature, and it operates from the *a priori* assumption that in the mind of God, in the starry heavens of Ouranos, the whole thing has already been worked out in principle, starting with number

----

and then gradually working down into the multiplicity of manifest forms. When we look at a chart in this way, we are availing ourselves of Prometheus' stolen fire.

Ouranos is a very elusive character in myth. He hasn't really got a character in the way that Zeus or Aphrodite has one – he doesn't possess a "personality" as the anthropomorphised Olympians do. We don't have any stories about the extramarital escapades of Ouranos. But we have a few very relevant motifs. First, he is extraordinarily fertile, as we might expect of a celestial creator-god; every night he "covers" Gaia and another child is conceived. Second, when Gaia gives birth to these children in all their variety, he finds them utterly repellent. They are not perfect; they are not what he had in mind. He didn't take into account the fact that his children would inherit her earthiness, with all nature's capacity for generating a vast variety of forms. And these children are not pretty, not lovely and symmetrical like a geometric design.

First she produces the Titans, who are huge, hairy, and rugged, and stomp about gracelessly; then she produces a few giants, who are even bigger and clumsier; and then she produces some monsters which have a hundred hands. This isn't quite what Ouranos had envisaged, and in a fit of repulsion he casts them into the underworld so that they don't offend his sight. Because of this act of repudiation of her offspring, Gaia is deeply offended, and encourages them to rise up and rebel against their father. To her favourite child, Cronos-Saturn the Titan, Gaia gives a sickle or scythe. Cronos quietly approaches his father when Ouranos lies sleeping, exhausted after yet another night of child-making. He grasps his father's testicles in his left hand, chops them off with the sickle in his right hand, and seizes the throne as the new king of the gods. The blood dripping from the wound seeps into the earth, and the Furies are born. Cronos hurls the severed genitals into the sea, and from the fertilisation of the waters by Ouranos' sperm, Aphrodite emerges from the sea-foam. Two extraordinary feminine images arise from this act of castration, one associated with beauty and harmony, the other with vengeance.

The castration of Ouranos

Audience: One story says he was actually making love with Gaia when Cronos crept up on him. So his separation was from Gaia as well as from his testicles.

Liz: Yes, it is a separation of the divine parents, the divine marriage of heaven and earth, and the beginning of separative earthly reality. It's a little difficult to imagine the actual mechanics, and who is doing what with whose right and left hands and so on, but never mind. We can view the castration on many different levels. As you say, it is an act of separation which Cronos performs, severing spirit from matter, and leaving human beings with the belief that the two realms are eternally irreconcilable. The castration also implies the ending of the creative potential of Ouranos, which we need to bear in mind when we think about the astrological Saturn's relationship to Uranus. Saturn destroys the Uranian potential for endless creation, so the visionary Promethean spirit can no longer generate new possibilities once Saturn has got hold of him by the short-and-curlies. He is no longer fertile. The potential for perfection is chopped off, limited, curtailed. We must then live life in the earth-world, which is a world of defined forms which cannot evolve into what they are not.

And so, in myth, the reign of Ouranus ends. Unlike other deities, his power has a finite lifespan. He doesn't die, but he is no longer a potent force in the cosmos. It is unclear just what does happen to him. When Cronos is overthrown by Zeus, we are told Cronos is banished to Tartaros, or to the Blessed Isles. At least there is a forwarding address. But nothing is said of the whereabouts of Ouranos. He exists within his progeny, of course – the most important of which, for our purposes today, is Prometheus – and he also exists in the deities who spring from his wound, Aphrodite-Venus and the Furies. We might say that he goes into the unconscious, and is no longer accessible to human beings except through his offspring. We get a glimpse of the starry heavens of the vanished creator-god when we explore Venus' world of beauty and harmony, or when we collide with the "minions of justice" who, according to Herakleitos, keep the Sun from overstepping his boundaries.

If we look at this world of myth as a spontaneous portrayal of human psychological processes, then Ouranos and his perfect geometry are a vision of life which was lost long, long ago, before human beings even walked the earth. We have existed only since the rule of Cronos and Zeus, and therefore our perceptions of reality are limited and earthbound. Although Zeus might seem a better bet than Saturn as a ruler of the gods, Zeus too is limited, for he did not create the cosmos, and has no idea how it was done. He seizes rulership of it, but it is not his creation. Uranus can only exercise his creative power from an invisible place, from the depths of the collective unconscious. This is a place we don't have access to, unless we are shocked into awareness by inspirations which erupt as though out of nowhere, and remind us that once upon a time the whole of the universe was conceived as a single perfect design. And when that happens, we might not always be able to handle it very well.

Uranus as Frankenstein

Some of the other associations in the diagram should be fairly obvious to you by now. Kenneth Branagh notwithstanding, you are no doubt all familiar with Mary Shelley's *Frankenstein* – hopefully through the novel, which is subtly and beautifully written, and not just through the often crass film interpretations which have been made of it. Dr. Frankenstein is a Uranian figure, created by a woman with the Sun conjunct Uranus in Virgo. Mary Shelley certainly had a taste for eccentric men – which is one of the more traditional interpretations of Sun-Uranus in a woman's chart – but the figure of Victor Frankenstein is a brilliant embodiment of her own inner creative vision, as well as an enduring portrait of the Uranian spirit run amok in human nature. She was born in 1797, just eight years after the French Revolution and thirteen years after Uranus' discovery, when the Enlightenment was really beginning to break forth. My feeling is that her natal Sun-Uranus conjunction made her acutely attuned to the new collective *Zeitgeist,* and she saw only too clearly where it might lead. Frankenstein is a modern Prometheus gone astray, whose spirit of invention is ostensibly dedicated to scientific good, but who instead creates a monster which ultimately destroys its creator. I don't think I have to comment any further on the continuing relevance of Mary Shelley's theme.

Alice Bailey and other Uranian pastimes

The best early example of the Uranian world-view that I can think of is the Pythagorean system, which heavily influenced Plato and all the Greek philosophers and mathematicians who followed. In contemporary esoteric thought, the idea of a plan in the mind of God is most clearly expressed in Alice Bailey's work, and perhaps her most Uranian piece is *Esoteric Astrology.* Rudolph Steiner is another important figure in this century who seems to have expressed the Uranian world-view in his work. You will also find it elsewhere, particularly in the work of people who claim to channel. The business of channelling is very interesting, and it is especially relevant to our theme when the message comes straight from Uranus. This is not always the case.

The *Seth* books of Jane Roberts are another excellent example of a Uranian cosmic system, transmitted through what the author defines as a higher spiritual entity. But the information which the psychic Edgar Cayce communicated, ostensibly from the "Akashic Records", was much more personal and specific, related to people's past incarnations. Certain people seem to be inclined to experience what they deem to be information or wisdom received from a higher source, and with some, the higher source may be chiefly concerned with matters of the heart, with messages from the deceased, or with a more Neptunian all-you-need-is-love vision. But some people, like Bailey, tell us about a meticulously ordered cosmic system.

Neither Bailey nor Roberts was especially Uranian in terms of the planet's prominence in the natal chart. Mary Shelley's creation was conscious, and therefore an artistic expression of her own inner world as well as a prophetic vision of the world in which she lived. So it isn't at all surprising to find that natal Sun-Uranus conjunction. But Bailey and Roberts are not in any way consciously identified with the entity they "channel". Uranus appears in subtler ways. Roberts had it in the 3rd house in 9° Aries, sextile Mercury in 8° Gemini, which is certainly applicable to her extremely Uranian world-view and way of communicating.[8] Her books are revelatory, and enormously powerful because of this, whether one accepts their premises or not.

The same might be said of Bailey. Uranus is in 5° Virgo in the 2nd house in her chart, forming a trine to Neptune in Taurus and another, out-of-sign trine to Saturn at the end of Aries. It is also square Pluto in Gemini. There is an absence of major contacts with the personal planets, but Uranus is involved in powerful configurations with the other two outer planets, as well as with Saturn.[9] Perhaps this is in some way connected with the strangely dissociated nature of her revelations, which seem to have nothing at all to do with her personality, but which, from the look of these configurations, reflect powerful movements in the collective psyche at the time of her birth in 1880. We know something first-hand about Uranus and Neptune together, because we have just experienced their conjunction, with its extraordinary mixture of social and political upheaval fired by mystical yearnings for redemption. A good example of this kind of thing at work in an individual is Marx, who was born under a Uranus-Neptune conjunction in Sagittarius, square Pluto in Pisces. This conjunction is quite disconnected from his personal planets. I don't think Marx would have approved of the idea of channelling *Das Kapital*, but it is a similar "transmission" of something straight from the mouth of the collective psyche. Bailey was born under a trine between Uranus and Neptune, suggesting a deep collective need – and

[8]Birth data for Jane Roberts, from Hans Hinrich Taeger, *Internationales Horoskope Lexikon,* Verlag Hermann Bauer, Freiburg, 1992, p. 1288: 8 May 1929, 23h27m EST/S (GMT 3h27m), Albany, NY, USA, 73°W45', 42°N49'.

[9]Birth data for Alice Bailey, from Hans Hinrich Taeger, *ibid.,* p. 96: 16 June 1880, 07h32m WET (GMT 07h32m), Manchester, GB, 02°W14', 53°N29'. For those interested in harmonic charts, it is worth noting that, in Bailey's 7th harmonic chart, Uranus is placed in the 9th in Aries, trine the Sun and closely opposition a Mars-Moon-Venus-Saturn conjunction in Libra in the 3rd.

potential – to synthesise Promethean knowledge and vision with spiritual redemption.

If you try to read Bailey's work without any introduction, it is often extremely difficult, because it is like reading a scientific or technical manual. It describes the intricate spiritual-mechanical workings of the plan in the mind of God as though it were an instruction book telling you how to take apart the engine of your BMW. The language is sometimes impossible, and one can easily come away feeling either utterly spiritually unevolved, convinced that God is actually a giant computer, or certain that the woman needed a bottle of Prozac. Bailey's work is full of incomprehensible jargon, but through it all comes the enormously powerful theme of the geometry of the cosmos, and the evolutionary plan in the mind of God.

We may well say, "Where did she get all this stuff? What evidence is there for this?" Of course there is no evidence, not in the Saturnian sense. But in Uranus' domain, it is irrelevant whether the rational ego defines the doctrine as false, purely mad, partially mad, drug-induced, a Monty Python send-up, or full of deep truths. What is relevant is that it arrived full-blown, a revelation from the starry heaven of the collective psyche, and it is up to each reader to work out what it might mean to him or her. It is Uranian because it is Promethean, full of the theme of human and cosmic potential, and it appears as a complete, seamless system without being worked through an individual set of conscious values and feelings. If you want to get a good flavour of Uranus, read Bailey.

The Kabalistic Uranus and ritual magic

In Kabalistic thought, the Sephira – the emanation of God – which is connected with the planet Uranus is called Chokmah. On the Kabalistic Tree, Chokmah is male energy, the flash of lightning which emerges from Ain Soph, the One, and which fertilises Binah, the feminine principle, to bring the manifest world into being. Binah is the Bitter Sea, and Chokmah, the Uranian lightning-bolt, is the spirit of God moving over the face of the waters. The lightning flash is the revelation of the plan of the cosmos, and the fertilisation of Binah is like the fertilisation of Gaia by Ouranos in Greek myth. Binah is associated with Saturn as a feminine earth-force, which relates to the Greek myth as well, because Cronos-Saturn is Gaia's favourite son, an image of her phallic power. In the same way, Hades-Pluto is an image of the phallic power of Mother Night, and Poseidon-Neptune represents the phallic power of the primordial sea.

In some ways Kabalism itself is a Uranian system, because once again it portrays the workings of the cosmos as an orderly, perfectly functioning design. I am not well versed in the Kabala, and it is a study which requires a deep commitment as well as intellectual understanding – not unlike astrology. But I felt I should mention it, because Chokmah is an important dimension of the Uranian network of associations.

Uranus is also related by Bailey to ritual magic as a science, and for those of you who are familiar with her scheme of the Seven Rays, Uranus is related to the Seventh. This is not magic in the sense of Dennis Wheatley's *The Devil Rides Out*, or voodoo spells and black chickens sacrificed in the basement. It is magic as the application on the material plane of those inner laws by which the invisible dimensions of reality work. In this sense, science is also magic, because it attempts to do the same thing. In order to change, transform, or create on the manifest plane, the laws by which things operate must be studied and implemented.

Psychology too has a relationship with this definition of magic, because once again we are seeking to transform manifest reality through a knowledge of how the inner laws work. We don't have much traffic with magic in astrological and psychotherapeutic circles, and that is just as well, since it usually comes in an unattractive package with some very unpleasant power issues tucked into the corners. Individuals who are involved in magic of the common or garden variety often seem to have dreadful power problems, and deep emotional wounds which impel them to try to control others and the world around them. Yet much of psychotherapy, as well as science, involves Uranian magic, which is one of the adjuncts of Promethean vision.

Any ritualising, systemising, harnessing, or deliberate patterning of natural energies, in accord with clearly defined laws and in order to produce an effect on the material plane, is magical. Seen in this way, we can recognise many alternative healing practises, such as homeopathy, flower remedies, or acupuncture, as magical. So is the kind of thing Hitler did, when he very deliberately utilised the power of archetypal symbols such as the Swastika and the black-and-silver panoply of his SS in order to produce an effect on the collective psyche. I think I mentioned earlier that Hitler had Uranus closely conjunct the Ascendant, and we can see it in operation in his ability to work magic on the collective German psyche.

Heretical though it may sound, the Church, in both Catholic and Protestant forms, has always availed itself of this kind of magic, since the calculated use of ritual and symbol in order to affect the psychological state of the believer is nothing more nor less than the application of inner laws to the outer world. Science and religion both employ magic. Once upon a time the two were the same, and the nature of magic was recognised for exactly what it was. This is what the Rosicrucian Enlightenment was all about at the beginning of the 17th century. It was an extraordinary Uranian synthesis of scientific research and magical experimentation, focused on translating God's "footprints" in the natural world. By discovering the secrets of nature, one could master nature, and during this remarkable time in history, magical rituals were as important as an empiric knowledge of how substances were made. Nature was perceived as a kind of hieroglyphic writing, a set of encoded images which, properly read, revealed the divine pattern at work underneath.

Uranian control

Audience: Where does control come in? I think Uranus is very controlling, and all the things you are talking about – the use of magic in science and religion – have to do with control.

Liz: Whether you perceive Uranus as controlling depends on how you react to its particular perspective. Because Ouranos in myth repudiates his earthy children and locks them up, there can sometimes be a powerful negative reaction to this planet, both within oneself and also to other people who carry strongly Uranian energy, If one has an emphasis in water and earth, for example, combined with aspects such as the Moon in Pisces square Uranus in Gemini, or Mars in Scorpio opposition Uranus in Taurus, Uranus can appear extremely dogmatic and tyrannical, and may be projected onto suitable hooks outside, human or otherwise. Uranus in the 7th or 8th house can sometimes be projected onto the partner, who may then seem very controlling and demanding. The child of a Uranian parent may perceive that parent as extremely controlling; this is often the case when the planet appears in one of the parental houses in the chart. But the Uranian person may not perceive it as control, nor wish to be controlling. A Uranian parent may perceive his or her insistence on certain high standards as positive, constructive, and civilised, and there may be intense frustration and anger in both parent and child because the parent has a perception of the potential of the child, whereas the child simply feels put down and criticised.

Audience: But that involves not accepting the child as he or she really is. It means imposing a set of values or standards on the child which might or might not fit.

Liz: Yes, that is quite true. Uranus is not very good at accepting things or people as they really are. Idealists never are; they are incurable meddlers. Prometheus couldn't leave well enough alone. He had to give human beings fire, because he thought they ought to have it. Maybe they would have been perfectly happy living in caves and eating raw meat. But the Uranian person doesn't perceive this as a violation of others' reality. The reforming spirit recognises that people or groups who don't wish to develop their potential can create a great deal of suffering and chaos for those around them. Therefore they must be taught how to work with the system. We are straight into *Brave New World* here. Of course it is controlling. But at the same time, declaring, "I'm like this, and I don't want to be any different, and the rest of you can go and sod off!" is also very controlling. We can justify a great deal of barbarity in the name of "being ourselves".

This is a very difficult issue. I am not trying to justify Uranus – it doesn't need my justification, after all – but I think it is important that we can step into the world-view of all the planets, and understand that, from within that framework, the aspirations and needs of each planet are absolutely right and appropriate. Only in this way can we really put ourselves in the place of another person, and grasp something of who they are and what is right for them, rather than what we would like them to be according to our own values and standards.

If you want a very disturbing image of Uranus at work right now, consider the fraught issue of genetic engineering. Think about it, and think about it hard. What does it invoke in you? What do you feel about it? What are its implications? At present, science is rampaging about identifying genes which, according to this model, "cause" alcoholism, depression, schizophrenia, and aggression. In this Uranian vision of a Brave New World, we could rid the world of most of its problems, by either aborting foetuses which carried antisocial or psychologically unstable genes, or by replacing or eradicating these genes. You can all work out the implications of this, I'm sure, without my having to spell them out. People no longer have problems or conflicts of an inner kind; their behaviour is caused by an illness determined by a rogue gene.

This allows them to avoid taking responsibility for their own emotions and motives. Instead of projecting our conflicts directly onto others, they are projected onto genes, and of course eventually they will be projected onto anyone suspected of carrying those genes. One can see the nobility of the vision – we could rid the world of terrible diseases such as Altzheimer's, and spinobifida, and other genetic sources of suffering. But where do we draw the line? And what if genes carry creative psychological components as well as potentially malefic physical ones, combined in one heady mix? When is a disease strictly physical, and when it is a combination of physical and psychic? And is there even such a thing as a strictly physical disease?

You can see why Hitler was so preoccupied with genetic experimentation. "If we could just get rid of these inferior types," he no doubt said to himself, "we would have a perfect race." (No prizes awarded for recognising the problems his own physiognomy must have caused him.) All one has to do is to remove anyone with a predisposition for... Well, you name it. The rogue gene is defined according to the particular personal tastes and unconscious complexes of the genetic engineer. Indeed, we could have a race of perfect human beings. We wouldn't age, we wouldn't fall ill, we wouldn't drink or smoke or get violent, we wouldn't have moods, we wouldn't do anything to upset the smooth and efficient working of society. Did any of you see an old John Boorman film called *Zardoz,* in which Sean Connery starred? It must go back fifteen or twenty years. It is a wonderful film, reeking of Uranus, and it is also coming true, as many science fiction novels and films tend to do. Are there any questions or comments at this point? I think we have pretty well exhausted our diagram, and we can move to Uranus in the natal horoscope.

Uranian fundamentalism

Audience: Is religious fundamentalism related to Uranus? It has so much rigidity of thinking, and fundamentalists seem to believe in a watertight, perfect system.

Liz: Rigidity of thinking can certainly can be an attribute of Uranus. When one receives a Uranian idea in its pure form, it is right and true in the absolute sense because there is nothing that can interfere with it. It is seamless and perfect. Earlier, I was talking about geometry in relation to Uranus, and how the Greeks saw it as a magical revelation of the structure of the cosmos. When you take your compasses and draw a circle, and then repeatedly mark the radius along the circumference, of course you will always get a hexagon. You will never fail to get a hexagon, unless you have bent the compasses, because due to some mysterious property of number, each face of the hexagon equals the radius of the circle. There is an inevitable rightness about such principles; they always work. Uranian truth has that quality. Whether it is related to religious fundamentalism is a more complex issue. What we ordinarily understand as fundamentalism relies on an *a priori* religious authority, usually in textual form, and this is not necessarily derived from Uranian revelation. More often, it is a conventional religious dogma, handed down over many generations. But some fundamentalist sects, such as the Mormons, do rely on Uranian revelation from one charismatic leader. Interestingly, Joseph Smith, the founder of the Mormon Church, had a very close Saturn-Uranus conjunction in late Libra, sextile the Sun in early Capricorn, square natal Mercury in late Capricorn, and square a late Cancer Ascendant.

I think there is a great deal of Saturn in fundamentalist thinking, and also a great deal of terrible inner insecurity and conflict in the individuals who espouse it. This configuration in Smith's chart also involved the Moon at the beginning of Aquarius, conjunct Mercury and square the Saturn-Uranus conjunction. Personal emotional issues obviously played an important part in his divine revelation. I think you are right, Uranus can be an important element in this kind of religious perspective. But I associate Uranus more with what I might call "esoteric fundamentalism". The authoritative text is usually extremely upmarket – channelled teachings from a Master, for example, or Smith's golden tablets. The rigidity of thinking is certainly there.

The Uranian vision doesn't take into account what happens when one applies abstract principles to something as fluid as the human heart, or to organic life, which is subject to many unpredictable shifts and changes. The dogmatism of Uranus is not really moral dogmatism. It is based on the fact that, if main principles are extracted from the general stuff of life, such principles always work. It is only when you apply those principles to everyday reality that they start going to pieces. But the Uranian nature doesn't want to look at that. The mind is focused on the general principle, and the general principle dictates that hexagons always come out of circles, because that is the law.

Audience: I think there is something quite childlike about these people. There is a huge amount of childlike excitement about genetic engineering. Then, when the ethics committee come in and say, "Well, we are not really not sure about this..." there is so much anger, because the energy they are involved with is like a child playing. "Don't stop our fun," they say. "This is exciting". There isn't any sense of where it's going. All they think is, "This is exciting."

Liz: Yes, it must have been exciting for Prometheus, while he was *en route* to earth with the fire hidden in the fennel stalk. He didn't think of the consequences.

Audience: It is terribly easy to go down that road. I find I can almost sympathise with the excitement these people are experiencing with Uranian discoveries.

Liz: So can I. That is what is so difficult about it; there is so much potential good and creative energy in Uranian vision. But there must be an individual ego which can mediate it, and consider the consequences on a human level. As astrologers, we have to face this issue, too, because astrology, as a means by which we can gain insight into the hidden workings of the cosmos, is a Promethean art. When we start learning astrology, we tend to go into it thinking, "Oh, this is wonderful!" because we are dazzled by its truth and the beauty of its symmetry. And the first time we have a client who dies, or goes down with a really serious illness, or loses a child, then the uncomfortable questions start arising. Is it possible to predict such things? And if so, how much can we tell people? And can prediction actually contribute to the actualisation of something? But if we see something unpleasant coming, and we don't tell the client, are we withholding important information? Could we have spared them?

Any astrologer with even a modicum of moral sense will begin to ask such questions as soon as the limits and the possibilities of astrology begin to be recognised. And in the psychological sphere too, these questions come up. A journalist recently asked me if it was "dangerous" to have the kind of self-knowledge psychological astrology can reveal. I replied that it was far more dangerous not to have self-knowledge. But at the same time, self-knowledge carries a price, which I talked about earlier. Prometheus suffers for the sin of his theft, and so do we. We may be exchanging blind pain for conscious pain, but it's still pain.

We astrologers work in an area where we tread through minefields all the time, and often we blunder in with great naivety and the highest possible ideals and aspirations. Then we realise we are dealing with something very powerful, as powerful in its own way as solar fire, and that raises a great many questions. The more we know, the more we are going to suffer, because our knowledge isolates us and also poses the dilemma of how much of it is valid and how much of it we are able to share. Whatever we do, we are not going to get it wholly right. Too much certainty of the starry-eyed Uranian kind may be quite a bad thing; it might be better to experience some anxiety and indecision, and also a healthy dose of self-doubt.

So never mind the scientists involved in genetic engineering – all of us in this room are dealing with the same kind of Uranian challenge in our own way. We say, "Isn't this exciting, look at the precision of this eclipse on the Ascendant/Midheaven midpoint of the Aries Ingress for the longitude of Bangkok when the Thai Airlines plane crashed! Look at this transit, exact within a minute of orb when Maggie Thatcher got booted out! Look at this precise Mars-Saturn conjunction at the meridian at the exact moment when the IRA bomb went off!" Then suddenly we see the same configuration in our child's chart, or our own, and we aren't quite so starry-eyed and eager any more. We play with Uranian fire too, and sometimes we don't realise how carefully and thoughtfully we need to approach it. We must never assume, because of this, that Uranus is malefic, or that its knowledge should be avoided. No planet is malefic or intrinsically destructive. But collective energies of this kind must be monitored, contained, processed, and articulated through an individual human psyche with an individual human heart and individual common sense. Without this, Uranus can unleash incredible destruction on a collective level.

Audience: What would we look for in a chart, to find these things? A heart and common sense?

Liz: I'm not sure such attributes are translatable into specific planets and configurations. But if I were trying to get a sense of who the individual is in essence, and what matters most to him or her on this deeper level, then I would look first at the Sun and Saturn. We need to be able to relate to, and express, these planets in order to have a feeling of being real and defined as individuals. Heart and common sense, whether they are solar, Saturnian, lunar, or a mixture of all of the planets, emerge from a defined individual; when these attributes are lacking, we usually find that the ego-structure is weak and unformed, and the person is still living in an infantile psychological state, and cannot make the best of the chart's potential. Then the outer planets, which represent the collective psyche, can move in and take over. But I am not sure whether the chart can tell us about ego-strength. Everyone has the Sun and Saturn, so everyone has the potential for developing these planets and what they signify on an inner level. Whether failure to develop them is due to chart aspects, poor parenting, innate character, social pressures, past lives, or a mixture of all these things, is a huge question which would take us at least two more seminars to explore.

The Sun and Saturn as containers of Uranian energy

We cannot really make sense of Uranus in the birth chart without looking at the Sun and Saturn as well, because these two are, in a way, the brackets around the individual's personality. They are the two planets most concerned with ego and ego development, and because of this they are the vessels for containing, grounding, and individualising the outer planets. This is why Saturn-Uranus aspects are so very powerful in charts. We often overlook these contacts, assuming that only people with Sun-Uranus, Moon-Uranus, or an angular Uranus are really Uranian in spirit. But people with Saturn-Uranus contacts are usually very close to Uranus, much more so than if the Moon, Mercury, Venus or Mars aspects it. Saturn-Uranus aspects are extremely important because the structure of the personality is being buffeted all the time by the collective Promethean vision of progress and potential perfection. This produces a powerful need to ground the Uranian spirit, but if the individual cannot handle the tension, he or she may polarise and identify wholly with or against Uranus.

Saturn, as you all know, co-rules Aquarius. He is the son and castrator of Uranus in myth. They are intimately linked and inseparable, and this is reflected in their joint rulership of Aquarius. The Sun is also intimately linked and inseparable, because it is solar fire that Prometheus steals, and this is reflected in Leo's natural opposition to Aquarius. Each needs the other; they are two halves of the same story. Without the fire, Prometheus would have nothing to do. He would be redundant, an unemployed Titan on the dole. Without Prometheus, humanity as a collective would have no direct experience of the Sun – solar fire would only be accessible through the artist, the ruler, and the priest, or, in other words, through the solar elite.

Modern applications of the Ouranos myth

Audience: Is there some significance to the fact that, in the myth, Cronos grabs his father's testicles with his left hand?

Liz: Yes, the symbolism is very specific in the myth, so it is telling us something. The left has always been associated with the dark, and with the subterranean realm, as well as with the feminine. Jung associated it with the unconscious. In Latin we have the word *sinister*, which has come through to us in modern Italian as *sinistra*, but *sinistra* just means "left", as in, "take a left turn at that road there". Sinister in English doesn't just mean left. It means dangerous, shady, threatening. Cronos approaches and grips his father through the unconscious side, the dark side. I could play about with this image and suggest that hard reality, represented by Saturn, curtails Uranian vision, not only through the direct confrontation of the right hand wielding the sickle of time and mortality, but through darker, more unconscious means.

The Uranian vision fails in part because of the unconscious Saturnian elements in human nature – greed, envy, feelings of inferiority, and so on.

Audience: What is the connotation of the fact that it is done with an agricultural implement? It seems to me ironic that what brings Uranian creation to an end is the abuse of a Uranian system of knowledge – agriculture is the most controlling system that we have on the planet. Maybe part of Ouranus' rejection of his children is that they are not only ugly, but too stupid to understand what they're doing. We take all these fine ideas and then invent ways to ruthlessly control nature.

Audience: That's a rather global statement. Surely there are some extremely good things about modern farming technology, especially the fact that it frees us to do things like study astrology instead of spending our lives working out in the fields.

Liz: This discussion could start getting very heated and political in a moment. That is what happens when Uranian energy is wafting about; everyone gets all fired up by abstract ideas. Yes, the sickle is an agricultural implement. It is associated with the Moon, which is sickle-shaped in its new phase, and it is a maternal gift from Gaia, so it is also a symbol of the cycles of nature. I don't think the Greeks pursued agriculture as a form of tyranny, because they hadn't yet invented pesticides, hormone injections for cattle, or monocrop culture, and in those days they didn't have any EU subsidies. For them, Cronos-Saturn was the wise and benign lord of the Golden Age, during which human beings worked in harmony with the seasons and enjoyed the fruits of their labours.

The sickle is a man-made implement which we use to harvest crops. The image of the sickle is both that of harvest – receiving the rewards of wise husbandry – and of death, of things being cut short in their prime. What seems to be making you angry is the human application of Uranian vision to practices which result in damage to the earth itself. And yes, in that sense his children are too stupid to understand. But the Titans weren't running as candidates for the Green Party, and according to Orphic teaching we all possess the Titanic nature.

Often people read the myth of Ouranos and think, "Oh, the poor Titans, they were rejected by their father." We instinctively sympathise with their rejection, because our own instincts are offended. I have even known astrologers and psychologists who have tried to make this story into a feminist issue, as though all the Titans were female, because they are earthy, and were being oppressed by a heavenly patriarchy. But perhaps the Titans really are ugly. Maybe Ouranus has a perfectly legitimate reason to want to avoid sitting down to dinner with those giants with a hundred hands.

I forgot to mention that Gaia also produced the Cyclopes, who had only one eye and ate human flesh. Ouranus had a particular dislike of them. I expect I would too, if I had to come home to one of them at night. Uranian vision can recoil from the genuine ugliness it perceives in human nature. It can do one of two things from this place of recoil. The Uranian spirit may set about trying to reform human nature, through science, psychology, sociology, or politics. Or Uranus says, "Thanks very much, I am getting out of here," and one retreats into the ivory tower of academic solitude, or tries to create an ideal community with no interaction with those horrible Titans out there. The ideal community is a very Uranian thing to do, in order to get away from the monstrous elements in human nature.

Audience: We seem to have a fear in this century of what we call subjectivity, although by subjectivity we really mean the irrational. It is as if we can't bear not having absolute material knowledge and control of the cosmos. Any perceptions which are strongly self-evident are considered subjective and therefore irrational. Is that Saturn or Uranus?

Liz: "Subjectivity" certainly seems to be a dirty word in some circles, especially to the more Uranian-minded. Depth psychology – whether Freudian, Jungian, or Kleinian – relies on an individual relationship and a body of knowledge based on individual observation rather than statistics. Because of this, it is often considered too "subjective" to be a science, and is therefore excluded from many psychology programmes at universities. For the same reason astrology is deemed "subjective", despite Gauquelin's efforts. But I am not sure it is only because subjectivity is "irrational". Uranus will often respect what is commonly called the irrational if general principles can be found which make sense of it – even if those principles are not yet acceptable to the orthodox scientific community. Uranus does not require things to be concrete. However, they must be logical, even if the logic is not corporeally demonstrable. Feelings, and imaginative perceptions, would be "irrational" to the Uranian person, unless laws can be defined to order them into a comprehensible system – thus we have psychology, as a direct result of Uranian efforts to order the irrationality of the human heart and soul.

But subjectivity is really anathema to Uranus, because it is the expression of individuality. When we are being subjective – that is, when we give voice to something which has not been agreed on by common concensus or statistical evaluation, and cannot be comprehended by logic – we are challenging the principles of the system. There is only an "I" behind subjective truth, not a "we". Uranian people can sometimes believe that truth is defined by the largest number of "we"s. Subjectivity is always on the side of the exception, not the rule. So when Uranus recoils from subjectivity, it is really saying, "Don't be so individual, because the system will fall apart if you have opinions and feelings and perceptions that are not part of it. That makes you dangerous."

In political terms, one can sometimes see the Uranian social vision getting very heavy-handed with writers and artists, who give voice to the subjective. This happened in Russia under the Communist regime. The dissidents were always the artists, who expressed a highly individual vision. They were taken away to psychiatric hospitals to be cured, because they undermined the doctrine of uniformity which is so dear to the Uranian heart. It is important to understand how paradoxical Uranus can be – or at least, how paradoxical it can seem to us, until we think more deeply about it.

On the one hand, Uranus will rebel against the norm, if the norm is perceived as stifling progress or conflicting with an ideal. But on the other hand, it will try to stamp out the dissident, if he or she does not conform to the norm – "norm" being the system which reflects the particular Uranian ideal. Try being a genuine individual, for example, within the framework of a Uranian ideal community, such as the hippie communes of the 1960's, which seemed so individualistic to the more conventionally minded. They were as collective as the collective which they so passionately opposed.

Uranus and the Enlightenment

We can now move on to that period of history which we call the Enlightenment. You probably all realise that Uranus was discovered right at the peak of the Enlightenment, and this important shift in human social and scientific perceptions is therefore a kind of materialisation of Uranus in the world, coincident or synchronous with its physical discovery. This discovery was bracketed by two political revolutions, the American and the French, both of which used as their rallying cry the concept of inalienable human rights. During the French Revolution, the goddess Reason was perceived as the highest good. If one has a black sense of humour, this could be seen as a great joke, when one thinks about the actual unfoldment of events. The French Revolution was one of the most unreasonable, chaotic, and barbaric events in the entire history of Western civilisation. It was a bloodbath. The guillotine might have removed a lot of heads, but the goddess Reason appears to have removed a great many more.

Nevertheless, a statue to the goddess Reason was erected in Paris, to celebrate this great and noble rebellion against social injustice, superstition, the power of the Church, the monarchy, and everything that belonged to the irrational side of existence. The French Revolution was born out of the spirit of the Enlightenment, which declared that human beings should not have to be subject to bondage through birth, social position, or the enslavement of nature. The ideal of inalienable human rights is without flaw. However,

----

attempting to make the omelette became exceedingly messy, and, after everyone had got heartily sick of the goddess Reason running amok, they flocked to Napoleon's thoroughly Leonine brand of subjective, unreasonable dictatorship, because it was such an incredible relief to have a bit of glamour, passion, individuality, and strong leadership again.

We tend to romanticise the Enlightenment, because we view it from the perspective of what it stands for, rather than what was actually unleashed on the human level at the time. Because the French Revolution happened two hundred years ago, we don't have to actually face what it felt like for the ordinary citizen. We can therefore say it was "good". Yet we still must ask whether the consequences were inevitable, or whether the truly liberating spirit of the Enlightenment might have been expressed on a social level in other, less destructive ways. The Uranian spirit of scientific discovery, which permeated the late 18th century, gave us a means of getting free of the awful sense of being at the mercy of irrational forces we cannot control – whether these forces are perceived as destructive human emotions, unfair social hierarchies based on wealth or blood, or the domination of religious institutions. When Uranus runs amok, one may adopt science as a religious doctrine. Only that which is logically and rationally provable constitutes reality. Anything which must be perceived through an "irrational" function of consciousness doesn't exist.

Audience: Then Uranus is opposed to mysticism.

Liz: Yes, I think it is very much opposed to mysticism. Within modern esoteric circles, we may sometimes hear a very funny cross-dialogue, because the incoming spirit of the time, the *zeitgeist,* is Uranian, and there is a strong need to develop cosmic systems which explain the laws of the universe. The inner motivating power behind many esoteric groups is Neptunian – the last gasp (or gurgle) of the outgoing Piscean energy – because beneath the pseudo-scientific surface, the ancient longing to be one with God is very strong. The devotional element of Neptune can be sensed immediately, even if one is showered with diagrams and theories. But there may be a great sense of shame about being Neptunian at the moment, because, of course, it means one is a raving loony. One is "irrational" and "subjective". So one must come up with a system which sounds scientific, in order to present one's mysticism in a form which is acceptable to an increasingly Uranus-dominated world-view.

Some very odd hybrids come out of this. If you go along to one of the annual "Festival of Mind and Body" events, or something similar, you will see an extraordinary mixture of Neptunians disguised as Uranians, and Uranians disguised as Neptunians. Equally, you may find them in the sciences, and astrology, naturally, is full to the brim with elusive, irridescent Fish pretending they are sober, rational Water-carriers, and Water-carriers brightly costumed in shimmering fish-scales. Uranus is the enemy of mysticism in the sense that mysticism is a direct, subjective experience of deity, for which there is no rational explanation. The mystical experience is a subjective, transient, inexplicable moment of fusion which cannot even be articulated, let alone proven or fitted into a system of logical principles. And it happens to one individual, a unique experience, unavailable to those who are not "prepared" or "evolved". This is anathema to Uranus. So the Uranian spirit comes up with systems – sometimes a highly creative system such as transpersonal psychology – to embed the mystical experience in a framework which makes sense to the intellect.

Uranus in the houses of the horoscope

Shall we start looking at Uranus in the houses? After exploring the mythic background, we need to get a sense of what happens when the Promethean spirit is incarnated in an individual horoscope. I know there are one or two associations I have not covered, but I think we should move on to the actual astrology, and if possible I will pick up these associations later, as we go along.

As a general approach to understanding the house placement of Uranus, I think it is useful to think of the houses as stage sets representing particular spheres of life. The houses are like the empty stage at the beginning of the play, before the actors appear, and each one has its characteristic decor, furniture, and objects, according to the domain which the house rules and the sign on the cusp of the house. We all have the same twelve houses in our chart, and they are the broad arenas in which we seek and encounter life experiences. A house in the abstract sense has no backdrop and no lighting; this is dependent on the sign on the cusp, which gives it its particular colouration. But then the actors come on stage, and these are the planets. Then we are going to meet something very powerful in this sphere of life, and we will have to engage in a dialogue, and involve ourselves in the drama.

One of the best sources I have come across for understanding the houses at a deeper level is the Roman writer Manilius, who, in the *Astronomica*[10], calls each house a *templum.* The Romans used this word both astrologically and to signify a place where people went to worship, just as we use the word now. But the Roman definition of a temple was any empty building or site which was designated for sacred purposes. The living presence of the deity wasn't in evidence until the cult statue of the god was placed in the temple. So one could find a temple without a cult statue, and such a building remained devoid of *numen,* and stood empty or was temporarily used for secular purposes. It was designated as sacred, but no experience of the divine could occur within, because the god was not present.

A *templum* of the horoscope is exactly the same. It is a designated sacred site, but we only encounter the gods – the archetypal life-patterns which we experience as our "destiny" – when there is a planet placed in the house. Without a planet, we experience this sphere of life primarily on the "secular" level – that is, we can more or less manage its affairs through the ego's functions, without feeling that we are encountering fated happenings. But when a planet is present, then we meet power, *numen,* or, in psychological terms, we meet an archetypal pattern which seems to take over in that area of our life, and pervades all our everyday experiences. Beneath the

---

[10]Manilius, *Astronomica,* trans. G. P. Goold, Harvard University Press and William Heinemann, Ltd., London, 1977, 2.856-967.

surface of mundane events can be seen the traces of a much deeper meaning and intelligence at work.

Uranus will be in one of the twelve *templa* in everyone's chart. So what is it that we meet in this sphere of life? One way or another, the Promethean spirit is going to find a way to colour and shape our experiences, whether we recognise it or not. When we encounter Uranus, it tends to fill us with anxiety, because it is so impersonal in nature. It is usually alien to the precepts in which we have been brought up, and it may threaten our security, emotionally and materially. At first, we don't know what to do with it. Often our early experiences of Uranus are the classic experiences of sudden separation or upheaval, at an age when we cannot bring any real consciousness to bear on it. Therefore we usually react by trying to control matters, strenuously attempting to keep things "normal" and stable in this sphere of life, and attempting to deal with the advent of the unpredictable in ways which preserve the illusion that the ego is in charge. But, of course, we can't get away with this indefinitely, because Uranus will keep on disrupting every attempt we make to deal with those issues of life according to the conventional attitudes and accepted wisdom of the world in which one lives.

Now, you might think that, if we understood this, we could accept Uranus' demand for change and new vision, and consciously make room for it. Then, in theory, we wouldn't have to suffer Uranian explosions. Let's consider, for example, Uranus in the 10th house. For the moment, we will leave aside the deeper psychological implications of the 10th and its relevance to the mother-image. If Uranus is in the 10th, what is the work one is called to do? What is one's place in society? Those of you with this placement will undoubtedly know that, with Uranus breathing down one's neck, one can't just go out and get any old job with a nice established business or company, in order to earn a secure living. One can try, and one might be able to struggle on for three weeks, or even three years. But sooner or later, either the individual with Uranus in the 10th, or the people around him or her, will ensure that it all blows up.

Deep within, there is a vision of potential, of new possibilities, that makes it impossible to live with what is conventionally accepted as "proper work" or a "normal" place in society. Usually this is an archetypal quality which comes down through the mother and the mother's line, although the mother may not have been able to live the Uranian spirit creatively, and may have acted it out through mental instability or erratic behaviour. But the mother is not to blame for the individual's problems with "normal" society. The sort of difficulties which Uranus often encounters with authority, when it is in the 10th, are related to a deep-rooted sense of inalienable human rights, which will rebel against hierarchical structures if they have no genuine inner authenticity. And Uranus will fight against the humdrum and the banal, because it carries a vision of a Brave New World to which one can make a meaningful contribution.

In the area of life ruled by the house in which Uranus is placed, we all long, consciously or unconsciously, to be Prometheus and offer the world the gift of fire. The classic job difficulties of Uranus in the 10th don't occur because some nasty fate has imposed it. It is because there is a Promethean spirit within the individual, that is impelled to strive toward a different, freer place in a different, freer world. This spirit perceives society as imperfect and in need of change and reform, and the individual will seek, consciously or unconsciously, to be part of the vanguard which ushers in new social possibilities. Anything less is likely to be incredibly boring, soulless and depressing.

Any good textbook will describe a range of concrete manifestations which may be associated with Uranus in the 10th. You will probably be familiar with these. Disruption at work, an unconventional job, difficulties with authority or with work colleagues, the need to find independence in one's work, an eccentric or disturbing public image – these are all typical expressions which are usually mentioned in the books. I can think of lots of good examples to illustrate these expressions; I am sure you can think of some as well. On the less attractive side, the American politician, Joseph McCarthy, had Uranus in Capricorn in the 10th, conjunct the MC and opposing Neptune.[11] As some of you may know, he initiated the virulently anti-

---

[11]Birth data for Senator Joe McCarthy from *Internationales Horoskope Lexikon, ibid.,* p. 265.

communist, anti-semitic socio-political climate in America in the 1950's, which inspired Arthur Miller to write *The Crucible* and compare McCarthy's tactics to a 17th century witch hunt. Every artist and writer with a high public profile was suspect, particularly if he or she was Jewish. Before we assume that the Uranian social vision is always on the side of democracy and liberal thinking, we should remember Senator Joe McCarthy.

On a brighter note, Charles Addams, the ghoulish-minded cartoonist who created the Addams Family, had Uranus exactly at the MC, also in Capricorn.[12] I have always had a special fondness for him, because he attended the same school I did, although a good thirty-five years earlier, so I never met him. But stories were still circulating, when I was at school, about the dreadful tricks he played, such as putting dead rats in the ventilation system. Uranus in the 10th does love to shock.

We also have classic "mundane" examples, such as the founding of the American Federation of Astrologers under an exact Sun-Uranus conjunction at the MC – no doubt an elected chart. But all these examples are the external manifestations of a culminating Uranus, the outer result of an individual meeting the god in the temple. What is the nature of the god? And what does it demand from us? Wherever Uranus is placed in the natal chart, this is the place where the *zeitgeist* is going to erupt into one's life, and the more one clings to the known and the conventional, the more trouble one is likely to have.

Now, it is all very well to say, "Jolly good, here is Uranus in the 10th, I'll become an astrologer." Or one might think the solution lies in involving oneself in social causes or progressive new ideas. But it may be emotionally very difficult to follow this good advice, unless the time is right and the individual is ready. With the outer planets, we need to always bear in mind the fact that they are impersonal and in many ways threatening to the ego's sense of security – even if they look great on paper. The nature of Uranus is antithetical to the solar sense of individual aspiration, and usually, even if one has a very airy chart and lots of nice aspects to Uranus, it will hurt to pursue the

---

[12]Birth data for Charles Addams from *Internationales Horoskope Lexikon, ibid.*, p. 34.

Uranian vision. The potential suffering and isolation of Prometheus are always there in the background, and we sense this, and usually only come to follow the path of the Titan when we have found that all other paths are closed to us.

Of course there are exceptions. But what usually happens is that, during the first half of life, we do our best to pretend Uranus isn't there. We may unconsciously project it and have it firmly pasted on someone else, and if we encounter Uranian disruption, then we may feel we have been subjected to a kind of psychological terrorist attack by that other person. Someone abandons us, or tears away our security, or overturns our existing structures, and we can't any longer hold on to the thing we were trying so hard to preserve for the sake of stability. And at that point there may, with a little luck, be some dawning recognition of the fact that one actually needed the explosion, even if it is a parent, partner, child, friend, colleague, or external collective situation which lit the fuse. Very often people fight desperately against Uranus because they want so badly to belong.

The issues that mitigate against our ability to acknowledge Uranus are varied. Obviously we must consider aspects to Uranus from the other planets, and some of them may be harmonious. But, in general, one very important factor that makes us fight our Promethean spirit is our need to feel emotionally bonded and secure within a family, community, or group based on emotional affinities and a sense of roots. It is, if you like, our lunar needs which make us resist Uranus' gift of fire. To pursue the Promethean vision may mean being cut off from family and community, and one may wind up feeling isolated, different, and outcast. One might not be able to enjoy the "normal" luxury of marriage, children, and a house in the suburbs. To steal fire with Prometheus may mean living with chronic instability. Not surprisingly, we may try to refuse Uranus' call, because of the suffering it may create on the emotional level.

Another thing that may mitigate against our ability to honour Uranus is that one may be required to gamble on an idea, without any guarantees. This threatens our Saturnian need for certainty and reliable structures. Uranus is the enemy of earth in more ways than just a disapproval of earthly imperfection. Uranus may threaten earth's

----

fundamental reliance on material structure and stability, and many people are not prepared to trust the intangible promises of the ideal world which Uranus offers as an alternative. If we pursue a principle or an ideal, then the instinct to make everything safe is constantly going to be challenged. There is something in all of us that is animal-like. We like to know where our bed is, and where our food bowl is, and what time they are serving dinner. Those of you who keep pets will know that animals are creatures of habit. Your cat wants its water bowl in the same place every day, and its litter box must never be moved. If you start moving these things around the house in an unpredictable fashion, the cat will suffer enormous anxiety, and will begin to act very strangely.

We too are creatures of habit. When we go to our front door, we want to know that the door is where we last saw it, and the stairs are the same and haven't suddenly moved. Our toothbrush handle is the same colour that it was yesterday, and we take out our credit card and there is our name on it, not somebody else's. We have countless little rituals that are the same every day. Usually we take these for granted. Although we rarely think about them, they allow us to feel safe, because these rituals give us an earth-identity, a sense of continuity in the world of form. But if one is being driven by the Promethean daemon of progressive vision, then these little rites and rituals are likely to be ignored or bypassed, because any opportunity to promulgate the vision, any opportunity to create change, must be taken; and to hell with stability and structure.

Uranus can generate terrible anxiety. It is the most characteristic emotional reaction to this planet's advent by transit or progressed aspect. It is also characteristic of certain natal placements involving Uranus, especially Uranus-Moon contacts, which thwart instinctual needs and turn them in new directions. More than any other response, Uranus provokes anxiety, even in a strongly Uranian person who can also see the exciting possibilities. This anxiety comes from the animal part of us, the instinctual part that wants our earthly rituals to be safe and secure. We want to know where we are on the earth plane, and where to find things, and how to navigate. We want to know that everything will be as we last left it, and this applies

----

emotionally as well as materially. So any change of a Uranian kind –
which usually means a change in basic structures – is likely to be felt
as threatening. Often people will react to this anxiety by refusing to
deal with the thing that is upon them. This is why Uranus has such a
bad reputation for creating explosions that one didn't ask for. We may
make the mistake of fighting too hard against Promethean fire,
because it makes us feel so dreadfully unsafe.

Audience: Could anxiety be the reason why the Uranian person is
driven to be inventive?

Liz: Uranus is inventive because that is its nature. It is not a reaction
to something else. But Uranus is one of eleven planets in the birth
chart, and the other ten may not be quite so enthusiastic about stealing
fire. Uranus has got some friends among the planetary pantheon –
mainly Mercury and Jupiter, and sometimes Venus, if she is in a more
cerebral mood. But the Uranian vision arouses terror in the Moon and
Saturn, and it can get the Sun and Mars pretty angry and worked up as
well, because they are made to feel selfish and unimportant. The
anxiety we feel in the presence of Uranus is experienced at a gut and
feeling level, because we know instinctively that we will have to let
go of something on which we have been emotionally or materially
dependent. The Uranian person may fear the symbolic castration
caused by too much structure, because then potentials may be stifled.
Uranus may often be heard to say, "I feel trapped." But this isn't the
same kind of anxiety that the lunar/Saturnian side of us feels when
confronted with Uranian transits and progressions. Uranus itself
generates a fear that one's vision will be destroyed by the density and
finality of the mundane world.

Uranus is not, in itself, "creative" as the Sun is. It reflects our
capacity, as human beings, to attune ourselves to the larger system,
and the sudden recognition of this bigger universe often has the effect
of shattering our existing world-view. This can make us either run in
panic, or leap forward without regard for the consequences. Uranus
symbolises our capacity to perceive a cosmic order which exists in life,
an interconnected network which is *a priori* and stands behind

material manifestation. This is why it can move into scientific, political, psychological, and esoteric directions with equal ease. The inventiveness of Uranus is not the same as the Sun's magical ability to create something individual out of the imagination. It is the capacity to "tap" the workings of the system, so that a sudden inspiration appears full-blown. The person has not created this; he or she has received it.

As long as human beings have recorded their perceptions, they have described some kind of cosmic order. We don't know whether they are describing an objective universal order, or are projecting a psychological order onto the cosmos. But in practice it doesn't matter; they are describing something that is a fundamental part of human life experience. The revelation of the system, or of some part of the system, inevitably reveals potentials for collective evolution and eventual perfection that haven't yet been fulfilled. That is when Uranus starts banging against the bars. When it does this, the Saturnian and lunar sides of us get very panicky, because if this thing breaks out, all hell might break loose. Often it does.

The sphere in which all hell is likely to break loose will be described by the house in which Uranus is placed. Hell may break loose because one has opened the door and let the daimon out voluntarily, the moment one hears it knocking, in which case one can, to some extent, consciously participate in and work with what emerges. But hell may break loose also because one has tried to nail the door shut, just at the moment when the daimon was intending to come out. Transits and progressed aspects tend to tell us when that time has arrived. But even if we know about transits or progressions involving Uranus, we may think we can trick the daimon and bend it to the will of the ego. This is usually a great mistake. How many of you have had Uranus smash down the door without your conscious consent? I see that a good many hands are up. Afterwards, did any of you have the sense that maybe there was something within you that needed the explosion? Ah, I see many nods and smiles.

This is hindsight, of a special and particularly important kind, and it is also connected with Uranus. It isn't the sort of hindsight which comes from painstakingly mulling over an experience and extracting conclusions. The revelations of Uranus often follow on the heels of disturbing experiences, and it is hindsight which allows us to put them in perspective and realise what they are showing us. In myth, Prometheus had a brother called Epimetheus, whose name means "hindsight". After Uranus has wreaked havoc or wrought major changes, we usually recognise what has been in operation, and this is the moment when our world-view is changed forever. Before and during its activity, we often don't understand what is happening, because we are in such a state of panic. We think this planet comes at us as though it were a random blow of fate. But it isn't. It is our own Promethean spirit, but it isn't an individual spirit, and it may not ask permission from the ego before it begins to move. It is moving on the collective level, and impinges on our personal lives. It is something that we share in common with other people, but we experience it as though it were uniquely our own experience.

So the person with Uranus in the 10th is not going to go blinding off into the blue to deliberately become someone whom society may pillory. Individual values usually pull the person in another direction, unless the Sun is conjunct Uranus, but a voice intervenes, which says, "You might not like this, but you are an example of a particular kind of rebellious spirit, and whether you like it or not, you are carrying this for other people. You are carrying it for your family, and especially for your mother, who probably had the same spirit, but couldn't live it. You are also carrying it for your generation, and the worldly arena is the area where you have got to enact it. You are a mouthpiece, on however small a scale, for certain new ideals and visions which the collective is presently seeking. Pursue your personal hopes and dreams elsewhere, but in the eyes of the world, learn to steal fire gracefully, because if you don't, you will be caught with it in your pocket anyway."

Whereas one's best friend may get to enact the Promethean story through the 2nd or the 5th or the 7th house, the person with it in the 10th is carrying the collective spirit of the time on the world's stage; one's work is not for oneself, but for the collective. I mentioned Senator Joe McCarthy earlier, as an example of a rather unpleasant manifestation of Uranus. But he no doubt believed he was giving voice to the wishes of the people, and indeed he was. He would never have been listened to if the American public had not been shaken by a need to be aware of the wider world.

However, McCarthy had Neptune at the IC in opposition to Uranus, and internal conflicts connected with his own background probably made him seek a "subversive" Neptunian scapegoat on whom to unload all the imperfections he perceived in the society around him. And the same might be said of the American public, who, at the time, could not really cope with an alternative ideology such as communism without reacting in a rather paranoid fashion. We don't really have the time to go into either McCarthy's or America's chart to understand why the Uranian vision became so dogmatic and destructive. But in its nascent form it was truly Uranian, and its object was a perfect society.

The consciousness-raising function of Uranus often collides with personal values. It is often not what we would have wanted as individuals. It is also often not what we would have wanted as a collective either, because it may collide with collective feeling values as well. We may not like what has happened, or what we are doing, or what we wind up representing. We may deeply oppose Uranian change, but in this area, our individual values may be mown down, and we may have to recognise that we are part of something in the collective that is seeking to change.

Uranus in the 1st house

How many of you have Uranus in the 1st house? What is this house about?

Audience: Self-image. A sense of personal identity.

Liz: Yes, this is the house of one's personal image. It is also concerned with our perception of the environment. It is often called "the environment" because it is what we project into the environment. The signs and planets connected with the 1st house are what we see when we look out of the window of our enclosed little psychic houses, so it is our view of life, which in turn shapes how we act when we are out in life. Our personal image is governed by how we define life. The 1st house describes what we think is out there, because it is the way we interpret our world. Therefore every time we step out into the world – from birth onward – we exhibit certain qualities which we define as outer reality, and we justify our own behaviour by what we experience as the world's response to us. On the deepest level, the 1st house represents one's view of life, one's world-view, one's perception of reality. So if Uranus is placed here, what do we see?

Audience: I have Uranus in the 1st, and I see life as unpredictable. But I also believe it ought to be unpredictable, and we should always be prepared for that. I also see myself as someone who tends to have the effect of waking other people up. I don't try to do this. But situations sometimes explode when I am around, and I suppose I see myself as a catalyst.

Liz: The 1st house is not only how we perceive the environment, but also what we bring to the environment. The 1st house is therefore concerned with our interaction with others. It is part of that horizontal axis which also involves the 7th house, and the 1st house is as relevant to relationship issues as the 7th. But the difference is that we think the 7th is other people, while we generally work out, after a while, that the 1st is ourselves. Uranus in the 1st may become the voice of a more enlightened or more inclusive world-view. Sometimes it's just somebody very disruptive, who has a Uranian effect on people around them.

Audience: I always used to feel I was abnormal. Now that I know I am a kind of catalyst, I feel I have a purpose.

Liz: With Uranus in the 1st, there may need to be a willingness to appear abnormal to the outside world. If one tries terribly hard to present an acceptable image to the collective, things often go wrong, and one is "suspect" anyway. People pick up the energy underneath the carefully maintained exterior, and they respond accordingly.

But there is something in what you are saying that makes me wonder whether such complete identification with Uranian energy is a good idea. Uranus is not a personal planet, and when you talk about a "purpose" in relation to being a Uranian catalyst, it makes me slightly uneasy. I don't doubt that you can sometimes act as a catalyst in situations where something has gone stale and needs a bit of shaking up. But it is the Sun, not Uranus, which is really the vessel for a sense of purpose in life. We need to look more closely at the role of the Sun in processing Uranus, which I would like to do a little later. Although you are probably deeply attuned to collective currents going on around you, it might be wiser to build a stronger sense of identity through the personal planets in the chart. Also, if you treat a propensity to be disruptive as a kind of cosmic life-task, then you are unable to take any responsibility for the effects. And unconscious personal issues can get mixed up with Uranian vision, just as they tend to do with everything. Then the disruptiveness may not always be creative or helpful, and you might not be able to discern what deeper and perhaps darker personal motives might be involved.

One of the things Uranus in the 1st seems to suggest, on the external level, is a very changeful life, in terms of lifestyle, environment, where one lives and whom one lives with. The moment one tries to nail everything down and create a nice secure environment, things tend to start erupting, because there is an inner need to live with a certain amount of flux.

Audience: Every time I try to make my environment stable, bang! everything is destroyed. Now I don't try any more. It's better to just travel light than to have everything constantly blowing up on you.

Liz: Uranus has a way of forcing us to rely on something other than the tangible world and the conventional definitions of normality. What you are expressing – travelling light – is probably the most creative way of working with Uranus. But this doesn't necessarily mean eschewing material security. It has to do with an attitude toward life.

If you are prepared to allow fluidity, and can accept changes in plans with equanimity rather than a ferocious determination to exercise control, you may not have to be uprooted all the time on the concrete level. This is learning to carry a light psychological suitcase. Uranus doesn't always necessitate material disruption when it is in the 1st house. Often this seems to be in proportion to the flexibility, or lack thereof, of the person's world-view. Sometimes change may be necessary, but I suspect that many people ignore the inner levels on which Uranian vision can be expressed, and therefore the planet has only the material avenue through which it can operate. We do have something to say about the level through which Uranus is expressed.

Such flexibility is revolutionary, and not only because it appears so in context of the prevailing social climate. It feels revolutionary to those lunar and Saturnian needs which I have been mentioning, and it probably always will, because these two planets, natural rulers of the 4th and 10th houses, are concerned with roots, stability, and an anchor in the past. Certainly in most Western countries we tend to equate a stable lifestyle with psychological health. We consider the "gypsies" and "New Age Travellers" abnormal, because they are always on the move. Our current definitions of normality teach us that, if one is a mature adult and relatively stable, one will live in one place with one person, and hold one job. But this is not just a recent social expectation. The desire for land, for possessions, for permanence, is fundamental to the earthy side of human nature.

If one is a wanderer, moving every year, with multiple partners or changeful relationships, or if one has an "eccentric" environment with a *menage à trois,* or one lives in a commune, or one's partner is the same sex as oneself – then one is suspect. Uranus in the 1st tends to kick against those patterns of behaviour in the outer world which are perceived as stable and mature – not because it is inimical to a good relationship or the enjoyment of a stable home, but because so often these things are used as definitions of the "right" way to be a human being. That is what the Promethean spirit rebels against. Uranus in the 1st says, "Sorry, but human nature is greater and more varied than that. It cannot be categorised by a particular code of behaviour. It cannot be judged by material standards. Many things are possible, and many kinds of human beings have a right to exist on the earth."

Now, this Uranian voice probably sounds very noble and democratic to many of you. But when one hears it inside, it can be very painful, especially if one has several planets in Taurus, Cancer, or Capricorn, or a strong Saturn. One may experience the awful feeling that one is bonkers, that something is seriously wrong. But one can't get therapy for a 1st house Uranus. It isn't curable.

Audience: I also have Uranus in the 1st house, and a couple of things have occurred to me. I was about to make some comments about what I thought about Uranus in the 1st, but then I heard this inner voice saying, "Shut up!" That reminded that I am of the generation with Uranus conjunct Pluto, so it is very difficult to talk about one without talking about the other. Pluto is the one that keeps telling me to shut up. This combination in my first house makes me try to live my life making sense of everything. I keep trying to make sense of some very impersonal, Uranian ideas, and at the same time I am strongly repelled by power issues which I find hard to deal with. It is difficult to differentiate whether it is Pluto or Uranus talking.

Liz: These two outer planets will operate together when in conjunction, and they will certainly reflect a powerful receptivity to collective movements and ideas, but I believe it is also possible to get a sense of their different voices. In some ways they are antithetical in nature, because Uranus operates on a cerebral level, while Pluto is connected with powerful instinctual drives. While Uranus is envisioning the Brave New World, Pluto is busy working out how to best defend itself from attack.

I did want to talk about this conjunction more fully later, because the Uranus-Pluto conjunction is a generational issue. There may also be quite a few people here with the Uranus-Saturn conjunction, which occurred during the early 1940's. And of course there was a long Uranus-Neptune square, starting in Cancer and Libra and then moving into Leo and Scorpio, during the 1950's. These major Uranian aspects

----

stamp entire groups of people, who seem to embody particular Uranian issues in their lives as a generation. Could we go back to this later? Are there any other comments from people with Uranus in the 1st?

Audience: I have Uranus in the 1st, but it's conjunct Saturn. I belong to that 1940's group you just mentioned. I am trying to understand how these two work together. I experience a lot of conflict between the strong ideas I hold, and a constant feeling of shyness and reluctance to express myself. I find myself thinking, "If only Uranus were free, and I didn't have Saturn sitting on it!"

Liz: We need to go back again to the importance of the Sun and Saturn in containing Uranian vision, because when Uranus speaks it is usually ideological, and often unrelated to how the person actually feels. It may also be unrelated to how other people feel. If a rising Uranus vocalises its world-view, it will usually be in terms of a system of some kind, and often there are strong political or esoteric allegiances, sometimes quite rigid. One has the Truth, with an upper-case "T". Now that truth may be the Truth for the Uranian individual, but it may not be other people's truth. And it might not even be true for all dimensions of oneself.

Saturn's shyness, which might be seen as a "bad" thing because it causes so much sensitivity and vulnerability, may serve to restrain the Uranian tendency to proselytise. The caution and reserve you feel may reflect the wisdom of recognising that your ideas might not be right and valid for everyone, and may need to be tested by experience. Saturn can also help you to recognise that the Promethean vision is not likely to come true at 3.00 next Thursday afternoon; it is an ideal toward which one aspires. The conjunction is likely to be quite uncomfortable, because Saturn will often interfere with your ability to express Uranus freely. But perhaps Uranus needs a little tempering, rather than blind unleashing. You may come to realise that Saturn is giving you some extremely valuable self-critical faculties, which can allow you to involve your feeling values, and adapt your ideas to the real world and the real people with whom you interact.

I keep mentioning Hitler because I believe much of his power was connected with Uranus on his Ascendant. Here is an ideology speaking, not an individual. That is the dark extreme of Uranus unleashed without containment, and there is no mistaking the fanaticism which comes through. So there has to be somebody home, a resident ego which can say, "Well, yes, this is a wonderful vision, but is it actually workable? And am I taking other people's reality into account? And what about my own reality? Have I thought this through sufficiently in terms of my own limitations?" This is what Saturn is asking, and you might be wise to see Saturn as a friend rather than an oppressor. Saturn, because it is related to self-questioning and self-doubt, keeps us humble.

Uranus in the 7th house

Let's look at Uranus in the opposite house, the 7th. We should always consider the houses in pairs, because opposite houses are related in meaning. How many of you have it in the 7th? Good, enough for you to give some feedback. As you will no doubt know, Uranus has a bad reputation in the 7th, because relationships tend to prove unstable. Divorce is sometimes associated with this placement. It is probably not a good idea, if one has Uranus in the 7th, to get married at twenty-one and assume one is going to live happily ever after. Why not?

Audience: The person's ideals may be too high.

Liz: Sometimes. But often the person has not consciously got high ideals. He or she may simply want a nice, normal, steady relationship. But Uranus in the 7th may explode, not because the ideals are too high, but because the person has been trying to live a collectively acceptable role in relationship, and he or she needs something much more flexible and progressive. As with the 1st house, the more one tries to nail down a 7th house Uranus and fulfill conventional definitions of what a normal relationship is, the more badly behaved the planet is likely to be. It will explode. It seems to be very important, with Uranus in the 7th, to allow relationships to be whatever they are, regardless of whether the sexual or social roles are "acceptable", and regardless of whether there is a signed and sealed promise of permanence.

Despite the apparently more enlightened attitude we presently have toward relationships which might not have not been countenanced socially thirty or forty years ago, we are not all that enlightened deep down. We may be marginally more tolerant, but we still think that normal people settle down with one partner, have families, and raise their children. If, by the time one has reached the second half of life, one has not fulfilled this set of expectations, clearly one is peculiar in some way.

We are superficially more accepting of homosexual relationships, for example, but one has only to hear some of the comments offered by the British Armed Forces to realise that nothing much has changed in Middle England since the 19th century. I believe it is much worse in America, where certain states are now overturning their laws to make homosexuality a criminal offence once again. A relationship between an older woman and a younger man still has the power to shock, although one between an older man and a younger woman is considered "normal"; and an older person who chooses to live alone and enjoys a lover without making a commitment to marriage and family is considered emotionally adolescent or disturbed.

We aren't enlightened at all, despite our newfound political correctness. All that has happened is that we now have a legal apparatus through which we can fight if we get thrown out of a job because of our gender or sexual proclivities. But although legislation may be necessary and constructive in certain spheres, it can do nothing to foster genuine broad-mindedness. Sometimes it even has the reverse effect, and entrenches deep-rooted prejudices. In many respects we are still rather Victorian about our personal relationships, and nowhere is this more apparent than when we encounter the often eccentric relationship patterns of Uranus in the 7th – especially if it is oneself. Do any of you who have it in the 7th wish to comment?

Audience: I have Uranus in the 7th. It seems to have disrupted all the best efforts of my Libran Ascendant. Uranus is also square my chart ruler, Venus, which is in the 4th.

Liz: I find it interesting that you say "it" has disrupted your best efforts, rather than considering that something within you might need or be attracted to such disruption. This is often what we do with Uranus – we disown it, as though it had nothing to do with with us, but is a kind of "ghost in the machine" which malevolently overturns all our plans. Uranus – or, more accurately, the Uranian spirit – will certainly disrupt all one's best efforts at partnership, if one's best efforts are modelled merely on what is socially acceptable, or on a desire for safety. Uranus strives toward a vision of partnership which allows for more flexible interaction than what is presently considered "normal". Sometimes this is extremely difficult to achieve, because "flexible" may involve sudden separation, or discovering that a relationship can exist even when the partner is absent. Yet unless we make room for such flexibility in our attitudes toward relationships, there may be some quite spectacular blowups.

Audience: Eventually I did end up happily married, although it took a while. But I also have Pluto opposite Venus, and my husband died.

Liz: It is sometimes extremely difficult to see where one's conscious participation could have changed things in a situation like yours, and Uranus is sometimes associated with the experience of sudden loss. Perhaps, in the end, all one can say is that somewhere deep within, there is a pattern at work which necessitates impermanence, because this tends to open up other, noncorporeal levels of relating. One way or another, impermanence is likely to affect one's attitudes toward patnership, and not necessarily through anyone's fault. That is the most difficult side of Uranus. Sometimes things happen which cannot be got round by saying, "All right, on some unconscious level I am responsible for this." Sometimes one isn't responsible. And yet somehow one's choices, even if they are the right ones and the happy ones, still wind up leading to that situation of impermanence. There is a great mystery around why what happens to us, happens.

Audience: Are you saying that, if a person has Uranus in the 7th, they need to accept impermanence?

Liz: I am saying something like that, although "impermanence" may not be as stark and literal as a death or a divorce. It may also involve shifting emotional states, or periodic times of withdrawal. The ability to cope with life's flux, through maintaining a vision of the pattern behind the flux, is one of Uranus' gifts, and it is worth working at. Without it, we may feel at the mercy of an unknown future. When the planet is in the 7th, the anxiety of not having absolute guarantees carved in stone may be something one has to learn to live with.

This really involves being open to behaviour patterns and ideas that are not part of the conscious collective canon. It doesn't mean that one's life must always be upheaved. But I think there needs to be a willingness to accept upheaval if it does occur, with a certain open-minded attitude toward the future and toward the potentially positive and releasing effects of change and loss. Putting it rather more starkly, Uranus asks us to put our personal feelings aside and look at the bigger picture. Loss, separation, and disruption are always painful, and we may feel we haven't deserved it. But if one can lift one's vision up to a more objective level, one might discern a pattern at work which has to do with a broader evolutionary process – not only one's own, but that of one's generation as well.

With Uranus in the 7th, a stable relationship may sometimes seem like living in a house in which all the doors are locked. Even if one is not conscious of one's psychic claustrophobia, something inside wants to start banging on those doors. The knowledge that they are all locked is very unpleasant, so one begins to rattle the handles and shout, "Let me out!" If someone opens a door and says, "Look, this door is open, you can leave when you like," the chances are that one won't need to leave. Because one knows one is free to go, one may well decide to stay around. But the moment someone says, "You are not allowed to leave. You have to stay. We have a marriage certificate, a mortgage, responsibilities toward the children, and your mother to look after, and what will people think?" then the impulse to get out can become quite compulsive. It is a question of metaphorically leaving a door open, which may be very difficult if one is too conventionally minded, or too identified with rigid relationship roles.

Uranus is a bit tougher in some houses than in others. It's very much at home in the 9th, for example. But it can prove to be quite painful in the 7th, because one's emotional needs may be compromised or even entirely overruled by the demand to find a new and more flexible mode of relating. The fear of loneliness, and the need for permanence, are very basic human attributes, and Uranus in the 7th may make it impossible for these needs to be met with any guarantee of safety. One may have stability for a long time, but one can never take it for granted. So a 7th house Uranus can be very challenging, because it requires us to leave a door open and accept the possibility of relationships whose longevity depends upon mental or spiritual, rather than emotional or physical, continuity. This is easier for some people than for others, depending on the aspects Uranus makes to other planets, and the overall balance of elements in the chart. It is perhaps harder for people dominated by earth and water signs.

Audience: What about Aquarius on the 7th house cusp?

Liz: A sign is not the same as a planet, although of course Aquarius will reflect Uranian, as well as Saturnian, qualities. A sign on the cusp of a house describes the stage set, the ambience surrounding a particular area of life, but it does not describe the actors or their interchange. Aquarius on the 7th house cusp may give a certain colouration to one's attitudes toward relationship – an appreciation of friendship, for example, or an attraction toward people who are intellectually exciting and emotionally self-contained.

One also interacts with others in Aquarian style, and this often means partnerships in which the element of intellectual and spiritual affinity is extremely important. Also, when Aquarius is on the 7th, Leo is on the Ascendant as a matter of course, and one's relationships might then provide a necessary restraint and detachment to balance the exuberance and self-expressive inclinations of Leo. But when a planet is placed in a house, it is like meeting a god. There is an archetypal pattern at work, a kind of vortex of energy in which one immediately becomes caught up. The moment one enters the affairs of that house, all the matters concerned are affected by the planet. A sign on a cusp doesn't have this kind of power.

Audience: I have Uranus in the 7th, virtually unaspected, and I have experienced quite unusual relationships with some very eccentric and difficult people. Does the lack of aspects mean I would be inclined to project Uranus on my partners?

Liz: Even if it were strongly aspected, there might still be a tendency to project Uranus. We tend to do this with any planet in the 7th – at least in the first half of life – and we are especially inclined to do it with painful planets such as Saturn and Chiron, and with the outer planets, because they can seem so impersonal and intimidating. Planets in the 7th often feel alien to the way we want to perceive ourselves. A lack of aspects to other planets might increase the planet's lack of connection to ego-consciousness. So the classic pattern of attracting Uranian partners may be called into play, and the instability may appear to come from the other person. Of course it isn't the other person's "fault" that a relationship doesn't work out, even if he or she really is very erratic and uncommitted. It is your own unconscious need which draws you toward such partners, who are acting out something within you.

Great flexibility is probably required of you in your interaction with others, whether you like it or not. I am not sure what you mean by "difficult" people, but you might be surprised to discover that you yourself can be quite difficult to pin down. If you find it too painful or distressing to acknowledge your own issues around freedom and resistance to commitment, then Uranian people will prove extremely attractive, because they will do for you what you are not prepared to do for yourself. But then you may feel like their victim, rather than recognising your own investment in the instability of the relationship.

Audience: Is it harder for me because it is unaspected?

Liz: By "harder" I assume you mean more painful. Yes, possibly, because it may be more difficult to take the Uranian spirit on board as something you can relate to personally. It doesn't mean that this is impossible, but it may be a long process, probably lasting at least until the time of Uranus' opposition to its own place. It is easier if there are strong aspects from Uranus to the personal planets; one then usually knows, relatively early in life, that the disruptive and rebellious spirit is at least partly one's own. When Uranus is unaspected, it has a way of laying quietly under the surface like a mine, and one doesn't know it is there until one steps on it, or until one chooses a partner who steps on it.

The 7th and 10th are angular houses, and planets in the angles tend to express themselves quite readily as "outer" events. This doesn't lessen the inner importance of Uranus in these houses, but often there is a corresponding external upheaval which matches the inner attitude. So Uranus in the 1st or 7th may tend to manifest in very clear ways, and one's environment, one's relationships, the people with whom one deals, may seem in a constant or intermittent state of flux. There isn't any nice, neat formula to get this planet to behave. Its very nature makes us recognise how little control we actually have over the unconscious psyche. And we should always remember the element of Promethean suffering, because if one does manage to find a position of relative flexibility, then isolation or social ostracism, from peer group or family, may be the result.

One way or another, Uranus confronts us with the issue of Promethean suffering, which is often experienced through a sense of being abnormal, strange, or outcast in some way. Because Uranus impels us to steal fire, we carry the feeling of doing something illicit. Uranian flexibility is a highly creative response to life. It depends on a vision of a larger pattern, rather than on conventional structures and social compliance. It opens up possibilities which people who live in more structured circumstances never glimpse. The abruptly changing environment, lifestyle, self-image, and relationships that so often accompany Uranus in the 1st and 7th mean that one's life can be

----

enormously enriched, colourful, and exciting, because one sees so much more of the larger pattern. Yet there is suffering attached to it, because one will never wholly fit into conventional definitions of the way people are supposed to live their lives.

Audience: Is the isolation inevitable?

Liz: Usually one doesn't choose it, but yes, I think it tends to happen that way, until one gets involved with people who have the same perspective. They might not share one's feelings, but they may share one's vision, in which case one may still be lonely in the ordinary sense, but there is enduring companionship on a mental and spiritual level.

Audience: Are people with Uranus in the 1st or 7th especially popular?

Liz: What do you mean by "popular"? Do you mean charismatic?

Audience: Do they attract lots of friends?

Liz: Uranus can be fascinating because it seems to confer a quality of freedom that many people envy – even though the person with Uranus in the 1st or 7th may not feel it's such a hot thing, because they might not have asked for the freedom and would prefer a tranquil, dependent, safe life. Uranus has a mind-expanding quality because of its inclusive vision, and the Uranian person can exercise considerable fascination over others because of the glimpse of celestial heights which he or she somehow manages to convey. This may be especially apparent when Uranus is in the angular houses. But on the emotional level, other people's envy is not especially pleasant, and Uranian people may be seen as a threat by the more conventionally minded. A 7th house Uranus individual set loose at a dinner party may strike terror into the hearts of the strenuously married, even if the individual is not remotely interested in playing about.

Although they may be fascinating, people with Uranus in the 1st or 7th often feel lonely a lot of the time, partly because they may not fit the suburban couple with 2.5 children routine, and partly through their inability to express feelings. Something inside keeps saying, "Don't get stuck in all that emotional glue, keep the door open so you can leave if you have to." Earlier, someone mentioned his rising Uranus-Pluto conjunction, and Pluto's propensity to shut Uranus up. But I think Uranus shuts itself up, because the expression of personal feeling binds us to other people, and the daimon wants us to be ready with our luggage packed and our tickets and passports in our hands.

Prometheus' liver and Uranian depression

Audience: I have a question about the Prometheus myth. He is punished by having his liver eaten every day by an eagle. What do you think this means in human psychological terms? Especially when Uranus is in the 1st or 7th?

Liz: I have thought a lot about this image of the liver, because it is such a very powerful and specific theme in the myth. In Greco-Roman astrology, the liver was considered to be under the rulership of Zeus-Jupiter. In Roman religious practise, sheep livers were regularly used in divination, because they were believed to describe destiny. The Romans inherited this from the Etruscans, who linked the different divisions of the liver to the divisions of the heavens. We know very little about Etruscan astrology, but it appears they understood the what-is-above-is-like-what-is-below correspondence to be demonstrated most vividly and accurately through the liver. So they would open up an animal and chart the liver in the same way that we chart the heavens, by zones. From this liver divination, the future of the state, or the future of the Emperor, could be foretold. To the cultures from which the Prometheus myth emerged, the liver symbolised the future, and the sense of connection with cosmic order. Jupiter is, of course, the Great Benefic, and the organ of the body ruled by Jupiter was understood to be the seat of joy and hope.

I believe that the eating away of Prometheus' liver is connected with depression. It is the erosion of hope and faith, the destruction of the sense of connection with cosmic order. I expect when Prometheus was first chained to his rock, he spent a lot of time muttering, "What's the point of being alive? Why did I bother with that wretched fire? Nothing has really been achieved, and now I shall always be miserable and in pain." All the joy, all the feelings of fulfilling a cosmic purpose, are being eaten away. I have noticed that depression is something that tends to follow in the wake of Uranian eruptions and inspirations. The collective voice within us says, "Well, you really cocked it up this time. Who do you think you are? You will never be normal, you will never be happy. There goes another relationship. There goes another secure job. Don't bother any more, because you will never get it right."

The eating of the liver may symbolise a sense of despair, which is something that I often see in people with a strong Uranus. They may have hope for humanity, but they often don't have it for themselves. They have given up on the idea that they can be happy, because they are guilty; they have stolen fire. They have done something which is against collective values. The theft of fire carries its own punishment. The eagle is Zeus' bird. The king of the gods, who is like a tyrannical father, is the one who resents the fire being stolen, even though it wasn't his fire to begin with – it was the Sun's fire. But Zeus is the one who inflicts the punishment. He is rather like Freud's superego, which says, "You have done something illicit. You have committed an act, or thought of an idea, that is totally unacceptable, and your punishment is going to be that you will never be happy. Give up any hope of personal happiness."

Audience: Could this come out as an actual disease of the liver?

Liz: Perhaps; that is a rather literal enactment, but there may be a link. One of the commonest diseases of the liver, cirrhosis, is linked with alcohol abuse, which is often connected with depression and loss of hope.

Audience: But you said that Uranus cuts off feelings. How can Uranian people get depressed?

Liz: One can be very deeply depressed and remain quite unconscious of one's feelings. And the characteristic Uranian cut-off may ensure that such feelings are buried and therefore doubly powerful. Clinical depression, by definition, involves not recognising that one is deeply miserable. Very depressed people usually don't know they are unhappy, and because they cannot express unhappiness, they exhibit the symptoms of depression. They go around forgetting to wash or look after themselves, and the mess accumulates in the kitchen, and they have no energy and can't get out of bed. They can't stop and say, "I am really wretched and miserable because I feel so lonely." They don't know how they feel. If they knew, they wouldn't be depressed. They might be desperate, and wretched, but they wouldn't be depressed. Depression is a state which is dissociated from feelings. And there is usually great rage involved beneath the surface of depression, along with feelings of being victimised, dominated, or thwarted in some way. But all these feelings are usually unconscious.

Audience: Doesn't the eagle in the myth have anything to do with Scorpio?

Liz: Not in the Greco-Roman world. It was the bird of Zeus. We have tacked the eagle on to Scorpio in more recent times because we keep wanting to change Scorpio and make it "transcendent". We seem to have a problem recognising that the underworld instinctual realm is numinous in itself, and doesn't need our feeble efforts to "spiritualise" it. Forget the eagle in that context, because it actually has nothing to do with Scorpio, except that it is a predatory bird and can be made to fit the sign in that respect. But tigers and piranhas are also predators. The connection of the eagle with Scorpio comes from a period of astrological study when astrologers found it very hard to value Scorpionic qualities. There have been many strenuous attempts to transform Scorpios into spiritual birds, rather than allowing them to

----

be full-blooded scorpions or serpents, both of which were originally associated with the sign.

The eagle, being the bird of Zeus, was perceived in Greco-Roman symbolism as the messenger of heaven. It carried the souls of the dead up to the Olympian heights. That is why the tombs of Roman Emperors always have eagles on them – Zeus comes down and brings the soul of the Emperor up to the stars. The Roman legions carried the eagle as their emblem because they served not only the Emperor, but also Zeus-Jupiter, the All-Father. When Zeus abducted Ganymede in myth, he transformed into an eagle to carry the boy up to heaven.

Audience: Do you think allergies could be linked with depression and the symbolism of the liver? I know someone with a 1st house Uranus who suffers terribly from a number of allergies.

Liz: The honest answer is that I don't know. This is an immensely complicated issue and would require another seminar to do it justice. Physical suffering of a psychological or psychosomatic kind, with all due respect to medicine, is an area about which we still know very little. I believe that allergies have a large psychological component, although there is undoubtedly also bodily sensitivity. Or perhaps bodily sensitivity and psychological sensitivity are not really two separate things. The psychological component is clearly demonstrated in the timing of an allergic reaction, which often has important emotional connections, and in the unconscious "secondary gain" element, which creates certain reactions in the environment.

It may be that the sort of depression that is peculiarly Uranian can result in certain kinds of physical symptoms, including allergies. I suspect this is so. But I can't really say more than that, because I don't have enough knowledge of the subject to give a comprehensive answer. And I am also aware of how important it is for many people who suffer from such symptoms to have their situation categorised as an "illness". To suggest that there may be emotional issues at work can often invoke great rage in the sufferer, because there is an implication that somehow one is causing the condition oneself. It isn't easy to explain what the unconscious is all about, to a person who can't or won't face the reality of the psyche. It simply sounds as though they are being blamed for creating their own misery.

Audience: Would you expect Uranus on the Ascendant to be particularly linked with physical symptoms?

Liz: Not necessarily. I don't think it is always, or even often, the body itself that expresses Uranian eccentricity. That may be more characteristic of Uranus in the 2nd or 6th. With Uranus in the 1st, it may be the way in which the person presents himself or herself – the body image, rather than the body. We could spend hours talking about the 1st house, because it also has a connection with birth, with the experiences at birth and immediately after birth. The 1st house can tell us a great deal about the actual birth process, and what was going on between mother and child at the moment of birth. Those of you here who have Uranus conjunct the Ascendant might think about your actual physical birth, and whether there were any complications or special circumstances surrounding it. How we were born is also how we "come out" into life every time we attempt to make an impact on the world as an independent entity. In this respect, allergies may be connected, on the psychological level, with a particular emotional response to the outer world.

Uranus in the 2nd and 8th houses

We must move on, because we are going to be hard pressed to cover Uranus in all the houses, let alone by aspect. Let's look at the axis of the 2nd and 8th houses. What lies at their core?

Audience: Values.

Liz: Individual values are usually associated with the 2nd house, But what links this to the 8th? What do we mean by "values"? We can understand these houses well enough through opposites – such polarities as stability versus change, building versus destruction, anchoring in form versus the disintegration of form. But I want to hear more, something which lies right at the core of both houses.

Audience: It has got to do with form. With material reality. The building and destroying of form.

Liz: Yes, what lies at the core of this pair of houses is the mystery of substance. This is the substance, not only of exchange, but also one's own substance, and therefore one's body as well as the inner substance which comprises our resources, talents, and values. I have always liked the definition of karma as substance, which suggests that the stuff of which we are made – the qualities we have accrued and anchored in actual life – is the real basis of our "fate". The 2nd house is connected with the life of the physical body, while the 8th is connected with its death. The 8th is also concerned with resources, values, and talents that one has inherited – the substance that is not only one's own, but is also in some way shared or part of others. When Uranus is placed in either of these houses, what are we facing?

Audience: No fixed address.

Liz: Up to a point. But I associate that more with Uranus on the 1st/7th axis. The individual himself or herself is changeable, or changes through changeable relationships. One's life is itself eventful. In the 2nd or 8th, Uranian instability has a different focus, and a different feeling.

Audience: What about loss?

Liz: Loss is very much part of Uranus' expression in these houses, although loss can occur on many levels, not just the literal one. When Uranus is in the 2nd or 8th, our definition of permanence is subject to challenge, and our understanding of attachment may need to alter radically. We have to learn to rely on resources other than the obvious ones, the conventionally recognisable resources, and discover that the only permanent thing in life is the eternal system. We may also have to recognise and respect those forces that lie beneath the surface of life, that do not permit things to remain the same.

Loss can occur with Uranus in either house. But the real loss is not so much of objects, as it is of our definition of what constitutes permanence and stability. In some ways Uranus in these houses is less obvious, and also more difficult than a 1st/7th Uranus, because the cardinality of the 1st and 7th can permit an active decision-making process which allows us to participate in, or even initiate, change. With all the potential instability of Uranus in the 1st, for example, one can decide to rent rather than buy a house, or live with someone without marrying him or her. But the 2nd and 8th are fixed houses, and their inclination is to hold on, to accrue, to establish and maintain. Change is experienced as a ripping apart, rather than a roller-coaster.

Any planet in the 2nd may be interpreted as a resource. It implies a talent, an innate ability, a positive inner fund from which we can draw capital to get on in life. This is why planets in the 2nd are sometimes associated with work; they may be expressed as talents which can be manifested and utilised to build stability. But it isn't easy to perceive Uranus as a resource, when it seems so inimical to stability. If Uranus is in the 2nd or 8th, those things which society generally perceives as one's most basic survival props, emotionally and materially, may fail to give us the security we seek. We may lose the objects and people to which we are attached, either through our own choice or through unexpected external circumstances.

Dealing with Uranus in these houses requires a spirit of non-attachment. When Uranus is in the 1st or 7th houses, which are angular, we need to cultivate a spirit of flexibility toward others and toward our environment – a willingness to allow events and behaviour which are eccentric or which fly in the face of conventional definitions of normality. When Uranus is in the 2nd or 8th, we need to remain unattached on a profound level. This doesn't mean we should not feel. But we may need to learn to let go no matter how deeply we feel, because if we try to nail our attachments down, whether material or emotional, they have a way of departing from our lives despite – or

---

sometimes even because of – our best efforts. Would any of you with Uranus in the 2nd or 8th like to comment?

Audience: I have it in the 8th, and I lost several members of my family before I was six years old. It has left me very mistrustful of life.

Liz: Yes, I have heard of this kind of experience several times, from clients who have Uranus in the 8th. There may be an experience of the death of someone close, and the psychological and material change that such a death brings, quite early in life. Even at a young age, one cannot assume that the people to whom one has become attached are always going to be there. The necessity to let go may not always involve the death of a loved one. It may be a separation through other means. I am thinking of the birth chart of Princess Diana, who has Uranus in the 8th, and whose mother left to live with another man when she was quite young. Uranus often shows its power to overturn existing reality very early in life, and it is the aftermath of such experiences which represent the psychological legacy, the "resource" of understanding life's essential unpredictability. Relationship disruptions and breakups are quite common in adulthood with Uranus in the 8th, just as they are when it is in the 7th, but the feeling is different, and usually so is the aftermath. Uranus in the 7th teaches us to be more flexible and unconventional in our definitions of relationship. Uranus in the 8th teaches us that there are patterns and forces in life which are beyond our control, and with which we must come to terms through a spirit of nonattachment.

Audience: In my adult life I also keep experiencing relationship breakdowns. It is as though the trouble comes out of nowhere.

Liz: If your relationships keep blowing up on you, it could be important to consider whether you might be clinging too hard to your attachments. It is possible that the early losses you experienced have made you determined to bind any person you love very tightly, and you could unconsciously be contributing to a partner's desire for space and freedom through being too possessive. On a deeper level, it is also possible that something in you, which is clearly not your conscious ego, needs a certain level of distance and detachment in relationships, and you might be denying this need. Your childhood experiences could be part of a deeper life pattern which requires you to allow people to move into and out of your life.

Perhaps Uranus in the 8th necessitates your understanding love and relationship at a more profound and less personal level. The 8th is concerned with the mysteries of life and death, and anyone with Uranus placed there may need to approach the great and inevitable cycles of life, death, attachment, and loss with a more universal and clear-sighted attitude. Wherever Uranus is placed, we have to learn detachment, which is not the same as emotional suppression or dissociation. This might be very hard for you to accept on the emotional level. If so, you could be choosing people who are temperamentally not really equipped to tolerate too much intensity or structure in a relationship, so there may be a kind of unconscious collusion between your Uranus and the Uranian people with whom you become involved.

In recent times some well-intentioned astrologer decided that Uranus was exalted in Scorpio. I can't imagine why. It is understandable that, since its discovery, astrologers have been wondering in which sign this planet is exalted, because we have inherited the concept of exaltations, falls, dignities, and detriments from the ancients, and such terms help us to feel we have a grip on the meaning of the planets. These categories may, however, have limited validity.

The old idea was that a planet is "weak" in its detriment or fall, and "strong" in its dignity or detriment. Usually we think of a planet being comfortable in its own sign – its "dignity" – in terms of what the planet seeks to express, and less comfortable in the opposite sign, its "detriment". To some extent this is true, since the signs are expressions of the planets which rule them. Venus is comfortable in Taurus because this sign is easily contented by the pleasures of physical reality (which is Venus' realm), whereas Venus is not so comfortable in Scorpio because this sign's taste for drama and crisis demands nothing less than everything to feel emotionally fulfilled, and contentment may be experienced by Scorpio as a kind of stagnation. But that doesn't make Venus "weak" or "debilitated" in Scorpio. It makes it different – less peaceable and more intense.

But I have many questions about the terms "fall" and "exaltation". Here we have what, in effect, is a social judgement – a reflection of the values of the time in which these terms were coined and developed. For example, Mars is considered "exalted" in Capricorn and is in the sign of its "fall" in Cancer, because Capricorn provides determination, concentrated energy, discipline, and an element of ruthlessness to Mars' drive to be first and best, whereas Cancer's emotionality and need of others make Mars too dependent on the right emotional atmosphere to express initiative. So Mars in Capricorn may be capable of achieving a great deal on the worldly level. But not everyone values such achievement, or the means by which the person acquires it, which may be questionable. Mars in Cancer, with all its moody sensitivity, may possess great imaginative gifts, and an ability to deal with others sensitively, tactfully, and gently. It is arguable whether this means Mars is "debilitated" or "weak" in Cancer. I don't think so. It is, like Venus in Scorpio, simply different.

The assigning of Scorpio to Uranus as the sign of its exaltation strikes me as very peculiar, and perhaps even downright inappropriate. I am not clear what sort of reasoning lies behind this choice, but I suspect it is the same reasoning which tries to turn the scorpion into an eagle – the idea that somehow Uranian cosmic vision "transforms" Scorpio's "lower nature". I am not convinced there is any wisdom at all in assigning exaltations or falls to the outer planets. We don't even understand these planets fully, let alone which signs they might do "best" in. Best for whom? And as far as Uranus in Scorpio is concerned, which is in some ways similar to Uranus in the 8th, it can be extremely painful to let go of emotional attachments in the way that the Uranian spirit requires. It isn't possible by an act of intellect or an act of will. Whether it is "transformative" is again arguable – this depends on how well the individual is able to process his or her experiences. Uranus can be transformative in any of the houses. When it is in the 8th, one is metaphorically dragged, kicking and screaming, into recognising the deeper necessity of nonattachment. But at the same time, it is also extremely important to honour one's basic human emotional needs, or serious dissociation can result. And that is not an exalted state.

Audience: I don't want to get too attached. I want to be in a relationship, but I don't want to be vulnerable or have to suffer the loss of someone I care about. From what you are saying, will this fear of attachment ever go away?

Liz: It may or may not go away. I can't answer your question. A great deal depends on how you work with the fear, and whether you are willing to take a psychological and symbolic, rather than a literal and concrete, approach to the problem. It is possible that some anxiety will always accompany any deep attachment; that is the usual by-product of the Uranian spirit, even when we are conscious of it. But I don't think any solution lies in trying not to feel. What often happens with Uranus in the 8th is that, after one experiences a few blowups, one says to oneself, "I will never put myself in that situation again." But this kind of rigid defensiveness may violate other important chart factors – for example, the Moon in a water sign, or Pluto in the 5th house, or a Venus-Neptune conjunction, or some other indication of emotional intensity and a deep need to be attached.

One may ultimately need to espouse a bit of Buddhist philosophy – letting oneself feel whatever one feels, but when it is time to let go, recognising that one may have to. Avoiding passion, with Uranus in the 8th, is not a good idea. But whatever one's passion may alight on – a person, an object, a system of beliefs – nothing can be guaranteed to be in one's life forever. In short, the deeper meaning of life, for Uranus in the 8th, does not lie in freezing time and fixing objects so that they do not go away. Have any of you read Goethe's *Faust?* Mephistopheles tells Faust that, if he ever says, "May this moment last forever!", at that moment Faust will be damned. Goethe himself did not have Uranus in the 8th, but he had it almost exactly square a Scorpio Ascendant, and no doubt he understood the problem

----

quite well. Uranus in the 8th calls for a middle way – a willingness to trust the cosmic system yet not expect favours from it, and a capacity to walk a careful path between dissociation and obsessive attempts to cling.

Audience: I also have Uranus in the 8th. I was thinking about this in terms of inheritance and karma, and it seems to have a lot to do with a sense of sexual guilt, which I am trying to deal with now.

Liz: The 8th house is concerned with sexuality because sexual passion, and sexual fulfillment through orgasm, are experiences in which the ego is no longer in control. During the sexual act we come face to face with something that is a raw and mysterious life-force, with a will of its own, and that deeper will can shatter many structures and existing attitudes which we thought were secure. Nothing is quite so effective at getting people to behave in ways of which they would wholeheartedly disapprove in saner moments. The experience of sexual passion is a kind of death. If one withholds at that moment, or tries to protect oneself, then there is no fulfillment. And we are also unable to dictate where our passions will go. That is why the Greeks imaged intense sexual passion as the arrow of Eros, shot by a mischievous god at an unsuspecting mortal, or as the frenzy of Aphrodite, which drives human beings into liaisons they would never normally countenance.

When Uranus is in the 8th, what is unleashed can be very disturbing, because one must not only contend with the overwhelming necessity of passion, but the passion may not accord with conventional ideas of sexuality. There are some very odd descriptions of Uranus in the 8th in older textbooks – one often sees references to "sexual perversion". I am not sure what that is supposed to mean, since definitions of sexual "normality" are highly subjective in any case, and can be especially stupid and inappropriate when dealing with the expanded vision and world-view of the outer planets. Uranus in the 8th may contribute to a guilty sense of being "abnormal" because one's sexuality does not fit into a particular set of precepts of how one is supposed to feel and act. Such guilt often accompanies Uranus in the

8th when the family background is particularly inhibited, and there are sexual skeletons in the family cupboard. Uranus in the 8th can reflect great fear of the vulnerability and loss of control that follow on the heels of passion, because something erupts which may not be listed on page 53 of the *Good Guide to Sex*. Through sexual feelings and sexual experiences, Uranus can disrupt or shatter one's image of oneself as a certain kind of person, opening the door to a broader and more flexible understanding of human passions.

Uranus can bring sudden insight as well as sudden foresight, and through sexual experience, Uranus in the 8th can sometimes provoke profound revelations about human nature and what is going on beneath the surface in any close relationship – emotionally as well as sexually. Such perceptions may be very disturbing because they reveal patterns and psychological dynamics which are usually deeply unconscious and may be part of the hidden family psychic inheritance. These insights are not usually available when the collective offers its given wisdom on what normal sexual behaviour is supposed to be about, or how relationships are supposed to work. I suspect that many people with Uranus in the 8th are appalled by the "return to family values and everything will be all right" stuff currently being offered as a solution to society's ills. The Promethean spirit erupting through the passions can unlock secret doors, like the doors in Bluebeard's Castle, and what we discover about ourselves and human nature in general may make us feel guilty, abnormal, frightened, or ashamed.

Audience: I have a feeling Uranus in the 8th is about the fear of death.

Liz: In many ways, fear of death and fear of the passions are the same fear. The Elizabethans called sex the "Little Death". For many people, sex is not profound; it is like a good meal, satisfying and nourishing, and a problem only when one isn't getting any. For a particular kind of earthy nature, sex is a pleasurable physical release. For other people, perhaps more watery in nature, sex is a way of getting close to another person. For an 8th house Uranus, sex may be a means of transformation, a kind of death which leads to a different

----

vision of life. Through passion, the ego's control is shattered. A world appears which is not what one thought, full of mystery and patterns and energies that stretch the mind as well as the heart far beyond its ordinary limits. It can feel as though one is dying.

Shall we look more closely at Uranus in the 2nd? We seem to have got lost in the depths of the 8th, and fascinating though this is, we must move on. The 2nd house is concerned not only with the physical body, the substance of which we are made, but also with everything that we usually define as security. To a great many people, security means money and all allied things – how one makes a living, what kind of mortgage one should have, one's Access and American Express cards, one's accumulation of possessions, and one's stable relationships. We are bombarded with admonitions and advertisements about how to plan for the future, protect our families if something should happen to us, and ensure that we do not have to depend on the mercy of the Social Services. We are taught to deal with the material world in certain "normal" ways. We are expected to contribute to a pension fund, retire at sixty-five, and save for a comfortable old age. We do all these things as part of the fabric of everyday material existence. We assume that security operates on a cause-and-effect principle, so that if we work and save, and make no wild leaps into an unknown future, our reward will be safety and stability.

But when Uranus is in the 2nd house, the "normal" way of dealing with security issues tends to go wrong, and efforts to create stability according to conventional wisdom usually don't work. Sometimes the person with Uranus in the 2nd is well aware of the inner Promethean spirit, and opts voluntarily to embrace instability. But this takes a lot of courage as well as foresight, and more often – at least in the first part of life – one plods along trying to do the right thing, and then discovers it isn't so simple. Uranus in the 2nd requires us to survive in the material world through the resource of vision, and teaches us to work with the energy of material reality without becoming too attached. Wise people with Uranus in the 2nd avoid working for companies or institutions. The person with a 2nd house Uranus may start off trying to find a secure job within a company framework, and then something blows up – the company folds, or one gets made redundant, or one begins to feel intolerably claustrophobic and must leave. For those with Uranus in the 2nd, the material world cannot be simply a means of establishing security so that one can pay off the mortgage. It needs to be understood magically. By this I mean that one may be required to utilise vision and foresight, combined with a deep knowledge of how the "system" works and how substance follows the flow of ideas. This is why the professions associated with Uranus in the 2nd are often called "unconventional".

Audience: I have Uranus in the 2nd, and I am a part-time nanny.

Liz: Perhaps "part-time" is the operative Uranian phrase.

Audience: I certainly can't see myself doing that work forever, let alone full-time.

Liz: With Uranus in the 2nd, you probably can't see yourself doing any sort of work forever. You may go through a great many job experiences during the course of your life; Uranus in the 2nd often does. The willingness to be flexible is extremely important. Over time, a pattern usually emerges, and one's varied experiences all contribute to a particularly astute understanding of how to survive yet remain free. For those who are determined to nail everything down, Uranus in the 2nd can be extremely distressing. If one is willing to travel with a light suitcase, and can enter into the spirit of exploration which Uranus requires, then it can reveal the secret of how to be comfortable in the world without selling one's soul.

Uranus in the 3rd and 9th houses

As there seem to be no other comments or questions about Uranus in the 2nd and 8th, let's turn to Uranus in the 3rd and 9th houses. What is the core of this axis?

Audience: Education. Knowledge.

Liz: Yes, the core is knowledge, derived from facts (the 3rd) or from intuition (the 9th). The approach to knowledge may be different, but the goal is the same – an understanding of the world, an understanding of life.

Audience: The 9th house is connected with the God-image.

Liz: That is certainly one of the concerns of the 9th. But the image of God that we carry is based on our knowledge of life, whether it is derived from an external spiritual authority or from our own inner experience. And our religious formulations reflect our efforts to comprehend what the world is made of, and what life is actually about. Not everyone with an emphasis in the 9th is concerned with God in the obvious sense. An agnostic scientist might have a dominant 9th house, if he or she is concerned with how the universe is made.

In many respects Uranus is at home in these two houses, because they are cadent and mind-orientated, and therefore associated with reflection and learning. Uranus is consequently less likely to present itself through unexpected events of an emotionally jarring kind (although this can happen), and more likely to be active through sudden, unsolicited revelations of an intellectual or intuitive kind. Nevertheless, although the activities of the 3rd and 9th are often internal rather than concrete, it can be just as shocking and disturbing. One may have started off with a world-view or a set of attitudes dominated by the family background and the early education, and then suddenly this world-view doesn't work any more, and one is left confused, floundering, and morally uncertain.

Sometimes there are great problems with early education when Uranus is in these houses. No matter how hard one's teachers try to drum their version of reality into one's head, Uranus keeps saying, "What a load of rubbish. This is nonsense. This is superficial, pointless information which has nothing to do with the big picture. I can see the big picture. I know the truth. These people haven't a clue." Because the Uranian revelation of the system is so complete and seamless, a person with Uranus in the 3rd or 9th may feel contemptuous toward any educational authority which lacks a global perspective. With a child with Uranus in the 3rd or 9th, what we euphemisticaly call "learning difficulties" are not uncommon. Resistance to mental discipline, rebellion against learning by rote, refusal to concentrate on subjects or tasks which seem boring, and a highly eccentric way of communicating and writing, may all be evidenced by children with Uranus in these houses.

These are in fact not "learning difficulties" in the sense that there is any lack of intelligence or ability. But such a child needs to learn in a different way, by understanding the world through connections which reveal the system, rather than through isolated pieces of information. If we remember the arts which Prometheus taught human beings, we can get some sense of the kind of knowledge which a 3rd or 9th house Uranus seeks and reveals. Uranian suffering may occur in the early part of life in connection with educational establishments, both at grammar school and at university. There may also be difficulties in the religious sphere, if the family background reflects a particularly conventional or rigid religious approach. Very often one's early spiritual convictions are shattered, sometimes unpleasantly, through circumstances which challenge one's faith, or through discovering that people who claim to be religious or spiritually enlightened are not practising what they are preaching. Uranus in the 3rd and 9th can also make a political ideology into a religion, because the Uranian spirit is inimical to mysticism and woolly-minded approaches to life. Uranus tends, sooner or later, to see through religious hypocrisy, and the whole structure may come tumbling down.

So Uranus in the 3rd and 9th may reflect a different way of perceiving the world, and a different way of learning which is not accommodated by our educational institutions. Orthodox science cannot really accommodate Uranus either, because it is often too Saturnian and rigid in its approach to the nonphysical aspects of life. And the Uranian spirit always seeks to connect different dimensions of reality to get a glimpse of the greater system, and we presently live in an era of specialisation of knowledge. Would anyone with Uranus in the 3rd or 9th like to comment?

Audience: I have it in the 9th house. I am German, and my parents came from a religious background, but they denied their background, and brought me up as an atheist.

Liz: Atheism is, of course, as much a religious ideology as Catholicism. The operative principle is the dogma, and the giveaway is the "-ism" at the end of the word. Atheism as a pragmatic denial of the invisible is no more attuned to Uranus than a narrow religious creed. Agnosticism might be more truly Uranian. But if atheism is coupled with a comprehensive political and social ideology, then one can see the Uranian spirit converting "God" into "humanity" or "society". Humanism, which was a powerful movement in the 16th century (especially in Germany), was essentially atheistic, but human beings were accorded the same awe and worship as the deity. Earlier today, the question arose about Uranus' connections with religious fundamentalism. Uranian people can be extremely rigid in their thinking, because of the tendency to receive truth as a revelation, and the irony of this is that the committed atheist and the committed fundamentalist – who see themselves as enemies – may be more alike than either realises. What are your religious views now?

Audience: I think I've exchanged one revelation of absolute truth for another. I am not an atheist, but I do not believe in a personalised God. My interest in astrology and esoteric "systems" is probably very Uranian. I suppose I am as rigid in rejecting the scientific, rational world-view as my parents were in rejecting God.

Audience: I have Uranus in the 3rd, and I like what you said about this placement. I have had problems in many courses of study I have undertaken here in England. I sometimes feel I have a mystical connection, or get understanding through intuition, but this causes many difficulties. Also, English is not my first language. I come from Sao Paolo, and I have lost my roots, and have left many friends behind.

Liz: You are expressing much of what we have been discussing, in relation to the loneliness and feelings of isolation which often accompany Uranus in the 3rd house. Although your English is excellent, I am sure you find it hard to express yourself with the same subtlety and complexity as you could in Portuguese. Yet it is you yourself who have decided to study in this country, perhaps because Uranus in the 3rd needs a broader world-view and you could only achieve this through travel and exposure to different ways of thinking. As you all know, the 3rd is concerned with communication and with one's interchange with the immediate environment, and with Uranus in the 3rd there is sometimes a dreadful feeling that nobody is going to understand what one is talking about. One feels one can't communicate one's perceptions to other people. So Uranus in the 3rd, although it is at home in this house in many ways, can also reflect a lot of suffering through a sense of intellectual isolation.

Audience: That is true. I have the kind of mind that sees the bigger pattern. But it is very difficult to communicate that. I couldn't do it at home either. I can't do it in words, but it seems so obvious. For me the truth is the Akashic Records.

Liz: You have used a word which is very redolent of Uranus in both the 3rd and 9th: truth. Truth usually arrives in the form of a revelation, when Uranus is in these houses. Understanding is not a process of building fact on fact, in order to come to a logical conclusion. Understanding arrives full-blown. For the person with Uranus in the 3rd or 9th, such truth is inarguable. For anybody who happens to be listening, it can be very difficult, because there is a quality of impermeability about the person's thinking. It is quite impossible to have an objective discussion with someone with Uranus in one of these houses, if the subject touches on one of these Uranian, self-evident truths. The system is complete, and needs no further alteration or moderation. For someone who doesn't have entry into the system, it can be infuriating. You have given yourself the additional burden of trying to communicate your truth in a language other than your native tongue.

Audience: I also have Uranus in the 9th, and my higher education was interrupted because I decided to move from France to England. I interrupted it myself. I felt as if everyone thought my world-view was mad. My university training was very rigid, very academic. I thought maybe I would do some courses in alternative subjects here. But people here think I am mad as well. I don't see why Uranus in the 9th is easier than in other houses.

Liz: This is getting rather funny. All of you who have commented on your 3rd or 9th house Uranus have come from countries where languages other than English are spoken. You have all adopted astrology as a universal language. Obviously Uranian loneliness and loss of social contact, and the feeling that one is a bit crazy, can be very disturbing and painful. But I think Uranus in the 3rd and 9th can sometimes be easier because of the communicative and inquisitive propensities of these houses. If one has got sufficiently fed up with being looked at oddly by conventionally minded people, one can go out and look for more interesting people, with whom one can share one's mad world-view. And one usually finds them, because Uranus is prepared to pack its bags and leap over national and linguistic barriers in pursuit of its vision. As though to prove my point, all three of you have found your way to an English astrology seminar on Uranus, in which people can talk about the truth of the Akashic Records without everyone rushing out of the room screaming or reaching for their cellnet to ring the local psychiatric hospital.

I did not say that Uranus in the 3rd or 9th was a piece of cake, or carried no Promethean suffering. But there are potential ways to alleviate much of this suffering through efforts which do not require a complete overturning of one's instinctual needs. When Uranus is in the 2nd or 8th, or in the 1st or 7th, finding creative resolutions may require giving up or compromising many of the fundamental lunar and Saturnian needs which are so important to all of us. When it is in the 3rd or 9th, one may be able to find a language – however esoteric – to describe one's experiences, rather than remaining mute and having one's large intestine unwound, which is often how it feels when Uranus is in the 2nd or 8th. If you are prepared to accept the fact that a lot of people will think you are bonkers, then you can really enjoy Uranus in the 3rd and 9th. If you desperately want to be accepted by a collective which thinks in more pragmatic or superficial terms, then you are probably going to suffer.

Audience: Does that mean I will never be in accord with collective thinking?

Liz: "Never" is an inappropriate word in relation to Uranus. This planet is not consistent, except in its inconsistency. Sometimes it sleeps quietly, and then erupts intermittently, in very specific areas. I think it is important to accept the fact that one may often be unable to think in accord with conventional patterns. There may be particular issues, or a particular subject, about which one becomes very Uranian. About some subjects there may be no problem at all in communicating. But when an issue is discussed where Uranus has revealed one of its cosmic truths, then there will probably be many people, perhaps the majority of people, with whom one will not really be able to communicate. This can be very painful, especially if one is quite extraverted. It may be especially painful for anyone with an emphasis in the water signs, because there is such a strong need to be close to others. One's intellectual eccentricities may alienate them, and one loses the feeling of closeness.

Audience: It can be tragic for a child with Uranus in these houses, if the educational system is too narrow.

Liz: Indeed, yes, it can be tragic, and sometimes the damage is permanent. When a child with Uranus in these houses is placed in too conventional an education system, he or she may be diagnosed as having a learning disability. In fact there may be nothing wrong whatsoever with the child's learning capacity, but the way of learning is very different, and often only a more creative educational environment reveals Uranus' real gifts. If one has been diagnosed with a learning disability, or with dyslexia, it can scar one's entire life, because one may be convinced that there is something irrevocably wrong.

As with psychologically based physical ailments, conventional wisdom collapses in the face of why some children appear to have problems learning, despite the clear evidence that there is no organic basis for the difficulty. In an ideal world, Uranus in the 3rd or 9th needs an enlightened parent and an enlightened teacher. Because education is reflected by the 3rd and 9th houses, these placements of Uranus have very special educational requirements. Of course our present system, in the main, is not capable of meeting these requirements. Often the individual must start anew, later in life. The tragedy is that confidence may have been destroyed very early.

Audience: I have a dyslexic son who has Uranus in the 3rd house. What you are saying comes as a great relief to me, although I also find it very disturbing and sad.

Liz: I find it sad as well, because he has been burdened with the label "dyslexic" when a little more understanding on the part of his teachers might have allowed him the freedom to discover his intellectual gifts in his own way. But hopefully, with time, you could help him to understand that the real failing may lie in the educational system in which he is embroiled.

Audience: I would like to ask a question about Uranus' foresight. Is this a kind of inner knowledge of the future, or is it psychic? And is it likely to be emphasised if Uranus is in the 3rd or 9th?

Liz: Foresight is one of the most creative dimensions of Uranus, even though it can sometimes have an unpleasant way of shattering all our existing assumptions and convictions. Uranus does bring a certain kind of intuitive vision, sometimes of the future, but more usually, of the bigger pattern at work, which may include the future as a kind of by-product. It does not seem to be especially emphasised in any particular house, although the sphere in which one experiences one's revelation may reflect the house placement. It is not the same as psychism. It doesn't seem to operate on an emotional level – Uranian foresight appears as a sudden revelation of how something or someone works. I have known many astrology students who have experienced this when they started studying astrology, and certainly I experienced it myself when I first encountered the subject, at a time when transiting Jupiter made a station conjuncting my natal Uranus. There was a sudden and powerful sense of recognition, as though I had known these things all along, but had stupidly forgotten them.

That is how Plato defined education, of course – a process of precipitating the recollection of universal truths, of "leading out" inner knowledge of the cosmic system, rather than an imposition of external facts. The interrelated subjects which Plato emphasised – music, astrology, geometry and mathematics – all comprise the Promethean revelation of the interconnected whole, the "eternal realities". Sometimes Uranian foresight will operate through sudden and profound insight into people. This may be characteristic when it is in the watery houses, and also in the 7th, where it may reveal the dynamics of relationships in a sudden, penetrating way. But it is no more "psychic" in the watery houses than it is anywhere else. The insight is usually a detached one, and does not arise from the kind of fusion-state and emotional identification that I associate with Neptunian psychism.

Uranus in the 4th and 10th houses

The next pair of houses – the 4th and 10th – are concerned with the family background and the parental inheritance. When Uranus is linked up with early life experiences, and especially if it also aspects the Moon, upheaval or stress may occur in the environment, or between parent and child, in infancy. This can leave in its wake the feeling that, any minute, everything is going to blow up. This anxious expectation of imminent disaster may carry through into adulthood, and may contribute to a state of chronic anxiety.

Sometimes the foresight of Uranus isn't foresight at all, but a memory of past upheaval, which may lead to recurring premonitions

----

of an explosion which is about to happen some time in the future. Sometimes, of course, the explosion does happen, because there is such fine-tuned sensitivity to the signals of approaching turbulence that the person foresees quite correctly. But more often the premonition of disaster is not a premonition, but a recall, triggered by a situation which may be externally or internally similar to the original childhood scenario.

There are certain Uranian anxiety states in which the person will go around expecting the gas boiler to blow up, or intruders to try to break into the house. The diffused anxiety of childhood focuses on a specific object or situation in the outer world in adulthood, and one goes around constantly fearing this thing, which is really a hook for the projection of childhood experiences. But there is also a highly creative dimension to the sense of uncertainty which originates in the family environment. It can make one develop a peculiarly flexible attitude toward the future, which entails finding intellectual or spiritual resources to cope with the possibility of imminent change.

Moon-Uranus aspects and childhood anxiety

Audience: I have Uranus in the 4th house, square the Moon. I have had a lot of experiences of intuitively sensing that something upsetting was going to happen. A lot of the time these things have happened. But sometimes they don't. I wonder whether I should trust my intuition, because sometimes it's so right and sometimes it goes so badly wrong.

Liz: It is a very difficult issue. There may not be any way of definitively working out which is which, and perhaps there is a creative element in never really knowing – it means you must learn to rely on inner resources, and put your trust in life rather than on the unchanging security of external reality. But I think you can assume, if you have got Moon square Uranus, that the thing you fear has already happened, probably before the age of 9 months. When you work out the Moon's motion by secondary progression, the aspects it makes to other planets, whether applying or separating, would have inevitably come exact during your mother's pregnancy (in the case of separating aspects) or within 9 or 10 months after birth (in the case of applying aspects). I am using an orb of around 9° to 10°. Is your Moon-Uranus square applying or separating?

Audience: The Moon is in 8° Libra, and Uranus is in 12° Cancer. I suppose that means it is applying.

Liz: Yes, there is a 4° orb, and the Moon is applying to the square. It would have come exact when you were between three and four months old, depending on the exact rate of motion of the Moon. The Moon moves between 12° and 13° a day, which in the symbolic motion of secondary progressions means between 12° and 13° a year, or roughly 1° per month. The experience of a sudden wrenching of the fabric of stability probably occurred at four months, and your fear of the future is really a displaced visceral memory of a past upheaval of some kind. The feeling of upheaval might not have been literal, in the sense of a concrete disruption (such as a parental separation), but it might have been caused by a particularly tense atmosphere.

Audience: My father left when I was four months old. He came back again, but at the time my mother didn't know he was going to return. I don't actually remember what happened.

Liz: You do remember, but your memory is encapsulated in your fear. The emotions you experience when you feel something upsetting is going to happen are probably heavily coloured by your early experience. Memory is not limited to facts or ideas; we have emotional memories, and our bodies remember things too. We don't always recognise when such memories are being stirred. The emotional and bodily level of memory are connected with the Moon, which is like a bowl or cup receiving the flow of life experience. Certain situations in your present life may trigger that visceral memory, and pitch you into panic, because in some way the essence of the situation resembles the original childhood constellation. Every time something that constitutes a symbol of security seems under threat through sudden change, the old fear is likely to be activated.

Situations which other people might not find so troubling might have a strange power to invoke anxiety in you, especially situations where something comes out of the blue and disrupts your feeling of rootedness. It may be especially bad in close relationships, since your experience is of losing your father and being exposed to your mother's extreme stress, albeit temporarily. This kind of chronic anxiety is one of the characteristics of Moon-Uranus contacts, especially the hard aspects. It can sometimes help if you look carefully at your intuitions of future upsets, to see whether the original shocking experience of parental separation is being triggered in some way. This may account for some of the "wrong" intuitions.

Of course, upsetting things may happen, since life is like that. They happen to everyone, with or without a natal Moon-Uranus aspect, and one way or another we all need to learn to cope with surprises and situations which suddenly slip beyond our control. But Moon-Uranus, because it reflects such an early experience of sudden change, may produce the urge to predict events, as a Uranian defence against life's unexpected upheavals. Compulsively trying to prognosticate disaster, whether intuitively or through systems such as astrology or the Tarot, often reflects a desperate need to second-guess the universe. This is really using Uranus to protect oneself against Uranus – developing Promethean foresight in order to cope with the huge impersonality of the cosmic system, which could slap us down any time.

It is why many people take up the study of astrology. This is often one of the results of chronic Uranian anxiety – searching for a means of foretelling what the gods are up to, before they come at you from behind. It can be extremely creative, and Moon-Uranus aspects can reflect a search for maternal security through Uranian pursuits, because the common or garden variety of material and emotional security cannot be trusted. The orderly workings of the cosmos, even if upsetting, provide one with a feeling of being contained and part of an intelligent and meaningful pattern. This is the deeper reason why Moon-Uranus, and also Uranus in the 10th house (which also has

----

bearing on the mother), are often associated with the study of astrology.

Although I don't think there is a formula by which we can distinguish between a genuine Uranian piece of foresight and the sort of anxiety which is really a memory of Uranian disruption from early life, we can sometimes get a feeling of where in the past the chronic fear lies. The more we understand that, the more it tends to mitigate the fear. This kind of understanding is itself Uranian – a knowledge of the complexity of the psychological "system" is the antidote to the terror aroused by the workings of that system on blind and unsuspecting humans. This is another dimension of the gift of fire. Moon-Uranus people will get such anxiety regularly, in certain situations which trigger the ancient terror of life's unpredictability. When this happens, it is likely to be the past rather than the future – although we can always recreate the past through "repetition compulsion", or unconsciously require its re-creation for deeper reasons connected with our inner development.

Audience: I feel that is the true Uranian foresight. Uranus has so much to do with understanding the patterns we act out. It is as if, when the clouds gather, it is likely to rain. It's so logical, but it's also foresight. So Uranian foresight has got to do with experience, and with the Sun as the conscious personality, recognising our life pattern. It has also got to do with understanding cause-and-effect relationships. It is as if we are studying the archetype. If you catch the gist of an archetype, you can foretell how it will operate, and the possible typical outcome.

Liz: Yes, and that is what we try to do with astrology. We relate personal experience to inherent patterns which are universal and applicable to all human beings – except that each human being interprets and lives the pattern in a very special and unique way. We are applying our knowledge of the system of the macrocosm to the workings of the microcosm. Because we know the archetypal pattern described by a particular planet or planetary configuration, we know its "outcome" in the broadest sense. But then we need to know something about the individual client, so that we can apply this broad foresight to a personal situation. As you say, Uranian foresight is impeccably logical. It pursues a logical pattern of unfoldment, because there is an intuitive understanding of the pattern. The speed with which Uranus arrives at a conclusion is blindingly faster than the intellect's cumbersome processes, but, although the knowledge may be built up of experience plus a deep instinctive understanding of the system, it is, in the end, logical.

Uranian foresight isn't really intuition in the colloquial sense; it is something else. It is an ability to plug into the larger system, so we immediately know the rules governing a particular situation. It is rather like the on-board computer which one gets on certain cars. If one is travelling at a certain rate of speed, and one's journey is two hundred miles, the on-board computer will work out the estimated time of arrival instantly, which will keep changing according to the fluctuations in speed. There is something computer-like about the way in which Uranus functions, which is why the planet is often associated with computer technology, and why people with a strong Uranus are often gifted at computer programming and engineering.

Uranus involves logical understanding, but it doesn't seem to be the conscious mind that possesses the understanding. Experience is indeed involved, but it may not be direct personal experience; it is a perception of the broader sweep of human experience, a kind of intimate dialogue with the archetypal realm. Through Uranus, we can arrive at a conclusion without having direct personal experience of a specific situation, because we understand the workings of the system and can apply the archetypal or general to the specific. Neptunian empathy is also collective, and it rests on a similar perception of an archetypal level of emotional experience, which allows the Neptunian person to somehow "feel" what others are feeling. But in the case of Neptune, the perception is not logical or related to the mental plane.

Personal experience, and a solar sense of consciousness, will flesh out what we perceive as a general set of laws, and this is why it is so essential for astrological students to keep track of their own transits and progressions, and relate the planetary patterns to events in their own lives and the lives of people close to them. In this way we see our art come alive, and can increase our ability to back Uranian foresight with a mature emotional and intellectual understanding. It is also why I keep going on about the importance of the astrologer experiencing psychotherapy of some kind; it is through direct experience of our inner world that we put flesh on the bones of our Promethean but impersonal understanding. But Uranus allows us to have the broad understanding immediately, without the direct experience. I believe Uranus can be related to those cosmologies which arrive full-blown in consciousness, as religious or scientific revelations.

Above all, Uranus is a mental planet, which works with mental energy. There is nothing psychic about it, although it is mysterious to us at our present level of awareness because it symbolises the creative power of the collective, rather than the individual, mind. This is a capacity of mind that we don't really understand. We know very little about it. Many of the fringe disciplines poke around this area, utilising this extraordinary power of the mind to arrive at a conclusion without following any of the acceptable steps that we have always understood as the route to achieving knowledge.

Sometimes Uranian revelations seem wild and cranky to "sane" folk. People use pendulums or dowsing rods, or they perform mental exercises which seem to have a direct effect on apparently solid and immovable matter. Or they peer at funny astrological symbols and seem to know everything about you. It makes no sense to the earthbound mind – how they are coming up with these answers? – but it is a faculty of mind which can move backward into the past or forward into the future with equal ease, and achieves its conclusions through insight into the whole system. It isn't really foresight, in that sense; but the rational ego experiences it as such.

Audience: It is a very well known phenomenon in science that very often the same discovery is happening in several places at the same time.

Liz: It is possible that Uranus is connected with this kind of synchronicity of ideas. When an idea's time has come, it sprouts

---

everywhere, like a weed. Although there may be only one mouthpiece, the collective is receptive to that individual's pronouncements, because the idea is occurring simultaneously everywhere – even if it is not conscious. When people hear of it, they respond immediately, because it seems familiar; it seems true; it is what, secretly, they are leaning toward themselves. This is why I have started off saying that Uranus has nothing to do with the individual.

There are always Uranian ideas in formation in the collective psyche – glimpses of new ways in which the cosmic system can be applied in space and time. It is not that Uranus "invents" the system; rather, it allows us to have a sudden creative revelation of how the system connects with a particular life state or experience *now*. Important scientific innovations are always a remarkable marriage of immediate practical applicability and a glimpse of the broader workings of the system. When an idea's time has come, it will always burst forth through people who are appropriate conductors. The idea erupts through individuals, who are then credited with the new "discovery". But whose discovery was it? Remember, Prometheus gave fire to all of humankind, not just to one man or woman. Of course, a great deal depends on the integrity of the individual who serves as Uranus' mouthpiece. We have touched on this problem already. But the idea has the person, rather than the person having the idea. This is why an innovative idea will often occur to several people at once, apparently unconnected with each other.

Very often, when Uranus speaks through us, we think we have been really individual, and then we discover to our horror that the same thing has been said or discovered here, there, and everywhere. It isn't that we have created an original idea. We may bring solar individuality to the shaping and expression of the idea, but it is not our creation. It is an original idea that has had us, and also anybody else that happens to be a suitable vehicle.

Audience: It is the same with music and art.

Liz: This is the way the collective psyche works. One of the interesting things about Uranus aspects is that, the more of them one has got, and the more powerfully it contacts the personal planets and the angles, the more likely one is to be a lightning conductor for new ideas that are being thrown up by the collective. The strongly Uranian person may be very powerfully affected by these ideas, and may become a mouthpiece for them, wittingly or unwittingly.

So it becomes very, very urgent to know what is going on; otherwise the power of such ideas, and their repercussions on the behavioural level, can knock the ego flat. We may believe we are great geniuses who have seen the truth, and nobody else is willing to recognise it. In that case, we are liable to get ourselves into a lot of trouble. Or we may become terrified by a vague sense of standing on a precipice, and may react by nailing everything down to the floorboards – at which point, naturally, everything tends to blow up, especially other people, who generally do not like being nailed down with such ferocity. Or we simply go around in a state of dreadful anxiety, not understanding what it is that we are afraid of.

We may also act Uranus out, caught at the unconscious level by an idea which does not register in rational awareness, but which precipitates compulsive and disruptive actions. A number of very unpleasant scenarios can take place, if we are getting these collective energies pushing through, demanding to be given form in personal life, and we do not allow it or don't know how to deal with it. Then Uranus can go out of control.

Possession by Uranus

One of the things that taught me a great deal about Uranus was a propaganda film that the Nazis made, called *The Triumph of the Will*. It is a terrifying piece of cinema. Hitler gets up on the podium to speak to the masses, and at first he seems like a human being. He shuffles and looks at his feet alot. One can see that he is shy, diffident, and uncomfortable, and one can glimpse the human pathology that fuelled his ambitions – the violent father, the invasive mother, the failed architect's career, the sense of social inferiority. Then he begins to speak, and it is almost as if something alien, something inhuman or non-human, starts coming in. His words become more and more staccato and disjointed. His gestures become jerky and spasmodic, and more and more exaggerated. His body language is that of a puppet being jerked about by unseen strings.

Watching this film for the first time, I thought to myself, "There was once a person there, however twisted and warped. After all, there are a lot of ambitious, hateful, bigoted people walking on this planet; one can meet them or read their pronouncements in the gutter press every day. But here the human being is not present any more. Something else is there, something huge and collective and impersonal, speaking through this man. And it has also possessed the audience; there is a *participation mystique*." It was as though pure Uranian energy, a pure Uranian collective idea, was trying to pour out, presenting a new world-view; but the idea was contaminated by personal hate, and the perfect world of the Promethean vision was tainted by the individual man's human pathology even as it emerged, taking on a dark and destructive colouration. I found it absolutely terrifying.

Dissociation and possession by a Uranian spirit are obvious in this film. The Nazis didn't see it that way, of course; it is a propaganda film, and it was well received by a populace primed to embrace the Promethean vision with its "final solution" to the problem of an imperfect society. It says something about why Hitler's speeches had such enormous power over the people listening to them. It wasn't one man speaking – it was the collective psyche of the nation speaking, with certain special flourishes of a personal and particularly nasty kind. Hitler was clearly a mouthpiece for something which was bursting forth on a collective level.

Audience: Would you say the same thing about Jesus?

Liz: I have never seen Jesus on film. But I would say the same for anyone who serves as the mouthpiece for an ideology. I don't perceive Jesus as a mouthpiece for Uranian ideology, but more as an avatar for the powerful energy of the incoming Piscean Age. I am inclined to feel it was the latter. But it would seem that, apart from the larger spiritual dimension, the historical Jesus also had some very strong ideological issues concerning the Roman rule of Judaea, which was why the Romans decided he was a trouble-maker. The Romans didn't really mind what god one worshipped, but they didn't appreciate a religious vision which became political and defied the authority of the Roman state.

It is also possible that the Church may have different ideas about what Jesus was and said than Jesus himself had, and what we have received over the centuries may bear little resemblance to the original teaching. Texts have been systematically censored and doctored, and internal as well as external Church politics have undoubtedly rendered the original message virtually unrecognisable. Certainly the behaviour of certain dignitaries of the Church, over the centuries, has little or no connection with any gospel of love and forgiveness, let alone the abjuration of worldly wealth. And one might be forgiven for questioning the behaviour of many modern "good Christians", who behave in a fashion that is horribly unChristian, and as full of bigotry and intolerance as the Nazi elite – although fortunately, at the moment, without their political and military clout. This is obviously a hot issue, and I am afraid we are not likely to find any answers, however long we discuss it.

When a Uranian ideology is being expressed in this way, one can often see its repercussions in mass political rallies. There are no individuals any more. Hitler expressed this understanding when he wrote in *Mein Kampf* that at a mass meeting, thought is eliminated, and therefore he would speak to the people only as a mass. I have no doubt that the yearning for a redeemer – the Neptunian longing for salvation – contributed to the extraordinary receptivity the Germans showed to Hitler's vision. Also, the unaspected conjunction of Neptune and Pluto which occurred at his birth suggests extraordinary receptivity to the yearnings of his generational group. But his special personal gift, his personal charisma, seems to me to have been largely Uranian in nature. Uranus on the Ascendant in his birth chart enabled him to articulate a collective vision that triggered the unconscious

----

Uranian vision in all the individuals listening. The idea of the Third Reich, with all its implications, was not created by Hitler. It was an idea whose time had come.

Because of Uranus' tendency to generate dissociation and possession by an archetypal idea, it is urgent that there is a person at home, a strong ego-consciousness that can contain the Promethean vision and hold on to it just long enough to say, "Wait a minute, this looks great on paper, but who is going to be hurt by it? And am I morally capable of implementing it without my integrity being destroyed?" Without such sober questioning, we are at the mercy of something which is not intrinsically destructive, but which is archetypal and collective; and it may mow us down as easily as enlightening us. Maybe it will not do so globally, in the sense of a Third Reich, but it can flatten our individual values and feelings in specific areas of our personal lives, and then we must live with the consequences.

Uranus in the 4th and 10th houses (continued)

Now, after that little digression, how many are here today with Uranus in the 4th or 10th? These houses are, amongst other things, concerned with family inheritance; both are parental houses. You can all argue amongst yourselves during the coffee break, about which parent belongs to which house. But both houses are related to our psychological legacy. They don't describe the parents objectively, in the sense of a statement of who the parent really is or was. Rather, they describe our perception of what we meet in our parents. Usually this is an archetypal pattern which comes down through the family, and a lot depends on whether the individual parent was able to give positive expression to the pattern. Because Uranus is an outer planet connected with future evolution, the poor parent probably won't have been especially conscious of the powerful collective forces at work in the family psyche. Otherwise, he or she might not have been a parent, since Ouranos in myth is hardly a prototype for an instinctively nurturing progenitor.

By its very nature, Uranus will resist the obligations, emotionally and materially, of parenthood. It may seem a bit cruel, but Uranus in either of the parental houses does suggest that one or other of the parents had difficulty in relating to children, because he or she may have been deeply ambivalent about being a parent. Uranus reflects a spirit that seeks to break free of bondage to biology, social structures, family structures, and emotional obligation, and it is this spirit which, when the planet is in the 4th or 10th, will have been at work within the parental psyche. This suggests the sort of problematic issues that people with Uranus in these houses so often describe when they talk about their parents.

Often, when Uranus is in the 10th, the description of the mother is of a highly strung, unpredictable personality – perhaps one who suffered breakdowns, or was always on the edge of exploding. Actual separation from the mother, through death or parental divorce, does not seem to be that common with Uranus in the 10th, although I have encountered quite a few examples over the years; but if the parents part ways, the child usually remains with the mother, however unstable she might be, unless she is clinically mad. More often I have heard clients talk about the mother as someone upon whom they could not rely, or as a "nonmaternal" mother who didn't seem to really like children, or who was inhibited in the expression of physical affection.

But it is not very helpful to say, "Ah, you have Uranus in the 10th, so your mother must have been bonkers." The characteristic instability, unreliability, and tension associated with such a mother – whether overt or covert – may be linked with the archetypal qualities associated with Uranus. In other words, a powerful Promethean spirit of revolution and vision was at work within the maternal line, but, given the limitations of the social role assigned to women in general and mothers in particular, it is likely that the mother would not have been able to give full creative expression to the dynamic collective energies working through her. The very fact of being a mother would, in itself, be sufficient to make her feel trapped and stifled on some level, and even if she was totally devoted and utterly self-sacrificing, she may well have suffered terribly through the emotional and material bondage childbearing and childrearing would inevitably involve.

When Uranus is in the 4th, actual separation from the father is fairly common, perhaps because of what I just mentioned – when a parental breakup occurs, we tend to give children to the mother, which, of course, means separation from the father. Also, it is often easier for a father to leave an unhappy marriage, because his life may be lived mainly outside the home and he is freer to go, with more opportunities to make a new life, if he finds his present life intolerable. Sometimes Uranus in the 4th reflects upheaval in the home in early life – for example, constant moves or relocations – or a father who seems very aloof or inaccessible. I have also heard clients describe a father who was extremely demanding in terms of expecting intellectual excellence from his children, or a father who found it difficult to show physical affection or emotional displays of any kind.

All these images, of course, fit our picture of Uranus as a mental planet, a radical Promethean spirit working within the paternal line – autocratic, sometimes intellectually brilliant but frequently unstable, demanding perfection, and often sadly ill-suited to interact with an ordinary, flesh-and-blood child. Once again, Ouranos' inclination to repudiate the emotional and physical imperfections of his children may mean that the father never really wanted to be a father in the first place, except on the plane of the ideal.

With Uranus in the parental houses, one may encounter all kinds of disturbance and instability, overtly or covertly, in the fabric of the family psyche. Because the 4th and 10th are angular houses like the 1st and 7th, the instability is often literal and enacted, not only in childhood, but also in later life. The Uranian need to break down existing structures, which begins as a parental inheritance but ultimately belongs to the individual himself or herself, may be regularly expressed in one's domestic environment in adult life, so Uranus in the 4th is often linked with the wanderer, the emigrant, the person who feels compelled to escape the place of his or her origin.

One may meet the fluctuating position in the world which is so common with Uranus in the 10th, where the person doesn't wish to be bound by the material and social structures that dictate what constitutes a "proper" job or a "proper" role in society. It is a psychological truism that children are often compelled to live out the unlived life of the parents, and if the parent was unable to express any creative Uranian attributes, or forcibly suppressed the Promethean spirit, the child become adult with Uranus in the 4th or 10th may be driven to become a social revolutionary or an eternal wanderer, giving expression to a family daimon which forever seeks a Brave New World.

With Uranus in the 4th or 10th, the Uranian parental inheritance will therefore demand expression in adult life, often against our wishes, until we begin to make sense of the collective spirit of revolution that was trying to express through the parents, and perhaps also the grandparents. The child who receives such an inheritance must find a way to deal with it in a more creative way than the parents did. Some of you had your hands up earlier, when I asked how many 4th and 10th house Uranus people were here today. Would anyone like to comment?

Audience: I have Uranus in the 4th house. I was evacuated during the war, so I am really alienated from the rest of my family. My father was Welsh, but my parents separated, and he emigrated to Australia before I was born. We have never even met.

Liz: This kind of total alienation from the father or the family is not uncommon with Uranus in the 4th. It is an extremely painful experience, and I don't doubt it has cost you quite a lot. But perhaps it has also freed you from the kind of unconscious identification with family and roots which keeps so many people's minds narrow and parochial. You are describing a Uranian experience which cannot be linked in any way with personal culpability.

The instability of war often seems to be reflected by Uranus in the parental houses, especially the Second World War, when Saturn conjuncted Uranus. Here the Uranian spirit of anarchy, at work in the collective, surfaces in direct and personal ways in the childhood of the individual. Children born during 1941 and 1942 have the Saturn-

----

Uranus conjunction in the birth chart, and the feeling of anxiety, threat, and instability is often a permanent feature of their psychic landscape. Any sense of structure and security is sabotaged all the time, in part by early memories of what it was like. Loss of the father is common for obvious reasons, and so is the experience of a mother living on the edge because her husband or son is away at the war. There is a constant feeling that, any minute, everything is going to be pulled apart. The atmosphere of the war is described very succinctly by that conjunction.

Audience: My mother resented the fact she had me as an extra burden, without any help. I am sure my evacuation was due in part to her wanting to be rid of me, and not just because she wanted me to be safe.

Liz: Your certainty may be misguided. Perhaps she didn't want to be "rid" of you because of lack of love; perhaps she simply couldn't cope. This seems to be a common theme with Uranus in the parental houses – the child may interpret the parent's behaviour as unfeeling or unloving, but in reality the parent may be on the edge of a breakdown and is quite unable to respond to the child's needs and feelings. The impersonal nature of Uranian experience is often hard for us to digest on the emotional level, especially when the disruption or separation appears to be undeserved and unfair. We assume that personal feelings must be to blame – our own or our parents'.

But usually Uranus describes disruption through collective circumstances such as a war, even though, when it is in the 4th or 10th, we still meet it through the family environment, in relation to one or other of the parents. Sometimes Uranus describes the temperament of the parent. But I have usually found, when this is the case, that the parent was caught in an intolerable situation, and the whole scenario has more of the flavour of a terrible cosmic mistake than of a deliberate intent to hurt. Either way, of course, it is still ultimately the individual's responsibility to find some way of containing and honouring the Promethean spirit.

Audience: I also have Uranus in the 4th, but mine is conjunct Saturn. My background is totally different. The war didn't intrude on my childhood. But I grew up in a single-parent household in a northern working class environment, and at that time this kind of setup was totally unacceptable. My mother was always under enormous pressure, and was extremely unhappy. The thing it left me with was that I don't believe there is a way into that tremendous feeling of anxiety. It is a nub of anxiety that doesn't really ever go away.

Liz: Do you have it aspecting the Moon?

Audience: Yes. The Moon sextiles Jupiter, but it squares the Saturn-Uranus conjunction.

Liz: I was talking earlier about the deep anxiety of Moon-Uranus aspects, and you have the additional challenge of the Saturn-Uranus conjunction and the Saturn-Moon square as well. The latter suggests the loneliness, oppression, and unease you must have felt in your early environment, and also seems to describe your mother's unhappiness as well. I get the impression that you expect very little from others, except rejection or alienation.

Audience: I have a tremendous sense of not belonging, yet desperately wanting to. I just have lived in America for ten years, and I have been trying to get back to England. Now I am in England, and I have a sense of not belonging in England; but I had a sense of not belonging in America either. It is a feeling of not being rooted anywhere. And I can't even say that I have chosen it. I don't want to be a wanderer.

Liz: Saturn in the 4th square the Moon certainly doesn't. But perhaps there is a deep internal conflict, because Uranus in the 4th, on some level, may seek to uproot and remain uprooted because of the freedom it brings. I think your past will always hurt a bit; you were robbed of a sense of real family and community in childhood, and once that innocent sense of belonging has been taken away, it cannot be replaced. Even if you were welcomed with open arms and a queue formed outside the door to celebrate your presence in the community, you would never wholly believe in it. But I also think you can come to the point where you can accept the fact that you will never feel you belong. "Belonging" in the instinctual lunar sense is not necessarily the pot of gold at the end of the rainbow, and your sense of fellowship with other people may need to be rooted in broader or deeper affinities than family or neighbourhood. Until your perspective changes, you will be constantly battling with your longing to belong.

Audience: I don't feel I battle with it. But I know that I have a legacy of anxiety from my beginnings.

Liz: You used the word "desperately" earlier, when you described your need to belong and your feeling that it never seems to happen. Perhaps "battle" isn't the appropriate word. But whenever someone expresses desperation, I wonder whether the desperation arises from an inner conflict which is not being dealt with on a conscious level. Your sense of no roots may also have given you something very valuable, in terms of genuine tolerance. This is another gift of Uranus, which often comes out of the shattering effect Uranus has on stable life structures.

When one doesn't belong, one learns to be very tolerant; the wanderer is in no position to feel superior, because he or she learns to be grateful for any sign of welcome, regardless of the social inappropriateness of the welcomer. Do you know the *I Ching* hexagram, "The Wanderer"? People who are used to belonging, who take social acceptance for granted, can be appallingly intolerant, because they have never experienced deep loneliness. Sometimes there is no one more smug and insufferable than the person who has always had the luxury of belonging to a certain community, and feels superior because of it.

Audience: What you say is true. Because I felt so isolated in my environment, which I didn't choose, I felt especially sympathetic toward the underdog. When I saw any kind of scapegoating going on, I immediately rushed to the person's defence.

Liz: One of the things you may have to take on board is the way you deal with your anger about it. Chips on the shoulder, which are not unusual with Uranus, aren't very helpful in the end, and that is an area where you might be able to fruitfully do some work. Personal rage at impersonal Uranian circumstances is a difficult issue to come to terms with, and it is a pretty basic human reaction. But it can badly distort the Uranian vision, and the fire one steals has no power to warm.

The thing with Uranus is that, in the end, there isn't really anyone that we can blame. Even Prometheus realised he couldn't blame Zeus. Somehow we need to accept the nature of a system which is in process of evolution and often gets it badly wrong. Uranus in the 4th can envisage a perfect society, a perfect community, in which birth circumstances and parentage should not be determinates of value. That is the Uranian ideal of perfection. But the material reality is not like that. It probably won't be for a very long time, if it ever is, because there is always a fundamental problem with human nature. The Saturnian elements of human nature, which we all have within us, are hierarchical, and will always oppose the loss of social structures which define our place.

So somehow, that past which seems to be generating a lot of rage in you may need to be viewed differently. A slow, simmering, victim's boil can be very counterproductive, and it might prevent you from tapping the most creative dimension of a 4th house Uranus. That is to be, very genuinely, a citizen of the world, rather than an outcast or a scapegoat. The two are not the same thing, yet they are both related to Uranus in the 4th. Whether you feel like a scapegoat or a citizen of the world depends very much on how small or large your perspective is.

Audience: I don't feel like a scapegoat now. But I still feel I need to understand the nature of my early scapegoating.

Liz: Uranus can be a scapegoat, but Uranus can also be the person who perpetrates the scapegoating. Again, I suggest you all go to your local video shop and get out, if you can find it, that film *Zardoz*. When all

----

the scapegoats get together, they create a society in which those who did not suffer from their particular woes are scapegoated. It's funny how often that happens.

Audience: I also have Uranus in the 4th, and no matter how hard I have tried to create a stable environment, I have always failed. My marriage broke up and my family life was destroyed, and I never seem to find the kind of security I want.

Liz: Sometimes that is the price one pays for fire, with Uranus in the 4th. Family based on blood ties may not always be possible, and this can apply not only to the family of origin, but also to the family one tries to create as an adult. When Uranus is in the 7th, one can have an unconventional partnership, or when it is in the 2nd or 10th, one can work at an unconventional job and expect to be at least partly fulfilled. But the 4th house is the natural house of the Moon, which is fundamentally inimical to Uranus. Our human longing to put down roots is threatened by Uranus. If one tries to make a blood-related family life the basis of one's sense of roots and emotional security, it may get taken away – and there may be something inside which wants freedom from such emotional bondage, and which helps to ensure that one's family is comprised of something other than blood relations.

Audience: Are you saying I can never have a family life?

Liz: No, I'm not saying that at all. Uranus in the 4th can have a happy family life, with children and extended family and a stable home. But I keep emphasising that it is one's psychological attitude that is so important with Uranus. Can you please try to distinguish between physical reality and an inner attitude? Shakespeare's Hamlet says, "The readiness is all." A happy family life, on the external level, is not the same as the psychological imperative of making blood-ties the basis of one's security. I have met many people who love their families dearly, but who have a sense of deeper and higher realities, and are therefore equipped to cope with the sort of changes that occur in every life – children leaving home, relatives dying, the necessity of uprooting, the breakup of a marriage – without feeling the purpose of their existence has been destroyed.

There are also people for whom the conventional family unit is the be-all and end-all of existence. No outside relationship is "good enough" to compete with the family; no place is as reassuring as the family home; no wind of change is allowed through the triple-glazed windows. Without the family, one ceases to exist. When family means these things, then Uranus may pose great problems in the 4th. You said that you couldn't seem to find the kind of security you want. Perhaps it might be worth looking at just what kind of security that is, and whether it is truly right for you, or whether it might be a compulsive compensation for something else. Issues around your early family background might prove relevant. Many people who have experienced disruption in childhood, particularly the breakup of the parental marriage, try to create a kind of "perfect family" in adult life, to mitigate against the pain of early life and the fear that the disruption will recur. That may not be the best way to work with Uranus.

Audience: It isn't really a fair deal that Uranus gives, is it?

Liz: It depends on how you look at it. Uranian fairness is impersonal and doesn't cater to our emotional needs, and Promethean fire doesn't come cheap. Uranus in the 4th can offer enormous inner freedom, and the capacity to form deep friendships which are far more binding, enduring, and fulfilling than the "I don't really like you, but you're family, so I'll have to put up with you over the Christmas holidays" syndrome with which so many people are burdened. The deepest level of the 4th is concerned with one's spiritual home, one's spiritual source, and Uranus can offer a powerful intuitive connection with that source. But we must always pay a price for such extensions of consciousness.

It is like the feeling of scapegoating which we explored earlier. Several of you have spoken about having to give something up, in the area of life ruled by the house in which Uranus is placed. There seems to be a feeling of wrenching or tearing, or of having

----

something forcibly taken away. This is how our lunar, feeling, instinctual side experiences Uranus. With all the outer planets, one does have to give something up, in terms of personal contentment based on a conventional or purely instinctual definition of security. Family bonds are part of our instinctual means of survival, physically and emotionally. Animals too can have very strong family bonds. The family is the first place we go, for a sense of community and belonging.

If the Uranian spirit takes that away, what do we put in its place? What Uranus offers is a sense of *cosmos,* divine order and harmony, which creates family of a different kind. The intuitive awareness of interconnectedness, and the capacity for contact with people on a profound spiritual and intellectual level – whether they are physically present or absent – are the basis for friendship and fellowship of a truly humanitarian kind. This is of course quite alien to going home for Christmas and having turkey with the family. It doesn't mean you can't have the turkey too. But maybe it needs to be eaten with more detachment.

We need to recognise what Uranus has to offer, despite that lunar feeling of unfairness. It is an unfair deal, from the perspective of our personal needs. Chronic anxiety, feelings of being scapegoated or victimised, and a gnawing sense of life's uncertainty, are frequent components of Uranus' price. But although it is a high price to pay, the rewards are equal to the effort. I would say that about Uranus in any house, not just the 4th – if we can let go of that nagging feeling that there is something "wrong" with Uranian vision, that it is not normal, then we stand a chance of reaching the other side. But I think it is a difficult thing to do. It is painful in the 4th, because it is a watery house, like the 8th. There is something about Uranus in all the watery houses that forces us to let go of attachments of an emotional kind. Perhaps once is sufficient, or perhaps a repetitive pattern might be required; one cannot know. It is the attitude we take that is critical.

Audience: I seem to swing between a feeling of martyrdom, and a strong need to control what is going on around me. I suppose those are reactions to anxiety.

Liz: Yes, I believe they are. They are characteristic human responses to the inhuman feeling that we attribute to Uranus. Either we feel victimised, or we try to mobilise Saturnian control to protect ourselves. But although these are natural responses on one level, they are unhelpful ones on another. When Uranus is configured with personal planets – even the "soft" aspects – we tend to carry a certain element of anxiety in that sphere of life, and we have to cope with it as best we can. The same applies to Uranus' house position.

There are many different ways of trying to cope with anxiety, some more destructive than others, and some more workable. All are highly individual, and not really open to judgement by others – unless the methods involve injuring other people. It would be unrealistic, and perhaps even downright foolish, to expect that there is a doctrine one can espouse, or a therapy one can undergo, that will altogether remove Uranian anxiety. By its very nature, it is beyond the ego, and is not amenable to the ego's efforts at control.

The ego will always panic when faced with something that threatens it with change that is not of its own choosing. The issue here is not "giving up" the ego, but learning to recognise that it is only one character in the cosmic play, and may often have to bow to the will of other, more collective characters. We need to engage in a kind of dance with Uranus – we have to be able to contain its energies and inspirations, and make the effort to shape and channel them, but we must also recognise that we cannot make this planet the servant of our personal selves. This requires a special kind of flexibility.

Audience: What orb do you use for aspects to Uranus?

Liz: I usually allow about 10°. The closer the orb, the more intensely one is likely to feel it; but an aspect is operable within 10°.

Audience: Only with Uranus?

Liz: I use this orb with any planet in a major aspect – conjunction, square, opposition, or trine. With sextiles, I would use a smaller orb, around 6°. I have worked with 10° orbs for a long time, because, over

----

the years, I have observed that the planets speak through the person, not only in his or her ideas and attitudes, but in behaviour, style, words, body language, and tastes. One can see it most clearly if a particular planet doesn't make any other aspects. With narrow orbs, one thinks it is unaspected. Yet each planet's voice is unmistakable, and one hears it loudly and clearly, and then one discovers a 10° aspect. Although such a wide orb may not be as intense and compulsive as a 2° orb, it will still find expression in one's life.

Uranus in the 5th and 11th houses

Shall we look at Uranus in the 5th and 11th? What is this axis of houses really about?

Audience: Participation. Creation.

Liz: These are excellent definitions of the 11th and the 5th as separate houses. But at its core, the axis is concerned with identity – whether it is the "pure" expression of identity through the 5th, or the development of identity within the collective framework to which the individual belongs, through the 11th. The issue here is, "Who am I?" Am I myself in the sense of a special, unique, solar individual, or am I part of a "we"? If somebody comes up to me at a party, and says "Who are you? Tell me about yourself," do I say, "I am an astrologer," or "I am a banker," or "I belong to the Church of Scientology," or "I am an Aries," or "I am an organic gardener," or "I am a feminist," or "I am a wife and mother," or "I am a single, white, middle-class female"?

How do we identify ourselves as ourselves? By our own creations, or by the group to which we belong? We are told in traditional textbooks that the succedent houses describe "values". They relate to the bedrock on which we build our stability in life. Identity is one of the most basic, fundamental structures on which everything else is built. Both 5th and 11th house means of defining identity are valid and necessary. Uranus placed natally in these houses may make it very difficult to experience and define identity in so-called "normal" ways. What are the normal ways by which we define ourselves?

Audience: Usually by work, or social position and background. But I'm thinking about it now, and I've just realised that I tend to always mention my children. I identify with being a mother.

Liz: This isn't unusual; many people define themselves first as parents. But surprisingly, this isn't a 5th house definition, although the 5th is traditionally linked to children – it's an 11th house definition. Being a parent is not an individual thing, although the children we bear are distinct individuals, and so is our style of parenting. Being a parent is a statement that one is a member of a family, and that one is therefore contributing to the next generation in the "normal" fashion. It is a subtle statement, and carries many meanings apart from the obvious one. Being a parent is a passport to normality in many circles. We define ourselves to others, not only by our family background, but by the family we have created.

    We also define ourselves if we create artistically: "I am a painter. I am a writer." That is more a 5th house definition – identity is equated with an individual creative talent. But it still uses a socially recognisable phrase to describe who one is. Like defining oneself as a parent, it carries many hidden implications on a collective level. By saying, "I am an artist," one is also saying, "I am creative, I do not belong to normal society, I don't have a proper job. I am a little mad, all artists are, and therefore I don't 'fit'." Even the artist, by describing himself or herself as an artist, has found a collective group with which to identify – even if it is anti-collective. It is really unavoidable.

    We define ourselves by what we have made, or we define ourselves by the group to which we belong, be it intellectual, creative, religious, emotional, racial, or social. But the moment we use a definition which evokes particular responses in others, we are declaring ourselves in relation to "them", and we have come out of the 5th and into the 11th. Obviously it varies, but we all have group allegiances, to describe where we feel we belong. Uranus in the 5th or

_____

11th, however, tends to say, "Sorry, but you can't use that group. You can't use your children to define yourself. You can't use your artistic talents. You can't even use an ideology. Even if you think you're one of them, it doesn't describe the whole truth about your identity." The 11th is, of course, Uranus' natural house, and the 5th its natural polar opposite. We can come closer to understanding Uranus in general by recognising that the issues around the 5th and 11th are really Sun-Uranus issues – whether the planet is natally in one of these houses or not.

The effort to be somebody who is recognisable according to normal social criteria may be difficult or even impossible with Uranus in these houses. Who here has got it in the 11th? How do you feel in a group situation?

Audience: Well, I have a feeling all the time, in any group, that I can't identify with it. I am always an outsider. I can understand this level now. But it was painful as a child, trying to take part in primary school, and always feeling as if I didn't belong. I have Uranus in Cancer in the 11th, and I suppose I was hoping to feel I had a "family", at school and later with other groups. But it never happened.

Liz: That is Promethean loneliness.

Audience: On the other hand, now I feel at home, in groups like this one. I think we're all outsiders here, in some way. I might never see most of the people in this room again, but yet I feel I belong. It has been a long struggle coming to terms with this feeling of not belonging in the usual way. I wouldn't want to belong any more, to the kind of groups I used to try to get accepted by.

Liz: It's rather like what Groucho Marx once said: "I wouldn't join any club that would have me as a member."

Audience: I was thinking of Uranus in the 11th as a kind of sports commentator, reporting the progress of a football match. He's not part of the team, and he isn't really involved with the direct action, but he has to understand the whole picture. He needs to know everything that's going on. He's outside, but he's also an important part of the game.

Liz: That is a nice analogy. So we are really talking about a different level of group involvement, a different relationship with the group – one who is involved but does not belong. What is a group? Normally we think of a group as a physical collective of people, who get together and discuss something, or meet for a specific purpose. The people within the group are linked by virtue of readily identifiable affinities – they are local residents who have formed a committee to repair the roof of the village church, or they are studying the same subject, or they have a shared political or spiritual vision, or their children attend the same school, or they all belong to the same profession.

We normally group together in a concrete way, for recognisable reasons. But Uranus in the 11th may find this kind of grouping difficult, if not impossible. The Uranian group may consist of both human and non-human entities, dead people, people not yet born. It may be based on a vaguely intuited sense of a certain kind of spiritual or intellectual alignment, serving a vaguely intuited evolutionary goal. Specific shared interests may not enter into it, nor may practical reasons or physical proximity. One might not relate at all well to one's professional group, yet one may feel special affinity with people scattered all across the world, who do totally different things in life yet who are somehow "aligned" or perceive the same holistic vision.

Audience: Yes! As a child, and also as a teenager, I used to have relationships with all the people that I met in books. I spent a great deal of time playing with my books. Others found this strange.

Liz: Others usually find Uranus strange. The other important issue with Uranus in the 11th is friendships. One's friends often wind up living in countries that are thousands of miles away. The nature of Uranian affinities pays no attention whatsoever to the practical convenience of making friends who live next door. One might not see one's real friends for many years at a time. Yet the friendships persist, and do not fade with time and distance. They exist on a level altogether different from the "Let's meet for lunch in town next week" level. The Uranian sense of "group" is not physical in nature. It is a group based on something much subtler, and often denies the possibility of finding a sense of fellowship near to home. You are virtually commuting from Austria to do the CPA course in London, which seems to reflect a need to pursue group affinities that transcend physical proximity.

Audience: I cannot feel affinity with the seminars and courses that are available to me at home.

Liz: I appreciate the compliment. But it might also be because those seminars and courses *are* at home, which is too parochial for Uranus. What about Uranus in the 5th?

Audience: I have it in the 5th.

Liz: Let's start with the obvious. Do you have children?

Audience: No.

Liz: Do you want children?

Audience: No. I've never really wanted children. But I do have a niece, who is primary school age. My niece relates to me as a parent-figure, although I haven't tried to come between her and her mother. In some ways it is harder than if she were my own child, because of the tension between me and my sister-in-law.

Liz: So you have established a parent-child relationship with a child who is, in fact, not your own. You say that your niece relates to you this way, but presumably you also feel the same toward her. That is very interesting. I hadn't thought of it, but of course, it is very

Uranian, isn't it? It breaks apart the conventional, biological definition of the parent-child bond. The 5th house is, in part, concerned with the divine child within us, the spark of creative life and new potentials which we project onto our own children. You seem to experience this with a child whom you did not bear yourself. The "normal" definition of "my child" is often irrelevant to Uranus. Sometimes the children of Uranus in the 5th are noncorporeal – they are often creative, intellectual, or spiritual works. It is probably inappropriate in this group setting to go deeply into all the potential issues you might have around children – unless you want to discuss them?

Audience: No, I don't think so. Not at this time.

Liz: That's fine. Is there anyone else here with Uranus in the 5th?

Audience: Yes, and I *do* want to discuss my issues around children. I have a Jupiter-Uranus conjunction in the 5th. I have always felt ambivalent, wanting children and not wanting them. I had my first child during my Saturn return, and I have really felt she was Saturn's child – not her personality, but the sense of responsibility and frustration I felt. I feared, and still fear, being trapped. My daughter actually has a Sun-Uranus conjunction.

Liz: What seems to occupy you as a personal conflict is also very much a collective issue. It is being dealt with in many quarters in a vociferously ideological way, which you don't appear to be doing – and that is to your credit. But whether a woman bears children or not is very much a hot issue of the time. The Uranian struggle against bondage to nature and instinct can create enormous conflict in a woman with Uranus in the 5th. One's sense of identity cannot be based on parenting, and sometimes there is a powerful impulse to reject parenting in order to establish a deeper or broader-based sense of identity.

Audience: I tried to be conventional, but Jupiter-Uranus didn't allow that conventionally to come through. I couldn't feel whatever "they" wanted me to feel.

Liz: It seems important that you can be honest enough to say, "I am ambivalent." I also believe that it is far healthier for your child, who would know instinctively if you were masking your ambivalence with a great show of self-sacrifice and strenuous devotion. There are many people who are not honest enough to say it. Uranus in the 5th has a reputation for problems with children, and sometimes this can be linked with the parent's inability to admit occasional feelings of ambivalence. The child picks these up unconsciously, and feels anxious and insecure. Children tend to cope with what is explicit, even if it is unpleasant, surprisingly well, but suffer psychologically much more from emotional deceit and dishonesty. I will risk offending the obsessively maternal here, by saying that any person with Uranus in the 5th, if honest with himself or herself, is likely to question the decision to have children, and may continue to feel ambivalent about child-bearing and child-rearing throughout life. As we saw earlier, "child" may mean something quite different to Uranus from what it means to many other people.

Occasionally Uranus in the 5th can be linked with one of those apparent acts of fate that we have been hearing quite a bit about, where the loss of a child, or an enforced separation (such as a divorce involving custody of the child given to the other parent), occurs. This may or may not reflect any personal ambivalence, but may be part of a deeper pattern, which requires the individual to find a sense of identity through creations other than the biological kind. Sometimes the inability to have children is reflected by Uranus in the 5th, and there may not be a lot one can do about it – other than adoption or surrogate parenting, which are themselves extremely Uranian resolutions. One may long for children, but the situation forces the person to reflect differently on his or her life.

It is as though Uranus is saying, "You cannot establish your identity through the biological channel of child-bearing, so you must find it some other way." I have met many people who have become very desperate because of this inability to have children. But I question whether this desperation, so often leading to painfully frustrating scenarios at fertility clinics, is really the most helpful way to work with Uranus. I believe it is always wise, when we feel thwarted by the outer planets, to ask ourselves, "Might there be a deeper purpose in all this? What happens if I think it through differently, from a new perspective? Could my desperation be fuelled by the compulsive need to belong, to be seen as normal?"

Uranus in the 5th may ask us to rethink our definition of what a child is, and what kind of children – physical or otherwise – we are best suited to create as individuals. As a collective, we don't really like to think about this; it can be very threatening, because it challenges our identification with parenthood as a passport to social normality. Many women tend to feel they are somehow less than women if they do not want children, and many men feel their virility is in question if they do not produce offspring. Yet the ability to parent – as opposed to biological reproduction – is a talent like any other, not a universal given, and there are many people who might do better to create on other levels and leave the child-bearing to those who truly, deeply, and genuinely want, love, and empathise with children. And there may be still more people, especially those with Uranus in the 5th, who are certainly good enough parents, but who can relate better to their children as friends. Such individuals might do far better, for themselves and their children, if they are honest about it. With Uranus, we may need to find the courage to question our age-old entrenched assumptions about the nature of "normal" parent-child bonds.

Audience: I am not very attached to my children. I don't ignore them, but I don't worry about them. I just assume they will be okay. You're right – I see them as friends.

Liz: That is an honest expression of Uranus. But at some point you must have suffered from the feeling that you were a bad or abnormal mother.

_____

Audience: Oh, I did.

Liz: Such feelings can afflict men as well, with Uranus in the 5th. This is especially prevalent if there is a divorce and the child goes with the mother – as is usually the case. And it can be even worse if the man has left because he has fallen in love with someone else. He may say to himself, "I am an abnormal parent, because I abandoned the children." But paradoxically, the existence of children may be one of the chief factors behind the man's leaving his marriage. The 5th house is also known as the house of love, and in this domain too, Uranus may seek a more visionary, unconventional way of loving which does not inevitably result in "normal" committed family life. For many, perhaps even most people, love is expected to lead to marriage and the establishment of a family. Even amongst homosexual couples, there may be a strong wish to participate in a form of marriage ceremony, or adopt a child, or, in the case of a lesbian couple, bear one through artificial insemination. But Uranus in the 5th may seek a less tangible kind of commitment, and may struggle against structures which define love in terms of its products.

Sometimes the rebellious, visionary element of Uranus is lived out by the child. The more the parent with Uranus in the 5th tries to cement a "normal" parent-child setup, the wilder and more "difficult" the child is likely to be. The child may carry the unconscious projection of the parent's 5th house Uranus, and may be a good hook because he or she also has a strong natal Uranus. If the parent does not own Uranus, such a child may be driven to act out the Uranian spirit in a compulsively rebellious way. Then the distraught 5th house Uranus parent comes for a chart reading saying, "I have a problem child!" The child is not the problem. The problem is the parent's sense – or lack thereof – of what it is to be oneself without identifying with conventional parenthood. There may also be issues around hanging on too tightly to what one creates. When Uranus is in the 5th, one cannot identify with one's creations. One needs to be able to let them go.

Audience: I don't have Uranus in the 5th, but my parents both have it there.

Liz: That could be taken as an indictment – although whether of you or them, I am not sure.

Audience: My mother has the Moon conjunct Uranus in the 5th, and whenever she was angry with me, she would say, "Go away, you are not my child, go and change!" That was from the time I was twelve. Whenever my father disapproved of me, he was always saying, "I am sure you can't be my son."

Liz: And this, ladies and gentlemen, is what is known as projection. It is clear that your parents both tried to lock Uranus in the basement, and got you instead.

Audience: Whenever I was a good boy, they would say, "This is my child. Look at my child."

Liz: Perhaps they switched you in the hospital.

Audience: No, but I was born under the Uranus-Pluto conjunction. They have the child they deserve!

Audience: Are some communities Uranian? A friend of mine married a Canadian Indian and moved up to the far north. Recently they came to England with their son, and explained to us that they could easily have left him behind – he wouldn't have missed them, because everyone was seen as family. Then, later on, they had a second child, because the wife's mother wanted a child. So they had one, and it was considered the wife's mother's child.

Liz: Yes, that sounds very Uranian. There are communities, just as there are individuals, which work along Uranian lines. They generally pay no heed to hierarchies based on blood-ties. This kind of system can work very well for people who feel an affinity with it. It may work far better for some individuals than our more "normal" family unit, which, since Uranus transited through Cancer, has been showing signs of serious rot. Historically, there have been many experiments with these Uranian types of community. The Israeli *kibbutz* is a good example in modern times. Unlike the Neptunian communities based on spiritual longing and devotion to a guru or messiah, Uranian communities generally have an ideological or political basis, with strong principles about equality and emotional detachment.

Uranus in the 6th and 12th houses

Let's move on to Uranus in the 6th and 12th houses. First of all, what is this pair of houses about?

Audience: Service. Order.

Liz: I am not sure about the first, but I would agree about the second – this axis of houses is concerned, on one level, with order and chaos. Service is only one means by which people seek to cope with an experience of something greater than themselves, whether this is the interconnected fabric of the physical universe (the 6th) or the sea of the collective psyche (the 12th). Both these houses are concerned with the integration of personal and transpersonal realms. They are interior, cadent houses, and they precede the two cardinal houses concerned with individual expression in the outer world. As usual, I am not equating "transpersonal" with spiritual, but with dimensions of life which lie beyond the individual's personality and immediate world.

In the 6th house we are faced with the task of integrating body and psyche, and of making a workable relationship with the cycles and rhythms of the physical world. In the 12th we are faced with the task of mediating the collective psyche out of which we come. Both houses are concerned with an interface, with boundaries or loss of boundaries. So they are both houses of synthesis. But the elements of life which must be synthesised, and the means by which this can be done, are different. The 6th house is connected with the creation of boundaries through the acquisition of knowledge and skills,

---

which can allow us to exist as part of the larger cosmos without losing ourselves. The 12th requires us to relinquish boundaries, in order to discover the source from which we come.

Audience: I associate the 12th with transcendence.

Liz: What does this word mean to you?

Audience: It means to climb beyond, to move beyond. I suppose that is what you just said – moving beyond personal boundaries to something greater.

Audience: The 6th and 12th are mutable houses, and to me they represent a turning point, the end of an old cycle and the beginning of a new one. So they are a sort of preparation. Something has come to a point where it is about to become something else. It is as though something is being cooked.

Liz: That is a lovely analogy, and also a very ancient one. When you cook something, its original components are broken down, changed, and integrated in a new way. Alchemy uses the analogy of cooking to describe the preparation of the stone, the enduring core of the personality. The 6th and 12th are houses which are concerned with a new quality of relationship, a new mixture of individual and world. They are houses of alchemical transmutation. It has always annoyed me to see these houses, especially the 6th, relegated to simple definitions like "work" or "self-undoing". They are extremely complex houses. The 6th deals with new relationship primarily on a physical level, the 12th primarily on a psychic level, although the two are not so neatly divided, which is why illnesses of both a physical and psychological kind are associated with both houses. During the process of cooking, poisons can rise to the surface, and things are broken down. The transmutation occurs when the individual experiences being a unit in a much greater system.

In the 6th, the experience of being mixed with something greater requires an earthy reaction. In order to survive, one has to differentiate. Rather than losing one's identity by encountering the complexities of the body and the material world, one creates order, structure, names for things, disciplines, skills – in short, all the Virgo rituals that ensure that, even though we are part of something greater and must bow to its necessity, at least we feel we can cope because we have boundaries. "Work", from the perspective of the 6th house, is not what one does as a vocation – that is more the concern of the 10th. Work in the 6th is the means by which we take our place in the daily order of things. It is work as a ritual, a means of establishing order in one's everyday life.

In the 12th, the experience of being mixed with the vastness of the collective psyche requires a watery response. We are asked to let go of all those things by which we have identified ourselves as separate individuals, so that we can feel what the whole of humanity is feeling. 12th house cooking dissolves all the boundaries we work so hard to acquire in the 6th. We lose ourselves in the experience of the unity of the collective. The 6th is very much concerned with the life of nature; it is the life of the physical world. The 12th is the life of the collective psyche, including its inheritance from the past. I associate it with ancestral inheritance, which stretches back beyond the parents to the national, racial, and religious roots from which the family has come.

Perhaps we don't fully understand the extent to which the 6th house, and also Virgo, its natural sign, are concerned with the experience of something greater, of which one is a part. This is why Virgo often relates very well to plants, animals, and the rhythms of nature. An emphasis in the 6th house of the natal chart will often require the person to develop a greater awareness of these rhythms, including the rhythms of the physical body. Our bodies function according to natural laws, which we share with the other kingdoms of nature. We are part of a huge interconnected organic life, which we often meet in the 6th through some illness or stressful situation which forces us to recognise these natural laws. The 6th makes us just as open as the 12th to the greater cosmos, but it is through the physical dimension of the cosmos.

Through the 6th house we create rituals, habits, and repetitive, safe patterns of behaviour which allow us to cope with the body and the world. When Uranus is in the 6th, collectively acceptable rituals, habits, and behaviour patterns tend not to work very well. Uranus in the 6th is sometimes associated with health problems of the kind that baffle one's doctor. It may be connected with illnesses or symptoms that don't appear to have an organic basis. Uranus may require greater or deeper knowledge of the synthesis between body and psyche, and the subtler effects of the environment and the mental attitude on the body may have to be taken into account. Those with Uranus in the 6th may not be able to ignore their bodies or treat them according to conventional theories. One's entire sense of what the body is made of may be forced to change when Uranus is in the 6th, sometimes because one becomes ill for reasons that nobody seems to be able to explain. Sometimes Uranus in the 6th is connected with disruption in our efforts to create a rhythmic and stable working life. As I said before, "work" in the 6th isn't what we do, it is the rhythms we establish when we do it. We get up at 8 in the morning, get dressed, brush our teeth, eat our breakfast, and go to work. We have a coffee break at 11 and then we have lunch, and then we work until the late afternoon, and go home and have dinner. But when Uranus is in the 6th, this neat, safe package tends to come apart at the seams. Things go wrong. Whenever there is an attempt to create this orderly, "normal" kind of life, problems usually ensue.

In work or health, or sometimes both, Uranus may make its presence known by saying, "Sorry, but you need to understand material life on an entirely different basis. Learn to look beyond the given wisdom of the society around you. Look deeper. Live with instability." Hence Uranus in the 6th is also associated with an attraction to alternative healing methods, and with the development of skills and knowledge in spheres that don't fit into what many people consider a "proper job". Uranus in the 6th may reflect something in the person which simply cannot work for anyone else, or fit into anyone else's routines and rituals. Who in the group has it in the 6th? Would any of you care to comment?

Audience: As far as routines are concerned, I have had to recognise that I am always going to have erratic routines. I go to extremes in doing things, all or nothing, with a sudden burst of energy or just as sudden a burst of lethargy. As far as the relationship with the body goes, I find I am very sensitive to electricity. Recently I had an amalgam filling for the first time, and I upset my dentist because I said, "I can't cope with this because I am conducting electricity."

Liz: How did that manifest? Could you hear Radio 3 through your teeth?

Audience: I couldn't sleep on a bed made with metal springs. I had to sleep on the floor, wrapped in a warm blanket.

Liz: A lot of people, of course, would listen to that and say, "You are completely mad."

Audience: Yes, they have done.

Liz: This is usually what people say about our behaviour in the area of life where we experience Uranus. But what seems clear is that you are forced to recognise aspects of the life of your body which go beyond, or are not fitting into, the conventional definitions of how the body is supposed to work. Probably you should not just sleep on the floor and leave it at that. You might try to learn more about various theories and methods of alternative medicine. We would do well to remember that Uranus is concerned with the system, and in the 6th it can reveal the workings of the body's system in highly innovative as well as disturbing ways.

Audience: My partner has Uranus in the 6th, and he suffers from irritable bowel syndrome. He doesn't know whether it's physical or psychological.

Liz: He may need to start exploring all the psychological, as well as physical, issues that may be contributing to the problem. I hope that

----

any medical practitioners in the group will forgive me, but "irritable bowel syndrome" is one of those wonderful labels doctors are always creating, which explains nothing at all, except that the area of the problem is the bowel. The causes are, at present, a complete mystery to orthodox medicine, although usually diet and stress are considered relevant.

Audience: Could it be connected with stress at work?

Liz: Perhaps, but the deeper issues may be concerned with why he has chosen the work he does, and how he interacts with his environment, at work and outside it. The work itself may not be the problem. Probably the whole way he lives his life needs to be overhauled, because the 6th reflects one's habits, how one structures one's time, how one arranges one's day. It may be that your partner is caught in a situation that makes him feel safe but is also making him feel trapped and frustrated. There could be many factors involved. I am reluctant to discuss his chart because he isn't here to answer back. But my gut feeling is that he may find the life he lives "indigestible", because he is trying to be somebody other than who he is. He may not realise how conventional his outlook is.

Audience: I think you are right. He has a "proper job", with all that goes with it, and I don't think it's his path in life.

Liz: Shall we move on to Uranus in the 12th? Planets in the 12th can behave in a mediumistic fashion – they are conduits for the collective psyche. Usually there is something inherited through the family line, and sometimes even further back, through the racial and national background – the "ancestors". This "something" keeps trying to speak, and gets passed down like a hot potato from one generation to the next, accumulating power according to the degree of its suppression. Nobody wants any part of it – it is generally deeply unconscious and reflects a powerful complex in the family psyche. Finally it arrives in someone's 12th house, and out it comes, encrusted with the voices of many generations.

The 12th house is thus concerned with inheritance, although on a very subtle level. We think of inheritance as genetic or material; we don't generally think in terms of inheriting gods, archetypal patterns, or psychic conflicts. When Uranus is in the 12th, one may be forced to understand inheritance very differently. The Promethean spirit has been moving down through the family fabric for many generations, unknown and unexpressed, and it can pack a very powerful punch because it has probably been ruthlessly suppressed in the past by family expectations, assumptions, and codes of behaviour. The 12th house Uranus person may wind up feeling very odd indeed, and perhaps even quite mad, because one is buffeted by this dynamic and revolutionary spirit, but the family are busy denying it and insisting everyone is "normal".

We might fruitfully remember that, when Gauquelin did his statistical work, he found that a planet in a cadent house, placed just behind an angle, was far more powerful than one that was already "out", so to speak, and in the angular house. The sportsmen with Mars culminating had it in the 9th, not in the 10th, and the writers had the Moon in the 12th, not in the 1st. This may be related, in part, to the fact that such planets progress over the angle during the early years of life – by solar arc motion in every case, and also, if they are personal planets, by secondary progressed motion, unless they are retrograde – and are thus intimately bound up with the person's development during his or her critical years of psychological formation.

There is a kind of energy field around this latter area of the cadent houses, a sort of "nearly ready" zone, in which something is clearly hotting up. Sooner or later it manifests itself through the angle, and emerges into the outer world. Obviously not every 12th house Uranus is within orb of conjunction of the Ascendant, but to some extent this applies to a planet anywhere in the 12th; and it is particularly apparent when Uranus conjuncts the Ascendant from behind. Sorry, that sounds vaguely obscene, but I think you get the picture.

Uranus in the 12th often feels its differentness far more painfully than Uranus in the 1st. The ancestral inheritance of Promethean vision and disruption is usually extremely strong, but the individual does not identify with it, as he or she might when it is in the 1st, because it is a kind of "family secret". The sense of being a misfit usually occurs on subtler levels, and one feels it inside, rather than showing it on the outside. Uranus in the 1st might dress and behave in an eccentric fashion, but Uranus in the 12th tends to go around trying to be conventional yet feeling a little crazy. It doesn't communicate itself in the obvious way, but one feels it like a coiled spring inside. There is often great pervasive anxiety, and sometimes a deep fear of incipient breakdown, which, in some cases, is justified. One may feel compulsively called to free the family, to redeem it, to carry and enact the Promethean fire that has been damped down and stifled over many generations.

Because we receive so little education in these matters, and so little real help with them when we are young, the psychological imperatives which planets in the 12th symbolise often result in breakdown states. Breakdowns are, of course, not always destructive or "bad"; sometimes they are healthy and necessary, so that the personality can renew itself in a healthier and more flexible way. But they can be dreadfully frightening and painful to those undergoing them, because the usual psychiatric approach is medication and a total absence of understanding of what is really at work.

The Uranian spirit, anarchic and collective and erupting out of the 12th, may be connected with sudden states of dissociation and disorientation – not because one is inherently unbalanced, but because there has probably been far too much family suppression of any real vision or connection with the greater cosmos. When that spirit starts to go on the rampage, it will challenge all the ego's familiar structures and landmarks. The person may become terrified, and the power of Uranian vision is so great that it can break apart the personality – for a time – if the ego is not tough enough, and flexible enough, to contain it.

Audience: I have had a breakdown experience, which sounds very like what you are describing. But I have Uranus in the 8th.

Liz: Uranus in the 8th shares certain things in common with Uranus in the 12th. Both houses are watery, and both concern unconscious inheritance. But the 8th seems to reflect the immediate family background as well as one's own hidden side, while the 12th goes back much further in time. The eruptions of Uranus in both houses tend to come through emotional channels, and they are often very frightening because they reveal a previously unrecognised dimension of reality which, potentially, transforms consciousness. The difference seems to be in the quality of the experience. Uranus in the 8th is linked with sudden loss or separation, or with inexplicable eruptions of passion or compulsive feeling which overturn one's perception of oneself. Uranus in the 12th has more of a swamping tendency; one feels one's entire personality is disintegrating.

Audience: I didn't experience a feeling of disintegration. It was more connected with uncontrollable rage.

Audience: Talking in terms of eruptions from the hidden side of life, I have Uranus in the 12th, and one of the things that has been happening to me since I have been coming to London regularly is that I have been having numinous experiences on the Underground. I got onto a train on Friday night, and was really surprised to see someone I recognised. In fact, I recognised a couple that I had seen a week ago. But I don't expect to meet anyone on the Underground. I don't come to London that often, and suddenly there they were. It felt strangely familiar and comfortable. I have had other experiences, very strong ones. What a strange place to find a connection, or a sense of family – on the Underground! I feel I am part of a community. Certainly with family issues, my story is typically Uranian – I feel alienated from my parents. I visited my brother and my sister last year as part of my therapeutic process. I thought it would be good to try to go back and rebuild some of what had collapsed. But no – forget it. Obviously they think I am a real weirdo when I show up, because they do things like run UK Towels or sell port, and I am an astrologer walking in the door, a bit odd.

Liz: If you have Uranus in the 4th, 8th, or 12th, that kind of effort tends to prove very disappointing, although it's always worth trying. The ability to create "normal" family links often fails; one usually doesn't get away with it, even if one works hard at pretence.

Audience: I know we are talking about Uranus in the 12th, but I wanted to ask something about Neptune in the 6th.

Liz: Don't worry, you're allowed. The contrast between Uranus and Neptune in the 6th might prove quite illuminating.

Audience: Well, I have Neptune in the 6th, and my experience of it is that things come out in allergies. Whatever I am feeling, it tends to manifest in allergies and psychosomatic illnesses. I am just beginning to realise that Uranus can do this as well.

Liz: Any planet in the 6th may exhibit a tendency to somatise unresolved psychological issues; the issue will, of course, be reflected by the nature of the planet. Mars, for example, is concerned with will and self-assertion, and if this is not being expressed within the sphere of everyday mundane life, then anger may build up, and find its way out through typical Martial symptoms, such as migraine headaches.

The outer planets are particularly prone to it, because they deal with energies that are beyond one's personal experience. They are collective, and therefore they can feel very powerful and intimidating. The sense of being overwhelmed by collective forces, or in touch with collective ideas and inspirations, may make the ego feel threatened and impotent, and therefore feelings and intuitions may be suppressed. This means they may come out through the body, because they are not being integrated, either psychologically or in material life. But the kinds of symptoms are different according to which planet is involved, and they may require quite different ways of handling the energies creatively.

Uranian symptoms are often linked with a feeling of being trapped within a life structure that is too confining and restrictive. Or one's outlook may be too narrow and materialistic, and there may be

----

insufficient understanding of the body on subtler levels. With Uranus in the 6th, one may need to stretch one's vision, to perceive the physical body as an intricate, interrelated system in which the psyche plays just as important a part as the flesh itself.

Neptune's issues are usually related to a feeling of not wanting to be in incarnation at all, and Neptunian symptoms often reflect a sense of helplessness and a powerful desire for fusion with a parental surrogate or divine caretaker. Neptune says, "I can't cope, it's all too overwhelming. Somebody please look after me, I just want to go home." All three outer planets have a bad reputation for somatising when they are in the 6th house. Somatising may be the first stage of a process which eventually leads to a greatly expanded consciousness. But initially these planets may not be able to express themselves in any other way, because the ego is locked in a very earthbound world-view. So they may erupt through the body, because that is the only way in which they can make themselves known.

Uranus and the body

I would like to talk a bit more about Uranus' relationship to the body. Looking at Uranian pathology as well as Uranian creativity may be very necessary here, although what we call pathology may be the incipient stages of a process of opening up new levels of perception, or the result of a deep conflict between what one is on the ego-level and what one is unconsciously striving to become. But one of Uranus' rather bad habits, in the realm of the body, is that this planet is connected with a vision of perfection, an ideal state of being. There isn't the remotest possibility that the physical body is ever going to meet that vision. Even if one starts off with the most wonderful, beautiful, perfect body, it will still eventually grow old. By its nature, the body is flawed, and doomed to its mortal *moira*.

Uranus doesn't cope well with the process of aging, or the body's ebbs and flows and phases of weakness and illness. The Promethean vision utterly rejects this level of life. On the positive side, this vision has led us, as a collective, to find ways of prolonging

life, and increasing its quality and vitality, especially in the later
years, through a constantly growing range of medical and
technological discoveries. But when Uranus is too dominant in the
chart, particularly if it is in the 2nd or 6th house, or strongly aspects
the Moon (which is related to body issues), there is often a feeling of
revulsion against the body. This may be experienced against one's own
body, or against flaws in other peoples' bodies, because, of course, we
can project our sense of physical imperfection.

In relationships, Uranus often causes havoc in this way. When
it is strongly configured with Venus, similar issues may arise, because
of Venus' 2nd house associations. One may find the physical reality of
a partner disturbing over time, because of the realisation of the
beloved's imperfections. Uranus may also be connected with certain
eating disorders such as anorexia, where there is an obsession with
bodily perfection.

If we go back to the mythology, we can see this pattern very
clearly in Ouranos' rejection of his children. Anything which is
flawed, or doesn't fit the perfect image, is repudiated, or there is an
enormous amount of effort, energy, and often money invested in "fixing"
the imperfect thing. A great deal of pain may be generated by this
attitude, both in oneself and in the people one loves, when this
dimension of Uranus runs amok. It is also not uncommon in people who
are strongly Aquarian, if there is not enough earth in the chart to
provide a balance.

Audience: Could I prove your point? I'm an Aquarian, and I have an
8th house Uranus. I never thought about these sorts of things, until
someone pointed out to me how disconnected I was from material
reality. I've always ignored the physical world.

Liz: In its milder expression, Uranus may simply not bother with the
body. In its more virulent expression, it may actively hate the body.
One might be able to get away with not bothering – that is, as long as
one is young, healthy, and attractive. Any strong emphasis in an chart
– whether by planet, sign, element, house, or type of aspect – means
that we generally don't bother with anything outside the field of that

----

emphasis. In the case of a strong Uranus, this naturally means repudiation of other factors in the chart, especially the lunar realm (although Neptune and Pluto get a pretty raw deal as well). When there is active hostility towards the body, then I don't think one gets away with it at all. The first planet to show its frustration with Uranian perfectionism is usually the Moon, which has a tendency to somatise its pain. When Uranus is showing this particular face, there may be compulsive body issues, such as eating disorders, or an obsession with changing some particular facial or body feature to create a fantasised perfection.

Audience: Can Uranus do this with feelings as well?

Liz: Yes, it can exercise the same repudiation toward the feelings – particularly primal emotions, which do not fit into the ideal image. Once again, it is usually the Moon, Pluto, and Neptune which suffer under such Uranian tyranny. There are many people who feel that only when the excesses of human emotion are weeded out or reformed, will we have a perfect society.

Audience: Does yoga have any relationship with Uranus in the 6th?

Liz: Yes, I think it does. In the creative sense, yoga is a form of magic. It is a discipline which involves psychic or psychological as well as physical energy, and it aims toward balancing the human being through a synthesis of physical and spiritual. The Eastern approach to health has always been more holistic, more attuned to the cosmic system, than ours has, and could therefore be seen as more Uranian, although our high level of technology in medicine is also Uranian, in a different way. In itself, Yoga can be enormously creative and healing. Yet I have met many people who are obsessed with it as a kind of dogma. Once again, we can see Uranus operating in both ways – as a creative and constructive force, and sometimes as a rigid world-view which rejects every other perspective.

Audience: I am getting an image of Uranus in the 6th as obsessively concerned with cleanliness and sterility.

Liz: That is one possible manifestation. It can behave like the people in *Zardoz,* where no one ever becomes ill, ugly, or socially disruptive. That is one particular Uranian sci-fi dream. One creates the ideal environment – free of the jungle, free of germs, free of savage animals, free of greed, free of everything except those elements which allow the system to work perfectly and efficiently.

Audience: Dealing with Uranus positively seems to involve walking a tightrope between the ideal and the reality. How do we do that?

Liz: With difficulty. I don't know how one "does" it, except to keep trying and falling off one side, and trying and then falling off the other. Gradually one learns balance, grace, and muscular control, and the falls aren't quite so frequent or catastrophic. Like all the outer planets, Uranus requires us to live with a fluid relationship between individual and collective. Uranus does not symbolise the personal mind; it is the collective mind. There needs to be a sense of "I" in the middle, in order to stay on that tightrope; or perhaps the ego *is* the tightrope.

The awareness of "I" is built on very small things. The development of the ego begins in childhood, with body recognition and an awareness of what makes me feel good, what food I like to eat, what colours please me, what environment I want to live in. The development of a strong container is bound up with personal identity, personal tastes, personal talents, personal ideals, personal desires, personal values, and a recognition of personal limits. I am, of course, describing the functions of the Sun, Moon, Mercury, Venus, Mars, Jupiter and Saturn. Unless this recognition of personal self exists, one falls off the tightrope.

There has to be somebody home in order to contain Uranus. If one is obsessively Uranian, then rejection of the body and feelings – the foundations of the personal self – may create many problems. Understanding why the body seems so abhorrent, and why it is perceived in such a negative way, may involve a lot of painful exploration into childhood issues, and perhaps the necessity of building a healthy sense of "I" from its rudiments, within a therapeutic situation. A powerful Uranus in the birth chart is not "curable", and it can be a wonderfully creative and exciting dynamic. But paradoxically, to get the best and most creative dimension of Uranus, we need to develop the very thing that Uranus tells us we ought to dispense with in the name of an ideal: an ego, a selfish little self. The Uranian spirit within us will tell us a personal self isn't important, because humanity and human evolution matter more. But unless that little self is there, Promethean fire can destroy.

Aspects of Uranus to the personal planets

When Uranus aspects another planet, that planet becomes a kind of a lightning conductor for Promethean fire. The Uranian vision will regularly strike that area of one's personal life, and jerk one's awareness into a state of nervous alertness. We have already looked in some depth at Uranus aspects to the **Moon**. The Moon becomes the receptacle for Uranian vision, and thus one's instinctual nature and emotional needs will be constantly buffeted and denied satisfaction by alien winds from the starry heavens. One's instinctual nature is challenged to extend beyond the "normal" sphere of everyday life and human relationship, and it may take a long time for the individual to come to terms with this as anything other than bad luck, malevolent fate, or other people's callousness. Because the Moon's nature is fundamentally alien to Uranian vision, such aspects – whether "hard" or "soft" – are liable to be very difficult, especially in the early part of life. The Moon keeps saying, "What's going on? Why can't I have any stability? I don't want to be separate. I don't want to be yanked out of my nice home and torn away from my family. I don't want to know about any of this 'cosmos' nonsense. I'm terrified."

If Uranus aspects **Mercury,** Mercury is likely to be a lot happier about it than the Moon – even with "hard" aspects. Mercury says, "Ah, *that's* what's going on! I can see! I have the truth! I know the answers!" Mercury likes being aligned with Uranus. Other people might not appreciate the alignment so much – especially one's teachers when one is young, or one's more pragmatic colleagues when one is older. The darker dimension of these aspects – rigidity of thinking, crankiness, opinionatedness, self-righteousness – are usually more disturbing to others than they are to the Mercury-Uranus person. The great problem is that Mercury, itself a wanderer of no fixed abode, can become badly overloaded with Uranian electricity, and it is extremely important to mobilise Saturnian pragmatism and a sense of mental and physical limits, to protect the body and psyche. But given sufficient containment and common sense, Mercury-Uranus can be marvellously inventive and open-minded, although often determinedly undisturbed by the burden of self-questioning.

Venus gets on better with Uranus than one might think. In myth, Aphrodite is Ouranos' child, who rises from the sea after it is fertilised by the sperm from the severed genitals of her father. Aphrodite Urania is an expression of Uranus in more personal form, and astrologically, Venus has far less relevance to emotional relating than we might conclude if we rely on traditional textbooks. We like to link Venus to relationship, but Venus has little to do with the heart level of relationship. As the ruler of Libra, it describes our impulse to define our values through the contracts we make with other people – how we adjust to them, how we define the boundaries between self and other. This airy side of Venus describes how we compromise, and the deals we make. This is relationship as a system, rather than relationship as an expression of emotional closeness. So Venus can be quite a comfortable conductor for the Uranian vision – provided one is not overly afflicted with conventional attitudes, and is able to detach from one's emotional needs sufficiently to understand the rules of fair play.

Mars can establish quite a productive and energetic relationship with Uranus, although the raw physicality of Mars may pose a problem to Uranian ideals. Uranus tends to make Mars more intellectual, and less instinctual in its expression; and while that may make a person more civilised and socialised, it can also create difficulties on the sexual level, and in the sphere of expressing anger and aggression. Also, Mars, when it gets electrified by Uranian lightning, tends to forget the limits of personal will, and can get itself in a lot of trouble because the Promethean vision of potentials and possibilities may be beyond an individual's physical capacities. There is a strenuousness, a rigorousness about Mars-Uranus which can result in enormous feats of courage and stamina, but which can equally generate a kind of blind stupidity about danger and risk. Mars-Uranus may find it hard to accept that the power of one person to actually change the world is limited. I think the euphemism we generally use about these aspects is "self-willed".

Expressing the **Sun** can be very tricky when it's involved with Uranus, because the solar urge for self-expression is inimical to Uranus in many respects. As we know, these planets rule opposite signs. The Sun says "Just a minute, this global consciousness is all very well, but what about me? Who am I? Never mind the evolution of humanity, and the ideal world, and all that abstract stuff. What about my personal fulfillment? How can I be special, how can I shine, if I am having to live a life that serves the *Zeitgeist?*" The Sun may struggle with Uranus, and sometimes the sense of individuality is crushed under the global vision, or under a peculiarly rigid and dogmatic vision of life. If the sense of personal ego is sufficiently strong, the person can find ways of utilising personal talents to make a contribution on a broader level, while still preserving a sense of self-value. Then life can become a bit like Odysseus grappling with Proteus. One struggles to shape the Uranian inspiration into creative work – artistic, scientific, or social – which is uniquely one's own yet embodies or channels a wider vision.

Of the personal planets, I think the Moon has the hardest time with Uranus, and Mercury the easiest. That is not to say that there are no problems with Mercury-Uranus; but the two planets are basically friends, whereas the Moon and Uranus are alien to each other, and have no common ground. However, this alienness can be enormously creative. The only place where they can find common ground is a system or vision which can serve as protection – which can be a kind of mother as well as a link with the greater cosmos. As we have seen, this is why Moon-Uranus has a reputation, more than Sun-

----

Uranus, for involvement with astrology – mapping the system provides a glimpse of a kind of cosmic mothering, freed from instinctual bondage and at the same time offering inclusion and surety.

Uranus aspecting the personal planets seems to reflect intense sensitivity to the greater cosmos and the potentials for the future that are revealed through such openness. This develops, in part, because the individual is usually denied comfort from a "normal" environment early in life. Or perhaps it is the other way around. Because Uranian-aspected personal planets sense a bigger universe right from birth, no environment is perceived as normal. Even with benign aspects, we are driven, consciously or unconsciously, to find something larger and more inspiring than the world we meet around us.

So, willingly or unwillingly, we begin looking for the open spaces of the starry heavens, and as a result, special gifts develop, as well as special problems in relating to ordinary mortal life. We could say this about any outer planet hitting the personal planets. Because we are forced to experience things that wrench us out of our very personal, earth-based identifications, we can develop the capability of seeing and experiencing a much greater universe. But most of the time, at least initially, it isn't by choice.

Audience: What about progressed aspects to Uranus?

Liz: Progressed aspects involving Uranus will generally bring a Uranian experience, inner, outer, or both, but the experience may not necessarily create the kind of ongoing openness which natal aspects describe. But one certainly gets a glimpse of the greater system at work – often through events which are deeply unwelcome at the time. It is like doing a kind of crash course in the art of stealing fire. If one is unused to it, one gets burned as a matter of course. Uranus transits and progressions tend to coincide with periods when one is kicked awake, into an awareness of what lies behind and beyond the tangible structures of life. But if the birth chart is weighted on the side of earth and water, or if Uranus makes many difficult aspects, then this awakening may be unpleasant and unwelcome, and there is no guarantee that the individual will learn what might be learned from it. Uranus can be quite traumatic by transit or progression, and sometimes people close down afterward, terrified that something similar might happen again. This, naturally, ensures that, when the next transit comes around, the impact will be even more upsetting.

Audience: I have Uranus aspecting every planet.

Liz: Then you have probably come to the right place. You should most certainly not go to work at the NatWest Bank. What do you do?

Audience: I work for the Local Authority.

Liz: That might be even worse than the NatWest. Did you go into this work because you had ideals about improving social conditions?

Audience: Yes, I did. But they didn't last very long.

Liz: If Uranus is aspecting every planet, then you will sooner or later need to make yourself at home in the Uranian world, and the Uranian world is, generally, sadly absent from local Councils. They would like to think that they are Uranian, but they are generally far more Saturnian and Neptunian, and any incipient vision gets buried under the weight of bureaucracy, with not a spark of solar fire in sight. In every area of your life you may need to keep doors open.

Audience: I have begun to realise this in the last year or so.

An example chart

Liz: We have enough time left to discuss a chart from the group. The placement of Uranus in Eva's chart is quite striking. It is on the Descendant in Leo, opposite Chiron rising in Aquarius, and trine the Sun in Sagittarius. It is also square Neptune, so we are looking at one of the generational outer planet configurations I mentioned earlier.

When I was talking about Uranus in the 7th, Eva, how did you respond?

Eva: Well, I was thinking that I always have an image of the perfect romantic relationship, and I am still waiting for it. It is so compulsive that I can't accept the fact that someone is simply human. There seems to be no way I can get rid of this.

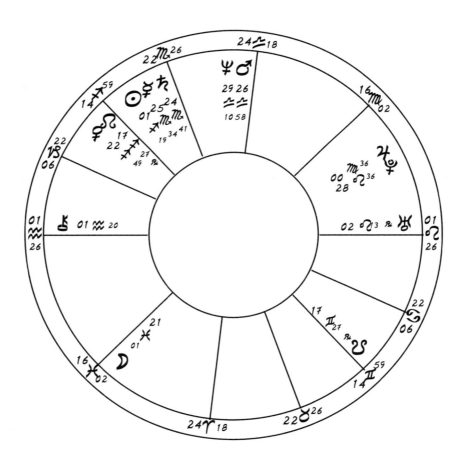

Eva
[Chart data withheld for reasons of confidentiality]

Liz: I wonder whether this image of the perfect romance is a defence against something. Uranus in the 7th doesn't usually go around with a perfect image of romantic love. It may seek unconventional bonds, or bonds which are free from the usual role-playing, with all the restrictions involved. But perfection in the romantic sense is a Neptunian longing, not a Uranian ideal. Uranus may demand a relationship which is more inclusive and flexible than the models of love and marriage which were available to you when you were growing up, and which you might have met in your parents' marriage. It is not impossible to find a Uranian relationship which is freer and more stimulating than conventional marriage; the social climate is increasingly favourable toward such bonds, at least in European countries. But because Uranus is opposite a rising Chiron, I would guess that deep personal feelings of inadequacy and insecurity might be making you avoid any relationship in which you fear rejection. I think you may be using these impossible ideals in order to protect yourself against hurt.

Because Aquarius is on the Ascendant and the Sun is trine Uranus, the chart ruler, your world-view and values are likely to be deeply attuned to new Uranian ideas arising from the collective. But the chart contains a deep dichotomy. On one side is the spirited, freedom-loving, Uranus/Sagittarius nature, with Venus also in Sagittarius. On the other side is a group of more emotional, instinctual placements – Sun square Pluto, Moon in Pisces, Mars conjunct Neptune, Venus trine Pluto. These two "camps" aren't likely to be friends. And Chiron, which is exactly sextile the Sun, is rising, opposite Uranus. This opposition forms a T-cross with the Mars-Neptune conjunction in Libra, itself very idealistic in the romantic as well as the spiritual, 9th house sense. Chiron's opposition to Uranus seems very important. What does it suggest to you?

Eva: I haven't really thought about Chiron.

Liz: It might be a good idea to start thinking about it. Chiron placed on the Ascendant suggests deep feelings of being wounded or damaged, and it is likely that, being independent of spirit and inclined to look forward and upward, you want nothing to do with such feelings. Earlier, we looked at the 1st house as the house of personal image, and with Chiron here, your image of yourself may, unconsciously, be a very low one. Chiron's feelings can be deeply unpleasant and uncomfortable, and not at all in keeping with the optimism and universal outlook of the Sun in Sagittarius trine Uranus. But rather than be seen as a damaged, needy person in a relationship where you might be hurt or humiliated, you may be ensuring that this can never happen, by espousing a set of standards that no one can meet.

If you want to work more creatively with what you call your "compulsive" behaviour in relationships, you may have to get more insight into whatever wounding Chiron is describing. This might also help to bridge the gap between the Uranus/Sagittarius side and the Neptune/Pisces/Pluto side. Uranus can provide you with an easy and positive line of defence because it is your chart ruler, and makes a friendly aspect to the Sun. So you are innately sympathetic to Uranus. Looking at life through universal spectacles would come quite naturally to you. But you may be identifying with an outer planet in order to avoid a deeply personal conflict, and that usually doesn't work very well in the long term.

Eva: Uranus is transiting my Ascendant at the moment.

Liz: This transit may bring a lot of revelations, particularly as it goes over natal Chiron and forms an opposition to its own place. This is the famous "mid-life crisis" aspect which generally brings all the unlived loose pieces to the surface. I suspect you will end up much more conscious of what this dynamic is all about, and certain old fears from the past may be less restrictive as a result.

With regard to your pattern in relationships, it might also be worth looking at the parental issues described in the chart, especially your relationship with your father. Our early parental relationships, and the parents' interaction with each other, are invariably involved in any compulsive relationship pattern in adult life. The Sun trine Uranus suggests certain things about the psychological inheritance from the father, and some of your Uranian values – particularly those involving repudiation of the "flawed" bits of the personality – are probably linked with him. Some of his values may be extremely positive, and you probably have a deep affinity with them, but at the same time, perhaps other sides of your personality are being shut out. Compounding this is Saturn at the MC in Scorpio, conjunct Mercury and the Sun, suggesting that he might have had a very repressive effect, not only on you, but also on your mother, who seems to be imaged as a frustrated, rather unhappy or downtrodden person.

Eva: Well, I have always tried to live up to the expectations my father had of me.

Liz: I think your father might not have expected a child with a rising Chiron, let alone one with the Moon in emotionally needy Pisces. This suggests a child who is complex, has certain emotional difficulties and conflicts, and is human, not celestial. In many ways you are expressing the themes we have been exploring all day. The Uranian emphasis in the chart can be enormously creative, but I think you are also hiding behind it, and your individuality is more than just Uranus. At the very beginning of the seminar I mentioned that Uranus can actually be inimical to individual expression. Your essential nature includes everything in this chart, which means the sensitivity of the rising Chiron, the excesses of Jupiter conjunct Pluto in the 7th, the vulnerability of the Pisces Moon, and the emotional intensity of Venus trine Pluto.

Eva: I didn't think Venus was trine Pluto.

Liz: Pluto is at 28° Leo, and Venus is at nearly 23° Sagittarius. Perhaps you just don't want them to be trine.

Eva: My computer only allows 6° orbs.

Liz: So your computer didn't want them to be in trine. How very Uranian of it. Why don't you adjust the size of the orbs in your programme? Six degrees is a small orb for a trine. Moreover, they are actually within 6° of orb. Your computer also clearly has Mercury square Jupiter, as you do, and seems to be editing out what it doesn't want to deal with. I should have a think, if I were you, about that Venus-Pluto aspect and all that it implies about your emotional and sexual needs, and ask yourself whether your father found such qualities acceptable in a daughter. You might even ask if he found them acceptable in a wife. This would, of course, affect your ability to find them acceptable in yourself. Uranus, with its impersonal cosmic voice, would probably dismiss that Venus-Pluto trine as Titanic, and therefore suitable only for banishment to the underworld.

An entire generation was born with the square between Neptune at the end of Libra or the beginning of Scorpio, and Uranus at the end of Cancer or the beginning of Leo. In this group there is an intense emotional longing for an experience of total unity in relationship. But at the same time there is a ferocious resistance to any dependence on other people, and in the case of Uranus in Leo, the quest for personal freedom can be quite compulsive. So those with this square are struggling all the time with a split – between an overwhelming, almost mystical vision of emotional unity with loved ones, humanity, or God, and an intensely independent energy that fights virulently against any form of emotional bondage. With each individual, the emphasis varies, depending on the overall balance of the chart and the involvement of personal planets with the square.

Usually, at least in the first part of life, those with this square tend to take sides. Your Aquarian-Uranian emphasis, supported by free-wheeling Sagittarius, is likely to try to shut up not only the Venus-Pluto trine, but also the Mars-Neptune conjunction. Such qualities may seem too clinging, dependent, demanding, passive, and needy. If you had Pisces rising, and the Sun were trine Neptune, then probably you would identify with Neptunian ideals, and Uranus would be the enemy. Then you might express your emotions in a very uninhibited fashion, and be unashamed of being a flawed human being; and then you would have an entirely different sort of problem. We can't win, you know.

Audience: The problem about always wanting to find the perfect partner is that years and years can be spent looking, and then at the end of it, you find what you think is the perfect partner, and that person doesn't think you are perfect for them.

Eva: I am in a relationship at the moment, and I enjoy it, but I go on looking for my perfect ideal. It means I can't commit myself.

Liz: This protects you from other feelings, which might be very uncomfortable and painful. One of them is the fear that you might be seen as imperfect, and also that you might start needing too much, and then get humiliated, as I suspect your mother was. The Uranian spirit may also protect you from binding yourself in a relationship in which you might have to sacrifice your individuality as your mother probably did. Here is the Moon in Pisces, suggesting that some issue of sacrifice surrounds your image of your mother. In that sense, Uranus' insistence on avoiding commitment may serve a positive function, because it has helped you to escape the repetition of a family pattern in which a conventional female role proved stifling to a potentially creative woman. But there may be options other than simply being opposite to your mother.

Some of your resistance to such commitment is probably perfectly appropriate. It is your Uranian spirit saying, "I don't want to wind up like her." Saturn is in the 10th house in this chart, and this house is associated with the experience of the mother. Uranus in the 7th may be saying, "I don't want to be trapped by convention like her, and have all my creativity destroyed." So Uranus is also fighting for freedom of spirit and creative expression, by rejecting the conventional maternal and wifely role model. That may be absolutely appropriate for you. But perhaps this fight is too compulsive and dominant, and Uranus is not allowing other planets to express themselves.

Eva: I find it a bore watching the dance of life and not taking part in it. I am getting very tired of this pattern.

Liz: Don't worry. With Uranus approaching the Ascendant, and moving into opposition with its own place as well as conjuncting Chiron, I don't think you will be bored for much longer.

Audience: One last question, please, before we finish? What about the fact that the Moon in Pisces is the only planet below the horizon?

Liz: A singleton, whether by element or by hemisphere, is always extremely important, because it moves against the drumbeat to which the rest of the chart is attuned. It represents a powerful focus of energy that keeps challenging the other planets, not allowing them to settle into habitual patterns of expression. The Moon, the only planet in the "subjective" or personal half of the chart, emphasises what I would interpret as a powerful drive to be emotionally fused with others, and this could invoke a very great fear of emotional dependency. It is in the 2nd house, which might reflect a deep need for stability and security, especially in your relationship life. This Moon in Pisces suggests an extremely strong emotional nature, full of imagination, yearning, and dreams of fusion; but this powerful emotional force may operate primarily at an unconscious level, or perhaps through artistic work.

Eva: I am an artist.

Liz: Then you have an important outlet for the expression of the Moon, although artistic work alone may not be sufficient for the entire range of the Moon's needs. The Moon in Pisces echoes both the Mars-Neptune conjunction and the Venus-Pluto trine because of its emotionality, underlining the importance of close emotional involvement. This is not a detached Moon, and separateness is likely to be very painful for this side of you. It is another statement of how extremely important it is for you to start exploring those vulnerable feelings which Uranus, busily stealing creative fire, is doing such a good job of silencing.

Thank you for giving us the chart to discuss, Eva. We have come to the end of the seminar now, and thank you all for attending.

Bibliography

Addey, John, *Harmonics in Astrology,* L. M. Fowler & Co., Romford, 1976.

Aeschylos, *Prometheus Bound,* in *The Tragedies of Aeschylos,* trans. E. H. Plumptre, David McKay, Philadelphia, 1931.

Bailey, Alice, *Esoteric Astrology,* Lucis Press Ltd., London, 1965.

Harvey, Charles and Harding, Michael, *Working with Astrology,* Arkana, Londn, 1990.

Jung, C. G., *Psychology and Alchemy,* Vol. 12, *Collected Works,* Routledge & Kegan Paul, London.

Jung, *Alchemical Studies,* Vol. 13, *Collected Works,* Routledge & Kegan Paul, London, 1973.

Jung, C. G., *Mysterium Coniunctionis,* Vol. 14, *Collected Works,* Routledge & Kegan Paul, London.

Manilius, *Astronomica,* trans. G. P. Goold, Harvard University Press and William Heinemann Ltd., London, 1977.

Plato, *Timaeus,* in *The Collected Dialogues of Plato,* ed. Edith Hamilton and Huntington Cairns, Princeton University Pres, 1961.

Roberts, Jane, *Seth Speaks,* Prentice Hall, Englewood Cliffs, NJ, 1974.

Roberts, Jane, *The God of Jane: A Psychic Manifesto,* Prentice Hall, Englewood Cliffs, NJ, 1984.

Taeger, Hans Hinrich, *Internationales Horoskope Lexikon,* Verlag Hermann Bauer, Freiburg, 1992.

Tarnas, Richard, *Prometheus the Awakener,* Auriel Press, Oxford, 1993.

Part Two: The Transits of Saturn and Uranus

This seminar was given on 17 February, 1996 at Regents College, London, as part of the Spring Term of the seminar programme of the Centre for Psychological Astrology.

The meaning of transits

To begin our day, I would like to make some general points about transits, so that we have a framework within which to explore the transits of Saturn and Uranus. As with all astrological interpretations, we need to understand the core meaning of what we are dealing with – not only the nature of the particular planets involved, but also the nature of planetary cycles. We use the word "transit" in our work all the time, yet I wonder whether we are always clear about what we mean. We say, "Transiting Saturn is conjunct my whatnot," or "Transiting Uranus is opposing my thingey," and we then produce a string of assumptions about what this transit will "do" to us.

But what are we really talking about? Do we mean that a piece of rock, orbiting around the Sun through the force of gravity, is causing funny things to happen to us? It isn't at all a bad idea to remember, whenever we speak of transits, that we are dealing with cyclical movements within the psyche. We can't really understand transits except in terms of psychological dynamics, because everything we experience – however concrete – is perceived through the individual psyche. Even if we wish to restrict our interpretations to external events, nevertheless we still need to recognise that there is a human being who will respond to – and perhaps has even attracted or caused – the external event, and whose responses will be highly personal. The perception of an event is a highly subjective business. The event and the person are not separable. As Jung once said, a person's life is characteristic of the person. A transit, whether of

----

Saturn, Uranus, or any other planet, is both the individual and the event which he or she experiences.

Transit cycles

The transits of Saturn and Uranus are only really comprehensible as cyclical inner patterns, rather than as isolated transits which hit one thing or another in the birth chart. Most of us are likely to get Saturn going around twice if not three times in a lifetime. Even if one does not manage a Uranus return, there is still the opposition at mid-life. This cyclical pattern does not occur with the other heavy planets – they move too slowly. The cycles which they symbolise are larger than the individual. Our lives form part of their bigger collective cycles, but we do not experience their complete circuit around our birth horoscopes, and so we can only intuit the full import of the larger cycle within which we live. Neptune and Pluto never complete their cycles during an individual lifetime. Jupiter and the inner planets move much more quickly, and although they are no less important in their own way, they do not reflect the basic drumbeat of the individual life. The cycles of Saturn and Uranus form the underlying rhythm of our lives, over which the melody lines of the faster-moving planets are played.

So during the course of the day, try not to think of Saturn and Uranus making "hits" and then vanishing into oblivion until the next "hit". Every transit of these planets to a natal placement draws on our memory and experience of all the previous Saturn and Uranus transits to the same natal placement, and this cumulative fund of experience – including the associations and feelings we attach to it – in turn shapes the impact and outcome of the next Saturn or Uranus transit. If we see Saturn approaching the Sun by conjunction, trying to interpret it in isolation will not really tell us the essence of what this transit is about.

We also need to consider the square it made to the Sun roughly seven years earlier, and the opposition it made roughly seven years before that. We must really begin with the very first time transiting

---

Saturn made an aspect to the Sun, and then look at the chain of experiences which followed each time a subsequent aspect occurred. As astrologers, if we wish to understand the meaning of a transit and really make use of the insights, we need to go back over our lives and look at the connecting thread of meaning which links all the independent experiences like a string of pearls. One pearl at a time doesn't tell us much. But if we can see the entire necklace, or a large part of it, then we know what kind of underlying psychological pattern we are dealing with.

All transits are part of a cycle, and all planetary cycles connect with other planetary cycles and create repeating patterns in the birth chart. Nothing in a chart is isolated and nothing is really a "one-off". Even if we cannot keep all the various ongoing *leitmotifs* and themes in our minds, the realisation that they are there can make us view an individual transit from a more comprehensive perspective. Even if a transit only occurs once in a lifetime – say, transiting Pluto conjunct the natal Sun – nevertheless this apparently isolated transit is part of a greater cycle. Before one was born, Pluto may have been hitting various important points in the family charts, which link up with the degree of one's natal Sun. It may hit one's children's and grandchildren's charts later on, even though it has moved past one's own Sun. Even where an individual lifetime is not sufficient to see the completion of the cycle, it is still a cycle, and we are part of it.

Rather than thinking in terms of transits representing isolated events, or reflecting isolated inner experiences, we need to remember that they are always part of a continuing process which will never complete, because it is ultimately the process of the cosmos itself. Depending on one's particular philosophy of life, we might see this eternal process as something that pertains to the development of the universal as well as the individual soul; or we can understand it on the molecular level, or as a reflection of the great ongoing movements and trends of the collective psyche, manifesting on the social level.

Whatever it is we are going through at a particular time, we need to think how it might connect with what was happening the last time the same or a similar configuration occurred. The actual nature of the aspect between a transiting and natal planet – "hard", "soft",

----

tense, easy – is less relevant than the relationship between the two planets in the birth chart. This relationship is described not only by any existing natal aspect between them, but also by their respective house and sign placements, and how each of them "fits" into the overall birth chart picture. And we also need to look at the issue of psychological opposites, since certain planets are naturally friendly or inimical to certain other planets. Saturn and Uranus are mythically ancient enemies, but they are also a father-and-son duo, and their transiting cycles, regardless of the actual aspects formed to natal placements, will always retain this highly ambivalent relationship between them.

Transits as teleology

Transits describe a process which can enact itself on several different levels, inner and outer. For the sake of clarity, I will use a rough grouping of three levels. I have found that viewing transits in this way is quite a useful tool to begin the interpretation of a particular planetary picture. Each of us tends to favour one of these levels of interpretation more than the others, depending on the astrological orientation and psychological approach of the individual astrologer. Many astrologers interpret transits primarily from the perspective of what we might call ultimate meaning. In other words, transits are concerned with the unfoldment of a higher pattern or design, and reflect a spiritual reality underpinning external events. Jung used the word "teleology" to describe the ultimate purpose of a particular psychological experience or symbol. We can apply this word to transits as well.

We can ask ourselves what a transit is "meant" to teach us – what it can potentially offer in terms of our growth. This approach assumes that there is a deeper meaning inherent in a transit, an intelligent spiritual or psychological goal which the transit symbolises. This is essentially a positive and constructive approach (although often sadly ungrounded), because teleology usually implies a pre-existing cosmic benignity. We do not perceive teleology in terms

----

of evil intent, unless we are deeply paranoid or severely disturbed, because we could not otherwise bear life. Whether the meaning we perceive is truly implicit, or injected into experience through the power of human imagination, attributing teleology to the experiences symbolised by the transits gives us a strong container in which to deal with life's apparently random unfairness and suffering. There can be great healing in understanding transits teleologically, although there are also great problems if we use this approach to the exclusion of others.

Transits as psychological patterns

If we focus exclusively on the ultimate meaning of a transit, we may overlook how the individual actually feels, and what the experience is like for them at the time. Then we may fail to understand and communicate with the client who comes to us seeking help. Whatever the teleology of a transit, we also need to understand the psychological pattern which it represents, and the emotions and associations which are likely to be invoked when that pattern is enacted. Although we may define the ultimate "intent" of a transit, we may fail to appreciate that the emotional experience may be quite opposite. For example, a transit of Uranus over natal Moon may reflect the potential for freedom from old family emotional patterns, and a broader and freer expression of feelings and imagination. We can also interpret it as an opportunity to extend the sense of family to humanity as a whole, and we can talk about the possibility of a new environment and a new relationship with the body.

That looks really good on paper. But while the transit is going on, the individual may feel quite wretched. He or she may experience terrible anxiety, and a frightening sense that all the familiar landmarks are being swept away. Great insecurity may arise, and one may be pitched into a recollection of childhood memories and feelings which are extremely painful and disturbing. Talking about the ultimate meaning of a Uranus-Moon transit may prove very helpful. But equally, it may not be helpful except in retrospect, and it may need to be combined with a genuine empathy for what the person is going through right now. This may be particularly important for those people who are rooted in feeling rather than thinking, and who do not easily detach and view life from the cool heights of the Uranian ethers. The last thing such a person is likely to want to hear about is ultimate meaning, because the process itself feels so terrible. We all like the sound of the word "freedom", but sometimes we forget, not only the price we must pay for it, but also the deep reluctance we may unconsciously feel at having to grow up and take responsibility for the consequences of our choices.

Regardless of the positive meaning of a transit, the individual may be subject to apparently inexplicable emotional and somatic reactions which seem to bear little resemblance to our understanding of the teleology. A transit of Neptune square the Moon may suggest a wonderful opportunity to move beyond personal needs and achieve a deeper and more compassionate relationship with the whole of life. It may also describe a necessary process of separating from the parental background. But on the emotional and physical level, the individual may experience strange compulsions which defy rational explanation, and which cause considerable pain and distress. Such compulsions are likely to reflect the urgent longing for fusion and the loneliness and isolation inherent in leaving mother's womb, and they may baffle the more spiritually inclined astrologer who isn't equipped to make sense of the compulsive eating, the sudden horror of being touched, or the death-fantasies which invade sleep in the middle of the night.

Or we may say to the client, "Oh, Saturn is coming into opposition with your natal Sun, and that gives you a chance to crystallise your identity. How wonderful." But however wonderful the opportunity, the person may be so heavily depressed that the last thing he or she is interested in is abstract concepts like crystallising the identity. He or she may feel tired, depleted, discouraged, unloved and ugly, and may be so trapped in mundane responsibilities and parental complexes that the sight of the wood is lost for the trees. Talking about inner development may seem like a load of rubbish at that moment, because of the painful sense of inferiority and failure which so often accompanies the early stages of self-discovery.

We need to be able to respond to the person's present suffering, and reflect back how it feels in terms which offer psychological insight and human empathy, as well as enlightened interpretations of what can be gained from such a transit on the spiritual level. Many people experience transits through disruption in their close relationships, and how they feel matters as much as any ultimate transcendent purpose. The range of emotional experiences varies enormously, and may be quite diametrically opposite to the meaning implied. It is up to us as astrologers to be able to put the two together, and help the client to recognise the kinds of responses which are likely to occur in everyday life, as well as the deeper archetypal patterns at work and the potential inherent in what is being experienced.

These two fundamental levels of interpreting transits are both vitally necessary. If we try to escape our emotional suffering and conflict through an overemphasis on teleology, we are only saving up worse emotional effects for later. Even "good" transits may carry a high price tag. In order to take advantage of the opportunities on offer, we may have to leave something behind, or face something we prefer not to face. If we try to avoid an honest dialogue with the client by using ultimate meaning as a kind of shield against emotional discomfort, we are cheating at our work.

Understanding the likely emotional patterns of response which accompany a particular transit will not spare us having to go through the experience, but it may spare us making stupid choices which could have been avoided if we had better psychological understanding. Understanding the teleology of a transit can, as I said, give us a container in which to face the more difficult aspects of life, because a sense of meaning is a powerful tool for healing and growth. But we must ground this in how we feel now, in incarnation, in order to make the teleology something which can be embedded in actual life.

Transits as events

Transits may also reflect events, of both a physical and a psychological kind. Here I am differentiating between emotional responses (which I was describing above) and a psychological change of some kind – a "happening" which definitively affects the individual's outlook toward life. Internal events of this kind are not always identical with the external event which triggers them, and they may even happen independently of physical events. For example, the psychological event of separateness – the lonely realisation that one is an independent entity in the world – may occur under a Saturn transit, but it may not be accompanied by an outer separation, such as leaving home or the breakup of a marriage. Or it may be reflected by a concrete event which seems diametrically opposite, such as the birth of a child, which for many people triggers an unexpected awareness of aging and the passing of time, and the recognition that one is no longer a child oneself.

Events of both an inner and outer kind are the third basic level on which transits may be expressed. It seems that we need encounters with the outer world of a concrete kind, in order to recognise and process internal change and development. In the main, the events which happen to us are the ones which somehow mirror what is occurring inside. But it would be a mistake to overlook the level of manifestation and deal exclusively with the spiritual and psychological dimensions of a transit. Manifestation is also part of our individual reality, and often it is impossible to comprehend ourselves without this mirror of incarnation.

Even if we can't be precise about what kind of concrete events are likely to take place, we can still make some educated guesses about what kind of psychological events will take place, in addition to the emotional responses which might accompany a particular transit. We need to recognise and respect the fact that transits are likely to manifest in some way in our lives. They don't just go by and, through some clever sleight of hand or psyche, make no impact on our material reality simply because one has "psychologised" or "spiritualised" them.

If the transit's expressions are purely inner, this does not mean we have been exceedingly clever. I have sometimes met people involved in depth psychology who have the strange idea that, if they do enough internal work, the movements reflected in their horoscopes will cease to have anything to do with their outer lives. This is incredible *hubris,* to say the least, since it implies that the conscious ego can control the cosmos. We may be able to make more intelligent choices, and avoid silly decisions which get us in trouble. But that is not the same as psychologising a transit into ineffectuality.

Sometimes astrologers say, "Oh, such-and-such a transit went by, and nothing happened!" But what does "happened" mean? Usually, when people say this, they mean that no specific concrete occurrence coincided with the day the transit was exact. But I have never seen a transit where nothing happened, in terms of the psychological responses of the individual. Moreover, a psychological event can occur long before, or long after, the physical event. In other words, the impact of the event on the individual may be delayed because he or she has not caught up emotionally. Or the psychological event may anticipate (or even cause) the concrete event.

Take, for example, the situation of divorce. When does a marriage end? When the decree *nisi* has been passed? When the two people decide they have had enough? But what if the marriage is finished for one, yet not for the other? Sometimes the event of divorce does not occur for one partner until several years after the actual legal divorce, and often it depends on a new relationship being formed. One can sometimes see this clearly through transits over the composite chart. Sometimes the powerful transit which signals the real ending of the relationship (such as transiting Pluto conjunct the composite Sun or Ascendant) coincides, not with the couple's separation, but with one of them remarrying.

A transit picture which clearly suggests the breaking up of a relationship may occur years before the couple part, but family responsibilities or financial issues keep them physically together when, emotionally, both people know the marriage has died. I have no doubt that transits reflect events. Although I am known as a "psychological astrologer", I do not see physical reality as less

important than the psyche of the individual. But I often think that
our arbitrary division of psyche and matter is just that – arbitrary, and
not an accurate reflection of the true nature of reality. Our definition of
an event may need to be subtler, deeper, and inclusive of the inner as
well as the outer world.

There are schools of astrological thought which focus almost
exclusively on concrete events, and there are schools which focus
almost exclusively on meaning. There are also schools of thought
which focus almost exclusively on the individual's emotional
responses, but these are mainly psychological rather than
astrological, and, sadly, they often do not avail themselves of the
insights astrology might offer them. Such focusing is necessary and
valid, because we all have different areas of concern, and different
aptitudes as astrologers. But clients have different needs, in terms of
which level is going to matter most to them. Some people want to know
what is going to "happen" to them, so that they can plan sensibly;
others want to know the meaning of what they are going through. Still
others want to understand why they feel the way they do. It is not our
job to decide which of these levels is superior or correct for the
application of astrological insight, although we may have to be
honest about which we understand best and deal with most
effectively. We need to have at least some appreciation of the
importance of all three levels, even if we choose to spend our time
talking primarily about only one.

Orbs in transit

The last general point I want to make about transits is that
they have orbs. We don't wake up on Thursday morning and experience
the full import of a transit precisely at 08.23 hours, when we are in the
bath. Something may indeed happen in the bath, but something has
probably been happening for many days, weeks, months, or even years
(in the case of slow-moving transits like Pluto), and the entire period
will reflect the meaning of the transit. Transits reflect a process which
is essentially cyclical. They have a time of secret underground

----

development, a time of outer expression, and a time for digestion and integration. Subsequent transits of the same planet, such as those which occur under the Saturn cycle, flow into each other, so that the conjunction ebbs and flows into the semisextile, the semisquare and the sextile, which in turn lead to the square and the trine, and so on.

We can observe the same ebb and flow when a transiting planet moves through the houses. As it approaches the cusp of the next house, it begins to throw its energy into that house, while still affecting the affairs of the house it is leaving. It isn't as simple as saying, "Right, when you are fourteen and a bit, Saturn will be opposition Saturn for exactly ten days, and then it's all over until you are twenty-one." The same orbs we use in natal interpretation apply to transits, and I would allow 10° for major aspects. This means that transiting Saturn may aspect a natal planet for a period of up to two and a half years, not merely a few days when the aspect is exact.

Transiting Uranus may aspect a natal planet for several years, if we consider an orb of 10°. This entire period is likely to be full of Uranian energy, although most of the time the process is quietly working beneath the surface of consciousness. The so-called "sudden" events which so often accompany Uranus transits are not really sudden at all, when seen in this context. They are the eruptions of an underground process which, periodically during the course of the transit, produces effects which rise to the surface and are reflected in characteristic Uranian "happenings". There may be points during the course of the transit when we come face to face with the transiting planet in all its archetypal power. But more likely we will meet it in our dreams, our moods, and in the currents of our feelings and fantasies, until something is ripe like fruit, ready for the picking.

Recognising the importance of orbs helps to clarify why so many of the important shifts related to the inner process of the transit take place before, not when, the planetary aspect is exact. It is rather pointless to think in terms of an exact transit of Uranus opposition one's natal Sun in two years' time, when the planet is already within 8° of orb. That transit is already happening, while one is busy making a note in one's diary to plan for disruption two years hence. A little introspection may reveal that the feelings associated with the transit have already begun to influence one's life, although, as I said earlier, those feelings might not bear much resemblance to what we understand as the teleology of Uranus opposition the Sun. They may take the form of a creeping anxiety, a sense that something threatening is looming, and a strong urge to nail everything down. One may feel anything but Uranian during the buildup. If one is trying to understand what this transit means when it is within 8° of orb, one doesn't have to peer into the future. It is here, on the doorstep, right now.

Anyone here who works with depth psychotherapy will probably be familiar with the way in which transits throw their shadow before them, sometimes years before the aspect is exact. Images appear in dreams which are unmistakably related to the transit, such as the underground tunnels and dark, sinister figures associated with Pluto, or the bondage and heavy, earthy themes connected with Saturn, or the oceanic fusion motifs associated with Neptune. Transits also show themselves in the development of the transference, which begins to reveal qualities linked with the transiting planet long before the aspect is exact.

One of the things I have learned from doing analytic work over the years is that the transit has begun its gestation in the unconscious from the time that it moves within 10° or 11° of the natal planet. We may think we have nothing to think about until it gets within 1° of orb. But it doesn't work like that. It is a gradual process, a segment of an ongoing cycle, and the more understanding we have during the buildup period, the more creatively we can work with the energies operating within. What we are then doing is getting intelligent insight into our own psychic patterns – cooperating with them, participating in them, and creating a relationship between the ego and the larger psyche which has definite effects on the outcome of the transit.

Because we are dealing with orbs, we will also find that very rarely is a transit unaccompanied. This applies particularly to those transits whose cycles are linked by a particular relationship in time. For example, most of you will know that the Uranus cycle and the Saturn cycle are connected through multiples of around seven years. Neptune is also plugged into this time frame. When we have transiting Uranus opposition natal Uranus, we will also have transiting Saturn opposition natal Saturn within a couple of years, and because of the orb factor, these often overlap and are connected psychologically. Transiting Neptune will also be square natal Neptune at roughly the same time. When we have transiting Saturn making its second square to natal Saturn, we will also have transiting Uranus square natal Uranus at roughly the same time. Whoever orchestrated the planetary orbits has a very keen sense of rhythm.

If we think about this inevitable coincidence of transiting aspects, we will also realise that any natal planet involved by aspect with Saturn, Uranus, or Neptune will get all three hitting it by transit at regular intervals. In the first half of life, the progressed Moon may also join in the fun, since it returns to its natal place not long before the Saturn return. It's rather like a cosmic gang-bang. The important junctures when these transits cluster together are the times when we pass through the well-known critical stages of life – puberty, the mid-life crisis, retirement, and so on. We must take the whole picture into account, even if we begin by exploring the cycles one by one.

For example, a person who has natal Saturn square the Sun will always experience a Saturn transit to the Sun at the same time as a Saturn transit to natal Saturn. At certain junctures, particularly in the first half of life, he or she will also have transiting Uranus hitting both natal Sun and Saturn, a little before the Saturn transit. And sometimes transiting Neptune and the progressed Moon will hit natal Sun and Saturn at the same time as transiting Saturn and transiting Uranus. Although the exact aspects do not occur at precisely the same time, the relevance of orbs means that there will be an overlap. The two natal planets are wedded to each other, and every transit will always involve both, even if by minor aspect.

The meaning of the Saturn cycle

These general points about transits are meant to provide an introduction to exploring the specific transits of Saturn and Uranus. Although I have taken quite a bit of time on it, I feel it is important for us to recognise the complex fabric which transits weave. Let's start now with the cycle of Saturn, and try to get to the core of what it means and what its psychological as well as material repercussions are likely to be. What does Saturn "do"? What does it symbolise? What is in store for us at the important points in its cycle? We know that Saturn is concerned with crystallising things, with inner and outer structures, with autonomy and self-preservation. So what does the Saturn cycle represent, as an inner process?

Saturn and separation

   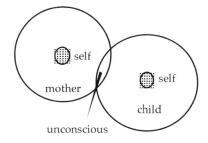

The young child   **The post-pubescent child**

This is a very simple – not to say simplistic – diagram, based on one by Edward Edinger, which many of you might be familiar with. It can be useful to understand the psychological level of the Saturn cycle, as well as its teleology in terms of the formation of the individual. On the left is portrayed the psyche of the young child – perhaps two to three years of age – reflecting the unconscious identity which exists between the child and the mother. There is sufficient difference for there to be emotional conflict, but insufficient distance for the child to have a distinct identity. The sense of self in the child is still virtually fused with that of the mother, although some separation is apparent. In early infancy, the two circles would overlap absolutely. In a newborn child, the sense of "I" does not exist. This is Neptune's world of psychological fusion, the pre-Saturn, preincarnation state. Freud called it primary narcissism – identification with the source of life.

The diagram might be seen as a picture of the psychic state before the first Saturn square. By unconscious identity, I mean that the child's feelings, thoughts and imaginings are heavily coloured by those of the mother, to the point where the child – and sometimes the mother too – cannot distinguish who is who. It is through this merged unconscious that children absorb so much of the parent's unlived life, and all the "inherited" complexes which lie within the family psyche.

It is through bodily and emotional frustration that we gradually move from the absolute fusion of the newborn to the left-hand diagram of the two-year-old, and on to the right-hand diagram of the teenager. Deprivation teaches us that we are separate – deprivation of food or affection generates fear, anger, and loneliness, expressed in a child's crying and raging tantrums. In the ordinary run of things, with a "good enough" mother (to use Winicott's phrase), these negative feelings shift into something more positive and substantial – the gradual realisation that we can survive, at least for a time, without mother. This is the beginning of self-reliance.

On the right is portrayed the adolescent – around fifteen, just after puberty, which means after the first Saturn opposition to its own place. While there is still some shared unconscious identification, there is a greater sense of separateness, and the awareness of an independent self exists. Of course, this is an ideal diagram, describing an ideal pattern of development. Naturally, there is no such thing. In real life, these perfect circles would be lumpy like potatoes, and the process of separating would be messier, and there would be bits stuck all over the place. Maps are useful, but they should never be taken as a literal description of the country through which one is travelling.

The process of separation which I have so briefly summarised is an archetypal human experience. We all undergo it, just as we undergo the inevitable physiological developments of childhood. Frustration – the denial of our instinctual needs – is inevitable even with the "best" of parents, and if it is embedded in a relationship of love, trust and acceptance, it is the formative tool of self-development. We are defined by discovering what we cannot have, and by running up against limits which, eventually, we internalise. This process gives us a sense of where we end and others begin; and thus we learn to adapt to life with a realistic recognition of our limits as well as our abilities.

The Saturn cycle makes us separate people. That is its meaning – its teleology, if you like. The cycle of Saturn builds, stone by stone and brick by brick, a defined, incarnate being. We are looking at a pattern of growth which is archetypal, and which applies to all living things; and we are also looking at a definition of mortality, because that which is separated from its source must one day die. Only in the realm of timeless fusion with the source is there eternal life. From the beginning of life, the burden of Saturn drives us to accept and make the best of the thorny road of mortal incarnation, and all the aspects it makes during the course of its cycle gradually crystallise a distinct and separate identity.

That looks great on paper – definitions of the teleology of a planet always do – but it should be immediately obvious that the process of individual formation involves separating from others on very profound levels, often including the physical one. We cannot become something distinct and solid without first separating ourselves from all those external and internal collective ideas, feelings and objects on which we have depended, and with which we have identified. And this will inevitably cause us pain.

Old Cheesefoot severs, castrates, confines, separates, crystallises, and creates barriers which prevent or obstruct fusion. On an emotional level, one of the characteristic expressions of the various junctures of the Saturn cycle is therefore loneliness. Loneliness is not the same as aloneness, which is an inner recognition rather than a feeling – the "existential" realisation of one's existence as an independent entity. Loneliness hurts, and can create desperation, which makes people behave in sometimes very destructive ways. And because of this crystallising, isolating, separating quality which accompanies Saturn transits, a sense of failure is also one of Saturn's characteristic expressions on the emotional level. Incarnation, on the one hand, means bringing forth into life. On the other hand, it means darkness, imprisonment, and separation from the source – whether we experience this source as maternal, cosmic, or both.

If you reflect a bit on this process of separation, and also think back to the critical junctures in your own life when this kind of psychological self-definition was most emphasised, you will see very quickly why it is so difficult to assign specific events to the stages of the Saturn cycle. How this cycle manifests is very much based on a person's character – or, in other words, on the whole chart and all the various configurations in it – and, equally important, on the level of consciousness which the person can bring to bear on what is happening. External circumstances usually play an important part, especially the family environment, the social and work milieu, financial issues, physical health, and one's personal relationships. In order to understand the kind of inner pressure which Saturn's transits symbolise, we need to have a lot of understanding of the client, so that we can see the transit in context. We are all different as individuals, and although Saturn's process is archetypal, it will be expressed differently in each person.

We respond to denial and frustration in very different ways. The sign in which Saturn is placed will tell us a great deal about the ways in which we deal with limits, and the kinds of defences and structures we build to protect ourselves from further experiences of denial later in life. The means by which we cope with separation when young is also the means by which we cope with future separations, and this forms the basis of how we defend ourselves when confronted with fear, loneliness, anxiety, and denial of our needs. A person with Saturn in Taurus, for example, will react to separation in an intensely physical way, for it is likely to be physical separation which hurts the most. So it is through defensive clinging to material security or physical contact with others that the Saturn in Taurus person may react to threat.

We need to consider not only Saturn's birth placement by sign, house and aspect, but also the world in which the person is living at the time of the critical stages of the Saturn cycle. There are "optimum" conditions for getting the best out of Saturn's transits, although usually we do not recognise what these are until we have learned the hard way what they are not. So if, for example, a young person of twenty-one is living at home with his or her parents, and has not really moved out into the larger world through university or a job, the Saturn square which occurs at this time is likely to be extremely difficult. The optimum conditions for this square need to provide room for extended worldly horizons and the opportunity for decision-making. At this age it seems to be a natural part of the psyche's impetus to want to explore wider intellectual and social terrain. The period between the first Saturn opposition at around fourteen and a half, and this second Saturn square at around twenty-two, is a period of preparation which, hopefully, culminates in firmer ego-boundaries and a new level of self-definition.

But a great deal depends on whether this young person is able to make the shift. If the family is too enmeshed, and the earlier stages of the Saturn cycle have not successfully contributed to the formation of a solid ego, then the person may experience terrible panic and a sense of intense ambivalence. He or she wants and badly needs to move out into the world, yet there is a powerful regressive pull to return to the earlier stages of life, when protection was provided by dominant parent-figures and no decisions or personal responsibility loomed on the horizon. This ambivalence and panic can occur even if the young man or woman has managed to get to university or finds a job. This is partly why so many breakdowns occur at this age, as well as glandular fever, that classic somatised signature of internal conflict and unhappiness.

If there is enough resistance to the inner dictates which such Saturn transits represent, then on the external level Saturn may appear to bring material difficulties, misfortune, illness, restriction, and emotional unhappiness. I believe there is a direct relationship between our willingness and ability to pass through these inevitable stages of separation, and our tendency to unconsciously draw disasters down on ourselves which force us into separateness through means we would never voluntarily choose. When we are younger, we may not be able to fully grasp the issue of accepting aloneness. But we can grasp it instinctively, if we have been given enough early support, and if we are prepared to support ourselves. Within many individuals, the anti-

----

separating lobby is vociferous, and drowns out the possibility of recognising the great inner opportunities Saturn presents. There is too much identification with parents and collective, and too little self-value.

The person may go through a crisis and yet learn nothing, and then, of course, at the next critical juncture of the cycle, the same issue appears again, but bigger and more insistent. The more time goes by, the worse it gets. But the person may become more and more defended, so that the size of the problem does not register in consciousness. One may crystallise, and appear well-adapted to external life. Through either utilising the support system of relationships, or relying on a tough and resilient shell, one may appear to get away with avoiding the profound issue of separating. The longer this goes on, the harder later Saturn transits are likely to prove.

We don't live in an ideal world and we are not psychologically educated, and so we generally have no idea, after all the schooling we receive, about the nature of the human being. Consequently, none of us ever gets it wholly right, or deals with Saturn's challenges in an ideal way. We always have unfinished business with Saturn, and usually our children must sort some of this out for us. That seems to be the nature of things. But I have also met many people who display such willful obtuseness with regard to these issues that it is quite staggering. On some level they know very well what is going on, yet they persist in turning their backs on the challenge – either because of a deep resentment toward life, or a deep conviction that if they exploit others enough, they will get away with it.

Saturn as "Lord of Karma"

In old esoteric teaching, Saturn used to be known as the Lord of Karma. As most of you already know, I have many questions about the uses and abuses of this word in esoteric circles. Nevertheless I have seen, over and over, the way in which Saturn's requirements do not go away, but are simply compounded, like compound interest, until such time as the person turns and faces what is waiting. In this sense "karma" reflects the consequences of one's actions during the course of one lifetime – although I am not discounting the possibility that these actions may themselves be influenced or spring from earlier roots, whether these are "past lives" or family inheritance. Sometimes this "karma" takes the form of a sense of meaninglessness and despair later in life. It is tragic to put off the day until there are no longer enough days to pay the bill in full. Yet over and over again people do this.

So Saturn's cycle reflects back to us the nature of the building we have built of ourselves – what gives us our survival capacities, what allows us to cope with external reality, and where our boundaries lie. From the teleological point of view, Saturn's "meaning" – its "purpose" – is to help us to become the individuals we are and fulfill the purpose for which we are born, through differentiating us from what we are not. In this sense Saturn is the servant of the Sun. This is the archetypal background of the process of separation. Saturn is also concerned with justice, which is reflected in its exaltation in Libra. Justice in this context means reaping the rewards of what we have sown, both light and dark.

The actual meaning of the word *karma* is "substance". We accrue substance through our actions and choices throughout life. Each time a critical point in the Saturn cycle is reached, we must face what kind of substance we have accrued. If we meet this challenge honestly, and work at what has been poorly built, then the next turn of the cycle brings us our "just rewards" in productive ways. If we avoid the confrontation, then the next turn of the cycle brings us a bigger bill, with accumulated interest; and eventually the bailiffs come to claim the debt. And Saturn's interest rates, unlike those of the Bundesbank, are never lowered because of political expediency. They remain fixed, because they are a reflection of our mortal limits.

Many of you will have had very positive experiences around the time of your Saturn return, and some of you will have had a pretty rough ride. So much depends on the overall balance of the birth chart, as well as on the attitude the individual takes to what is happening within. There are some striking "famous" examples, both reassuring and frightening, of the importance of this first completion of the

Saturn cycle. The frightening implications are nicely illustrated by two artistic figures: Nijinsky and the poet Novalis.[13]

Nijinsky, who was at the peak of his dancing career at twenty-nine, went into a catatonic state during his Saturn return, and never came out again. He died in a psychiatric institution. He was a Pisces, with a powerful Neptune opposition the Moon and conjunct Pluto. Saturn in his birth chart, although prominent in 28° Leo at the MC, was not his friend; it formed a grand cross with the Moon, Mercury, and the Neptune-Pluto conjunction.

Novalis died of consumption during his Saturn return. In Novalis' poetry there are many references to eternity, and to death, and to a longing for dissolution. His chart, like Nijinsky's, also reflects a powerful Neptune, this time in a grand trine with the Sun and Pluto. Saturn, placed at the Descendant in 23° Leo, was no more his friend than Nijinsky's, and seems to have reflected profound disappointments in love. I sometimes have the feeling, reading his poetry, that he never intended to stay on this planet very long; "home" was elsewhere. His reluctance to incarnate, as well as Nijinsky's, can tell us a lot about the difficulties of Saturn's challenges when the individual is too in love with the eternal, and cannot, or will not, accept the limitations of mortality. Both these figures are, in many respects, classic "tragic artists", dominated by Neptune – resistant to incarnation in the first place, and more than a little in love with oblivion.

On the "up" side, we might look at figures such as Steven Spielberg, who broke through from obscurity into international success at the time of his Saturn return with *Close Encounters of the Third Kind,* soon followed by *E. T.* Spielberg has a Saturn-Pluto conjunction in the 2nd house, trine Mercury and sextile Neptune, and he does not appear to have a problem in balancing the imaginal realm with making lots of money. For those who do not perceive the material world as the enemy, and have been prepared to pay Saturn's dues along the way as the bills come in, the Saturn return can be a time

---

[13]Chart data for these and other charts included in this seminar are from Hans Hinrich Taeger, *Internationales Horoskope Lexikon,* Hermann Bauer Verlag, Freiburg, 1991.

when one's role in life is defined in the outer world in solid, permanently rewarding ways.

Now, I am not suggesting that we should sit about waiting to go catatonic, or anticipate coughing up our last breath surrounded by white camellias when the Saturn return comes along. The two artists I have mentioned were driven by their own pathologies, and identified almost wholly with the archetypal realm. Both were inordinately gifted but severely damaged people, who had little ego-strength to cope with Saturn's challenges. The damage seems to have been proportionate to the gift.

But at the same time, some extremely unhappy psychological states can occur in any of us at the time of the Saturn return. Breakdowns are not uncommon at this stage, just as they are at the time of the second Saturn square. This may be, in part, because any deep disturbance, hidden from view at other times by the personality's defence systems, will usually rise to the surface in response to Saturn's inexorable demand for truth. When they are related to the Saturn cycle, such breakdowns or periods of severe depression are usually related to the issue of separation, and highlight unresolved issues going back to the first seven years of life, before the first Saturn square.

Psychosis has lots of clinical labels, most of them questionable and some of them frankly useless. There are many different experiences of this loss of connection to external reality. For many people it is an altered state which happens only once, and reflects the need for rebuilding one's basic ego-structure and re-evaluating one's attitudes toward life. This kind of breakdown episode can be extremely productive in the long term, although horrific in the short term, and is usually connected with Saturn's transits as well as Saturnian problems in the birth chart. By "Saturnian problems" I am referring mainly to hard aspects to natal Saturn, usually accompanied by a strong Neptune or a heavily emphasised 12th house. All of these may suggest difficulties around achieving self-sufficiency and self-definition, which in turn relate back to the central dynamic of the ability or inability to separate.

Many people believe they are strong emotionally because they have managed to avoid a deep relationship, either in an obvious way or by involving themselves with someone who acts out all the dependency issues for them. Relationship breakups, which are all too common at the times of critical Saturn transits, can then serve as the trigger for a breakdown. But the underlying suffering and inability to cope are generally linked to a much earlier experience of loss or rejection, at an age when separation feels like annihilation. Then, in adulthood, rejection or loss comes as a terrible shock, invoking the small child's pain and terror, penetrating the defensive walls, and revealing the unformedness and lack of identity of the person within.

There are some things about the Saturn cycle which are so obvious that sometimes we don't register them as related to the planet. Yet we ought to. After all, we know that Saturn is an earthy planet, that it is concerned with physical manifestation and the experience of incarnation, and that therefore it is intimately linked with physical, biological changes. The advent of puberty around the time of the first Saturn opposition is one of these shifts, and understanding this great biological initiation in context of the astrological symbol can give us many insights into the problems and conflicts a young person experiences at this time. The process of puberty separates us, finally and irrevocably, from identification with the parents, because we are now able to procreate in our own right. We may still be somebody's child, but we can now produce our own child, which means we have become equals and rivals to those who were previously our protectors. It is therefore not surprising that so many young people become intensely religious at this age. They are in full flight from the body which threatens to betray them into mortality, incarnation, sin, and loneliness.

The Saturn cycle is age-related through its relationship to the challenges of particular ages of life. The limits we experience are often body-related, and dependent on age and the passage of time. The final, most complete separation we can experience is the separation from the mortal shell, and because this is the ultimate teleology of Saturn, every critical point of the Saturn cycle reminds us, gently or forcibly, that one day we will die. A fifty-nine-year-old, going

----

through the second Saturn return, may be fit and well and far more confident than his or her younger counterpart going through the first Saturn return. But that older individual will not have the kind of stamina and physical resilience of the younger person, and if he or she ignores this, a painful reminder usually comes along.

The experience of limitation at the time of the second return may be a direct reflection of the recognition of the aging body and its increasing slowness and lack of energy. Saturn's transits always remind us of the nature of the mortal incarnation we are experiencing, on the physical as well as the emotional and spiritual level. We have to make sense of the boundaries that exist at the time of life we encounter the planet. To refuse to acknowledge the aging process is, in effect, a refusal to acknowledge Saturn, which is our most profound symbol of that process and all it entails. Anyone who doesn't take this into account is likely to end up with a nasty shock. It is like trying to build a house while stubbornly refusing to consider what raw materials are available on the market, and how they will weather, and how long they will last.

It isn't a question of getting it wrong; it is a question of time and experience. We only seem recognise that a boundary is a boundary when we cannot get past it, no matter how hard we attempt to push, manipulate, bleat, whine, connive, meditate, jog, diet, smash, psychoanalyse, or buy our way through. We should never be surprised by the immovability of Saturn, although it seems to take several critical aspects of the Saturn cycle for us to begin lose that surprise. Some people never lose it.

Yet failure seems to be a necessary part of Saturnian experience. This is one of the most profound lessons the planet has to teach us. There is no guarantee we will learn this lesson, although we are given opportunities each time transiting Saturn makes a hard aspect to its natal place. We may perceive failure as something which proves our "badness" or incompetence, or affirms the nastiness of the world and other people. Yet we cannot separate unless we have encountered the frustration of failure – the anger and disappointment of being thwarted by a person, a collective, a physical body, or an inner quality which, like mother, turns out to be imperfect, and unwilling or unable to give us exactly what we want when we want it. We expect unconditional love from mother when we are infants, because we are identified with her as an extension of ourselves. As adults we may also expect unconditional love and acceptance from those around us, albeit unconsciously, because we are identified with them as an extension of ourselves. Frustration at both stages of life is a Saturnian necessity.

The stages of the first Saturn cycle

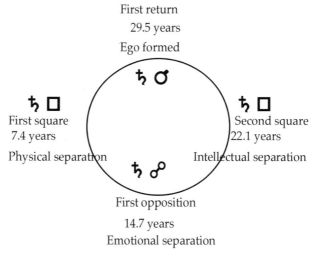

First return
29.5 years
Ego formed

First square
7.4 years
Physical separation

Second square
22.1 years
Intellectual separation

First opposition
14.7 years
Emotional separation

First Saturn cycle

In this diagram, which is as simplistic as the other one, but also useful if we work with it flexibly, the ages of the critical points of the cycle are given precisely. Of course we know they are not so precise, because we must take orbs into account, as well as the phenomenon of retrogradation, which may mean the transit repeats its exact aspect two or three times. So although the Saturn return is usually exact at twenty-nine and a half, it may come within orb of conjunction a year or more before, and not finish until a year or more after. It would be more appropriate, although messier, to think in

----

terms of a period of roughly two years, during which these critical points are operative. We would naturally like a neater package, but the psyche is unlikely to oblige.

At around the age of seven years and four months, Saturn transits to make the first square to its own place. As I have just said, we need to bear in mind that this time of the exact aspect is preceded by a year or more of buildup. So we must think in terms of the period of childhood between five and seven years for this first Saturn square. Interestingly, Freud saw this time as the period when the oedipal conflict comes to an end, and the child moves through a time of relative peace – "latency" – until the old struggles are reawakened at puberty. An important separation has been achieved by this time – a sense of having one's own body, of being a separate physical entity. By the age of seven, we think in terms of "I", and this is usually related to the physical body. We may still be emotionally identified with the parents, but we inhabit our own bodies. Frustration and the subsequent development of physical and instinctual control have achieved their purpose.

Between fourteen and fifteen years of age, Saturn arrives at the first opposition to its own place. Usually puberty has already taken place up to three years earlier, but the psychological repercussions of these bodily changes take much longer. At this great stage of initiation in human life, we discover that we are sexual beings, no longer androgynous, and capable of reproducing ourselves. The impact of hormonal changes, and the accompanying psychological changes, create a profound separation from the parents, and awaken the old oedipal conflicts in a new form. And because Saturn's transits always carry whatever is still left undone from the previous transits, this first opposition will awaken any unresolved issues arising at the time of the first square. In other words, if the process of separation in the early years has been interrupted, interfered with, or fraught with undue suffering, the opposition will awaken these feelings and memories, making the passage from prepubescent child to sexually aware teenager a particularly stressful and frightening one.

What kinds of things might interrupt or interfere with that earlier process? Just about anything. There is no such thing as a perfect transition from babyhood to adulthood. We all follow a winding route, full of wrong turnings and U-turns and apparent errors, and the route is circular rather than direct. But in a general sense, the relationship between mother and child – and, to a lesser extent, between father and child – can be full of unconscious hostility or invasiveness, making it much harder for the child to develop an independent spirit because the parent will not let go, or lets go too harshly.

Sometimes the child himself or herself will not let go, perhaps due to other factors in the chart – for example, a strong Neptune – which make it harder. Sometimes too abrupt a separation, or not having had enough containment early in life, can make this process frightening and unbearable. If we have not had something, we may not be able to let go of wanting it, and the child who has been forced to separate too painfully or too early may be reluctant to move away, still hungry for what he or she has never had. Such situations are usually reflected by chart configurations. In the case of reluctance to let go on the part of parent and/or child, we may see something like Moon conjunct Neptune or square Pluto, for example, and in the case of too early or abrupt a separation, Moon square or opposition Uranus, Chiron, or Saturn. Or there may be a mixture of the two.

The second Saturn square occurs just after twenty-two years, and as I have already said, it reflects a time of intellectual and social separation – a movement out into the larger world, and a time when decisions must be made about future direction. By this time one is expected to have made up one's mind about what one is going to do in life – even if everyone knows that the decision will be changed later. At twenty-two, we are are out in the world on our own. Before that, if we have no sense of direction, people say, "Oh well, you have lots of time." But by twenty-two we are expected to have some idea of where we are going.

Although by this age we may have our own bodies and our own sexuality, we do not yet have our own thoughts. We are dominated by the family background and family expectations in ways which we may not realise, but which circumscribe our ability to face and respond to life's challenges. This Saturn square to its natal place will bring to the surface any unresolved issues that belong to the earlier opposition

----

and first square. Many people rush from the parental home into a marriage at this time, perhaps because the emotional separation at puberty is still unfinished, and therefore the challenge of thinking one's own independent thoughts and carving a place in the world is too frightening. One rushes back into the family bosom, as it were, and sadly winds up choosing a partner who may display the least attractive qualities of one or both parents.

Saturn completes its first return at around the age of twenty-nine and a half. Although it is not a measure of either intelligence, capability, or talent, this first Saturn return is a measure of psychological maturity, if we assess this by the ability of the ego to stand on its own ground. Saturn has now made its circuit through all twelve houses of the chart, and one has acquired sufficient experience to form one's own values and attitudes, separate from those of the family background.

Those of you here who have not yet reached the time of the first Saturn return may feel vaguely insulted, as if I am suggesting that you are immature. On the ordinary level, this is not necessarily the case – a person in his or her late teens or early twenties may be extremely gifted, intuitive, insightful, and capable of important decision-making. But there is a level on which the ego is still pliable and fluid, and where some essential inner structure has not yet fully formed. Maturity in this sense does not occur until the Saturn return. For this reason, those who have not yet gone through the Saturn return may find that problems and conflicts are more readily solved in a therapeutic situation, and childhood wounds can be healed more easily – largely because one has not yet crystallised one's defence systems, and is still open to creative and healing input from parental figures and surrogates who might provide something more nourishing than what one got at home.

The Saturn return is a time of great challenge, potential rewards, and also potential shocks, if unfinished business from the earlier squares and opposition has not been dealt with. Some people find this period extremely satisfying, and feel they are reaping the rewards of earlier years of hard work. Others have a terrible time, and find that the structures they have built, especially at the time of the second square, come tumbling down. At the Saturn return we face our own reality, and have a good, hard look at who we are and what we have made of our lives thus far. The picture may not be very pretty if we have been avoiding earlier Saturn challenges. We may realise that we are fakes, or that we have made marriages to people who are really parental surrogates, or that we have cemented ourselves into financial or professional situations which are stifling the spirit.

A lot of people rush to get married at the time of the return. They don't like the uncomfortable feeling of being alone and separate out there in the world, so they try to lose this feeling in a marriage which may turn out to be a disaster if it is based on desperate insecurity and a need to find protection. Not all Saturn return marriages are built on such foundations. Some are made because of a clear sense of where one is going. These are likely to endure. But whenever we make commitments under powerful Saturn transits, our motives are usually mixed, and much more complex than we might realise at the time.

By the time of the first Saturn cycle, the ego is more or less formed – or is badly unformed, if there are strong elements of the personality fighting against separateness. If the latter is the case, the Saturn return is likely to be pretty rough. But with a reasonable degree of self-sufficiency and self-definition (rather like Winicott's "good enough mother" – perfection is not required, but rather, something workable), what you have is a relatively mature entity with a good enough sense of self and an adequate capability of surviving in the world. One might be neurotic, eccentric, and full of conflicts, but there is a capacity to stand on one's own ground, and a deep feeling of being someone real.

The manifestation level of the Saturn cycle – Saturn transits as events – varies enormously. This is because Saturn is placed differently in every birth chart, and the "X-factors" which the chart does not portray – the level of consciousness, the nature of the society in which one lives, and so on – are also completely different from one individual to another. Yet there is a kind of inexorable logic in the way each Saturn aspect to its own place builds on all the past aspects, according to the choices we make at each juncture. This inexorable logic can feel like fate when we are hit with a manifestation which, to a detached observer, is clearly the consequence of earlier choices.

We often do some very silly things at the important stages of the Saturn cycle, largely because we panic. As I have said, one of Saturn's chief emotional expressions is loneliness, because the process of separating is painful. We experience our existential aloneness – a profound recognition that, no matter how close we are to other people, they cannot ever wholly know us. Also, there is often a deep recognition, sometimes unconscious or only partly conscious, that, even though we may have an immortal spirit, nevertheless the body will die.

This sense of mortality and loneliness can make us very frightened, and we may reach out compulsively for anything which will alleviate those feelings. Hence, during the first Saturn cycle, there are many breakdowns, many rushed marriages, many hasty work decisions, and many compulsive childbirths which cluster around these significant ages – especially the second Saturn square in the early twenties and the Saturn return at twenty-nine. Sometimes the best advice we can give the client who comes at these times is to wait, and to make decisions and commitments only when the whole process, including its possible consequences, has been thought through. Impulsive action is not usually a good idea under Saturn transits, but reflecting on the inner process as much as possible can have positive consequences for many years to come. Otherwise, one may be compensating for a false structure – or a false self – which has now reached its full term.

A lot of you will have gone through the first Saturn return. Would any of you like to comment on how you experienced this, in the context of separating? How did it come out in your lives?

Audience: I broke up my marriage for a while, and left my family. It wasn't a permanent separation, but it was a separation.

Liz: That was during your Saturn return? How long did the separation last?

Audience: For around two years. I have Saturn in Taurus.

Liz: It sounds like you were acting out exactly what I was describing. Perhaps you were trying to get away from a process that you feared, by creating an alternative reality in which you didn't feel the uncomfortable feelings. Let's look at what these feelings might have been, based on the sign placement of natal Saturn. What are the basic issues of Saturn in Taurus?

Audience: A need for security.

Audience: Fear of change.

Liz: Yes, both are true, but we need to get beneath these characteristic defences and understand what Saturn in Taurus requires – what it feels like inside. The hunger for absolute security is very great, and there may be a strong sense of deprivation around security needs. Often the early home life felt materially shaky or unsafe, which a child with Saturn in Taurus cannot tolerate.

Audience: Well, we weren't poor, but there were a lot of financial worries, and several moves of house when I was quite young. I hated it every time. I need to get used to things and know where they are.

Liz: Later on, Saturn in Taurus, which remembers with a shudder every early incident of instability or undesired change, may cling very tightly to a familiar situation, even if it is uncomfortable or stifling to other aspects of the personality. That's the "down" side. The "up" side is that the great determination to establish stability can create enormous tenacity, strength, and patience in the face of adversity. Saturn in Taurus people are often able to endure hardships which would break other people. The trouble with this quality, which is in itself valuable and admirable, is that, if there are more freedom-loving and volatile attributes suggested in the birth chart, one can feel trapped by one's Saturnian needs. I have a feeling this is what happened to you at the time of the Saturn return. Did you feel as though life was closing in on you, that you had cemented yourself in a prison through your security needs, and that time was slipping by?

Audience: Exactly that. I have the Sun and Venus in Sagittarius.

Liz: Did you come back to your marriage out of a sense of duty, or was it because you felt in your heart it was the right thing for you?

Audience: Both. I have a strong sense of duty, and I didn't like the idea of throwing away something I had worked at for a long time. This was apart from my responsibility to my children, which also weighed very heavy. It seemed such a waste. I had a lot of conflict. But in the end I decided that I was someone to whom duty mattered a lot, and I had to accept that. If I wanted stability, and didn't want a guilty conscience tormenting me, something would have to be sacrificed. Once I accepted that, it seemed less imprisoning. I felt calmer, as if I had made peace with my fate.

Liz: So you paid Saturn's coin, by facing yourself and accepting your limits. I think you are describing your experience very honestly. I often wish more of us would cultivate this sort of honesty when facing Saturn's dilemmas, because it always pays off in the end. As transiting Saturn moves toward its natal place for the first time since birth, we get a sense of something heavy and imprisoning creeping up. We think it is "out there", and say, "I am getting out of here!" But as someone I know once wryly put it, wherever you go, you have to take yourself with you. We fear that a very great burden, a very great weight, is going to descend. On one level that is true. It often isn't burdensome on the concrete level, but that is what it feels like, and we may try very hard to escape. The weight is really the necessity of our natal Saturn sign, house, and aspects – our inner necessity, which might not accord with our hopes and dreams for the future. This limits all of us, in different ways. It is truly a great weight – the weight of our substance, our authenticity, our earthly responsibilities in incarnation.

Audience: There is a story somebody wrote somewhere. It's an Indian story. One of the gods is trying to escape the Saturn principle, and so he puts himself into a bottle for two and a half years, and at the end of this period, Krishna comes along and says, "What on earth are you doing?" The god says, "Well, my Saturn return was coming up, and I didn't want to have to go through anything dreadful and heavy, so I imprisoned myself in a little pot and buried myself in the mud." And Krishna says, "Well, you have had your Saturn return, haven't you?"

Liz: I know this story, but in a slightly different form. In the version I heard, the god turns himself into a hippopotamus, and sits covered in mud for two and a half years, so as to avoid his Saturn return. Clearly, attempts to avoid Saturnian mud simply create a different variety of Saturnian mud, which may be far worse than the mud one is seeking to escape.

You ran away from something hoping you could find freedom from the bondage of your own inner necessity. But the conflict you experienced was probably just as painful as what you would have met if you had stayed at home and fought it out. So you got Saturn anyway, in a different form. It would be quite impossible to judge such a situation from a moral perspective, and say, "You should have done this, rather than that." Leaving as you did opened up an inner conflict which has made you grow. Staying might have pushed you into a depression which would have required facing an inner conflict, which would have made you grow. Strangely, it almost doesn't matter which choice one makes, provided one chooses sincerely and takes on the conflict. Other factors – personal morality, damage to other people, material and emotional responsibilities, and so on – may make one choice preferable to another. But one way or another we fail, because there is always some limit we cannot pass.

The important issue is the facing of the conflict. Attempting to avoid this conflict is, to my mind, a major part of what the Greeks called *hubris*. This really means arrogance in one's attitude toward the gods. If we think about it, we can see that a refusal to face a conflict which life is thrusting upon us is tantamount to attempting to control life, to believing that we can exempt ourselves from going through something. We may think we are practising avoidance out of cowardice, but there is a powerful element of arrogance in it as well.

Audience: You don't seem to be mentioning the trines and sextiles as part of the Saturn cycle.

Liz: I haven't mentioned the trines and sextile for the simple reason that they are subtler and less challenging. They too reflect stages in the separation process, but they are more concerned with consolidation after an experience of separateness or separation. I have been trying to give you the main theme of the first cycle, based on the junctures which tend to register most powerfully. We often don't notice the transiting trines and sextiles of Saturn, because they reflect a time of internal stability and a coming to terms with the decisions one has made during the preceding hard aspect. Of course they are important. But trines are a completion of something, which is initiated at the time of a square and challenged at the time of an opposition. Sextiles are the interim between the conjunction and the square, and seem to reflect a seeding time, before the initiation of something in action in the outer world. We see Saturn's meaning and manifestations most clearly with the hard aspects.

The stages of the second Saturn cycle

Of course Saturn will go round again; fortunately or unfortunately, it doesn't stop in the heavens when we reach twenty-nine and a half. The underlying meaning of the second cycle is the same as the first. But we have time and experience on our side now. We have been there before, and have a solid base from which we can respond to whatever comes our way. It is the nature of Saturn to build self-definition through experience. We cannot do this with the intellect or the feelings in a vacuum, but must pass through some experience which makes an impact on us. Time is our friend when dealing with Saturn.

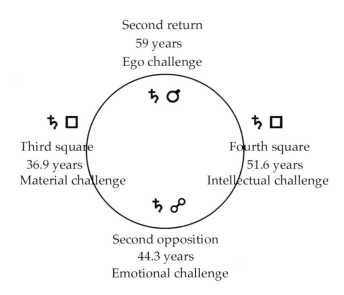

Second return
59 years
Ego challenge

Third square
36.9 years
Material challenge

Fourth square
51.6 years
Intellectual challenge

Second opposition
44.3 years
Emotional challenge

Second Saturn Cycle

We also need to keep in mind the different stages of life, and their different focal points in terms of where our energy is directed. Biologically as well as psychologically, we change as we grow older, and although on the inner level there are dimensions of human nature which are constant – or perhaps even eternal – there are also dimensions which alter according to experience and our interpretation of experience. In a woman, for example, the next Saturn square after the return, which occurs in the mid-thirties, often reminds women of what is sometimes called the "biological clock". It starts ticking very loudly. If a woman wishes to bear children but has not yet done so, this may be a critical time, when there is strong inner, and perhaps outer, pressure to establish a family. When we reach the mid-thirties we are "in our prime", but no longer in the "first flush of youth", and the body has begun to show signs of aging and slowing down – even if we choose to disregard this, or remedy it with an increased emphasis on physical fitness.

At the time of the second Saturn opposition, which occurs in the early forties, both men and women are expected to have reached the peak of their careers. A woman may not yet be in menopause, but it is late at this point to consider bearing a child, and children who were born during one's twenties are now approaching adulthood and are ready to leave the nest. The "biological clock" may not be merely ticking; it may be positively clanging and booming, and there is often a quality of desperation in people who want to start families when they are in their early forties. Sometimes this is a compensation for something else, which is not being faced. Sometimes it is a second family which seems to promise the elusive happiness, and often the consequences of this are not faced honestly. You can all see what kind of challenges may arise which, on the level of "events", reflect one's place in the world, one's sexual identity, and one's relationship with the collective. There are echoes of the crisis of puberty from the first Saturn opposition. On the inner level, we are still dealing with themes of separation.

The next square occurs between fifty-one and fifty-two years, and at this point the aging process has usually begun to exert a powerful effect, physically and emotionally. We are no longer young; we are euphemistically termed "middle-aged", although to our children, and perhaps even our grandchildren, we are simply "old". A woman will now be entering, or even completing, menopause, with all the powerful psychological and physical repercussions this involves. If she has identified her femininity with motherhood and the capacity to procreate, she may undergo severe depression and loss of identity, since such collective identification is now coming to an end and she must define who she is as an independent individual.

Both men and women may find it difficult if not impossible to move further in their work. They may be made redundant at a time when they cannot easily begin a new career. They may have to begin to think of retirement, which, although technically set at sixty-five, occurs in many spheres (such as the military) at fifty-five. A man may still become a father, but if so, he will find that, as his children reach adulthood, he will be in his seventies, and must take this into account.

The second Saturn return occurs in the late fifties, and on the collective level this is the herald of "official" retirement. For those identified with their work and their contribution to the collective, this can be a critical time, because the loss of one's place in the world may accompany a severe sense of loss of identity and purposelessness. There is a high divorce rate at this age, perhaps because the issues which have been avoided at the time of the first Saturn return come back to meet us at the time of the second – and they are much harder to deal with then, because our options have been reduced.

A marriage which has been emotionally and sexually dead for years may escape detection because of work and the responsibility of children, but at this stage of the Saturn cycle the children have grown up and gone away, and the work comes to an end; and then we must face our partners without disguise. New relationships are harder to find and sustain, and are invariably accompanied by the problems of ex-partners, existing children who may even have children of their own, and various financial and emotional obligations which have been accrued over the years – not to mention the loss of sexual confidence which often accompanies aging. At the time of the first Saturn return, the question is: "Who am I? What do I want from life?" At the time of the second Saturn return, the question is: "Who am I now? Who have I been? Where do my mistakes lie? And what do I want from whatever years of life remain to me?"

The second Saturn return, like the first, can be a time of reaping the rewards of one's efforts, and a renewal of confidence and self-esteem. It can also mark a profound turning inward, a coming to terms with oneself which accompanies a deep spiritual commitment. Equally, it can be a severe trial, especially if the foundations of life have been built on sand, and if one has been engaging in ongoing self-deception and avoidance of inner issues.

Emerging illnesses may make their appearance at this time, not only because the body's resistance is less, but also because the accrued inner conflict of many years may now begin to take its toll on the physical vehicle. Many of the dangerous health conditions which are common to this period – especially those involving the heart – may, in part, reflect a gradual accumulation of stress which the body can no longer handle with the same elasticity it did in youth. Sometimes Saturn's way of reminding us that we must bow to the laws of nature, inner and outer, is to tell us through our bodies. If we learn the lesson, then we may be rewarded with many years of good health

----

and vitality, as long as we respect the laws of conservation over which Saturn presides.

When we consider the third Saturn cycle, we are once again dealing with issues of separation and self-definition. But they too have to be seen in context of the stage of life we have reached. I won't spend any time on this now, because we must move on to Uranus. But it should be apparent that, as we continue on our journey, Saturn reminds us increasingly of our mortality, which in turn increasingly defines the meaning and value of the life we have lived and the identity we have built. The nature of time is a great mystery, and looking at life through eyes matured by time alters perception in profound ways which are virtually impossible to communicate to those who have not yet completed two Saturn cycles. The sense of aloneness in old age is often linked with this inability to share what one now understands about time. Time itself separates us.

Final remarks about the Saturn cycle

Before we look at the overall meaning of the Uranus cycle, there are some final things I want to mention about the Saturn cycle. When we make concrete commitments under hard Saturn transits to its own place, such as getting married or having a child or setting up a business, we need to remember that the thing we have brought into being – human or otherwise – will have its own birth chart, and its Saturn will be square, opposition, or conjunct our own. So these concrete products of our Saturn transits tend to be very binding, and we rarely succeed in removing ourselves from them, even if we sell the business, leave the marriage, or the children move away.

Within families, it is very interesting to look at the planetary cycles in operation when parents have children. Many people have children under the Saturn return, and they experience that child as part of the maturation process. That child becomes the instrument of Saturn. The child is part of the essence of separation and crystallisation. Sometimes limiting material circumstances are linked with this, such as in the case of a single parent who must raise the child herself, or a marriage which occurs because of pregnancy, where the child is the catalyst for the parents' bondage. Or the experience may be joyful and much desired, but inevitably limits the parents' freedom.

If one has a child at the time of the critical stages of the Saturn cycle, then this child's natal Saturn will conjunct, square or oppose one's own. This does not have to be a "bad" thing. It can be enormously creative, in terms of forcing both parent and child to develop as separate individuals with their own identities. But there is often a good deal of friction, usually of the defensive variety. Both parent and child feel hurt or rebuffed by the other's defences, which are mobilised to protect against hurt or rebuff. An emotional standoff is often the product of these Saturn interactions, especially the squares and oppositions. I have met many people who have been astonished to discover that they are themselves rejecting the parent whom they claim so vociferously is rejecting them.

Saturn, as we all know, is a major factor in any deep relationship, and therefore it is not surprising that so many important relationships form or break up at the critical points of the Saturn cycle. It is also useful to think of Saturn's transits, as well as its natal placement, in terms of synastry. If one is involved with someone whose Saturn is conjunct, square or opposition one's own, one has chosen to be involved with someone who is part of one's own Saturn cycle. Every time Saturn transits one's natal Saturn, it transits the other person's Saturn as well, and will trigger separation issues in both people. And if we also consider the composite chart, we will see that, if Saturn in one chart is conjunct, square or opposition Saturn in the other, the composite Saturn will also be triggered by a hard aspect from the same Saturn transit that hits both birth charts. This may be a semisquare or sesquiquadrate, but it is likely to be important in terms of issues of separateness and self-definition within the relationship.

Audience: Which house is more important, the house natal Saturn is in, or the one it's transiting through?

Liz: We need to look at both. Natal Saturn's house will describe the specific areas of life in which we will have to face the issue of separateness through direct experience. This is a constant. It is always with us, and we are never let off the hook. It is the place where we may suffer loneliness and loss, but also the place where we can develop very strong foundations and a powerful sense of survival. We get a lot of hard experience in that sphere of life, and if we are prepared to learn from it rather than becoming bitter and defensive, we can become extremely wise and competent over time.

The house through which Saturn is transiting is the transient (pun intended) arena through which apparent difficulties come, which trigger off the basic life-challenge described by natal Saturn. Later, we can look at some example charts to see how this works. The Saturn cycle is universal and archetypal, but it becomes individualised through the arena in which one experiences the challenge of separateness – the house in which it is placed in the birth chart. The house through which it is transiting matters too, but ultimately the most important issue is the natal house, because that is Saturn's essential life-theme.

The sign in which Saturn is natally placed will say a great deal about the way in which we deal with Saturn issues, and the defences we mobilise to help ourselves cope with the experience of separateness. The house will reflect the arena of Saturn's operation, but the sign describes something of our own personal "stuff". So if, for example, Saturn is in the 2nd house in Aries, the process of separating, distilling and crystallising will, in the main, come through security issues and material affairs. The experience of separateness will be connected with material self-sufficiency (or lack thereof), the acquisition of inner and outer resources, and the building of a sense of self-worth rooted in the security one is able to establish over time.

That is the sphere of life in which the process of separation will occur. But the manner in which the individual responds to Saturn's challenges will be Arien – in other words, with a powerful competitive instinct, a strong need to be first and best, a resistance to others' authority, and a compulsion to overcome feelings of personal inadequacy by proving oneself in the face of difficult challenges. As one gradually becomes defined as an individual through the phases of the Saturn cycle, the Arien attributes become crystallised as a defensive and self-protective behaviour pattern. There are many ways to establish material and emotional self-sufficiency with Saturn in the 2nd; but only Aries will do it by beating the competition and pursuing the heroic quest. And when Saturn in the 2nd in Aries fails on the material level, the feelings of failure will be linked with a sense of furious impotence, angry frustration, and thwarted will.

During the first Saturn cycle we tend to develop the qualities of Saturn and its sign and house through external channels. Saturn's inner strength and authority are not automatic. They form over time, through the hard experience of the critical stages of the cycle. For example, if Saturn is in Capricorn in the 10th house, at the time of the first opposition at around fourteen to fifteen, there may be problems with authorities at school, or battles with the parents over personal autonomy. Inner authority as an archetypal theme is concerned with authenticity and the honing and shaping of one's talents and energies. Ultimately Saturn in the 10th in Capricorn can translate outer authority – a position of responsibility and a long-lasting contribution to the larger world – into inner authority, and the two gradually become the same thing. But at fifteen, one has not yet reached the point where one can comprehend what inner authority is all about.

So at fifteen, one may fight authority outside, in order to establish one's inner boundaries. Defining the individuality depends on the establishing of personal authority, which one can only do after one has worked out what is intolerable about authority other than one's own. We each have a unique combination of Saturn in a particular house and sign, and with particular aspects to other planets. So no two individuals will meet, or deal with, the archetypal issue of separateness in the same way.

We must, of course, look at other planets aspecting Saturn, and in some respects this is the most important dimension of the individual expression of the cycle. Natal Saturn will be interlocked with other planets by aspect, or, if unaspected, by the dispositor of the sign in which it is placed. When transiting Saturn forms an important angle to natal Saturn, it will also activate a web of aspects in which natal

Saturn is enmeshed. There is really no such thing as a "pure" Saturn opposition Saturn, or a "pure" Saturn return, because other planets, and therefore other dynamic energies or drives within the personality, will be activated. If there is a natal Saturn-Jupiter square, each stage of the Saturn cycle will activate that square, and along with the issues reflected by the house, a fundamental collision between ideal and reality, between optimism and cynicism, between potential and limitation, will always recur. The more strongly Saturn is placed in the birth chart, the more powerful its cycle is likely to be, because of the involvement of other planets and perhaps angles as well.

These are general principles, and we need to see how they work in individual charts. But general principles can help us to grasp the basic meaning of the cycle, and the characteristic ways in which people react to it. The reactions are important, because we don't deal well with separation issues. Separation is not something that we do naturally; it is something we do under duress, through deprivation and frustration. The formation of the ego comes through denial, defence, and compensation. Friction and conflict produce something solid, as they do in alchemical symbolism.

Separateness doesn't flower of its own accord as a natural human state. It is like a piece of granite. Granite doesn't grow like a plant. It is created under enormous pressure over a very long period of time. It is not the product of a natural, easy flow, or a comfortable organic cycle. There are things that form in nature only under pressure, and granite and the human ego seem to be among them. One develops a sense of "I" by being forced away from those people and objects with which one instinctively identifies. Given the choice, we humans would much rather stay fused with the source of life. Then we could be immortal. We are forced to accept being in a limited body and being a separate entity through deprivation. That is how the ego is formed.

Saturn's process is always through duress, through friction and deprivation, through depression and denial. There are people who can do this better than others, because they understand the necessity of it. These are the Saturnian people of the world. That doesn't mean they like it. It is just as painful for them as it is for anyone else. But those with a strong Saturn or many planets in Capricorn seem to know instinctively the importance of aloneness, even if they kick violently against it in the early part of life.

Those with a strong Neptune, or an emphasis in Pisces or the 12th house, may find the Saturn process terrifying and extremely painful. They may do everything possible to avoid it. Jupiter isn't very good at it either, unless there is a very clear intuition of the meaningfulness of the process. Mars can cope with it if necessary, and gains strength and confidence through discipline – hence Mars is "exalted" in Saturn's sign. Mercurial natures can cope with Saturn, but tend to deal with separateness on the intellectual level, and may avoid facing the emotional suffering involved. The strongly Venusian person may find the stages of the Saturn cycle distinctly uncomfortable because of the loneliness. But at the same time, Saturn's exaltation in Libra suggests that Venus appreciates the sense of order and structure which boundaries provide. The strongly lunar temperament will naturally fight against any experience of separateness – hence Saturn is in detriment in Cancer, and the Moon in detriment in Capricorn. These are the natural affinities and dislikes amongst the planetary family. If we have a sense of the overall balance of the chart – by planet and by element – then we can also get some idea of how quickly one might get the hang of the cyclical process Saturn requires us to undergo.

Saturn-Neptune contacts

Audience: I have Neptune and Saturn in square. Does this mean the Saturn cycle will be particularly hard for me?

Liz: This is always an impossible question to answer. Presumably you mean "hard" in the sense of painful. You may feel deeply unhappy, depressed, and lonely at times, and you may experience a good deal of suffering through disillusionment and the compromising or shattering of your dreams when transiting Saturn hits this natal square by hard aspect. But we cannot really measure one person's pain against another, and say that the particular kind of pain you experience – loss

----

of contact with the eternal – is worse or bigger than the pain of someone with, say, a natal Mercury-Saturn square, who may experience intense intellectual isolation and an inability to communicate with others at the critical stages of the cycle.

Your square guarantees that the Saturn cycle will always raise Neptunian issues – longing for eternity, resistance to incarnation, desire for fusion – along with the Saturnian challenge of separation. That means you are likely to experience a certain special quality of emotional pain, because separation is so hard for Neptune, and there is often so much world-weariness and sadness involved in this combination of planets. Yet Saturn-Nepune is also known as the artist's aspect, because of the deep need to translate the eternal images into the world of form. I think this natal square, when triggered by a Satun transit, may make you intensely aware of the gap between imagination and physical reality, and could deepen and heighten your sense of a multi-levelled universe. It may impel you to do some kind of creative work to build a bridge across the gap. It sharpens the conflict between mortality and eternity. There is often a very acute sense of this divide in Saturn-Neptune people, even with the trine and sextile.

Audience: It's true, I have been severely disillusioned in the past when Saturn has hit this square. I tend to get depressed quite easily, and at these times I have become seriously depressed, with feelings of hopelessness. But I haven't always been clear about the inner issues. I always have felt hurt and disappointed in people close to me. I feel as if I have been building on sand-castles.

Liz: I think the image of the sand-castle is a very good one. The hurt and disappointment you feel are probably proportionate to the intensity of your idealism, and the unreality of your expectations. A natal Saturn-Neptune contact may reflect a tendency to swing from expecting too much to expecting too little. One moves from a state of ecstasy – "I have found the One!" – to a state of cynicism – "Sooner or later everybody lets me down." Saturn transits are guaranteed to invoke the latter response. One can, of course, stop trying to make the sand-castle permanent, and get into the spirit of building it for the pleasure of it and letting it go when the tide comes in.

But Saturn likes its castles to be made of cast concrete, with steel reinforcement. So one must find a compromise, where the ideal is not quite so high, and the disillusionment is consequently less. Castles made of simple but enduring materials, such as paint or clay or written words, may prove more effective than the most gloriously coloured sand. The moment you try to preserve a Neptunian castle, it tends to disintegrate and float away on the waters. But refusing to build any castles at all takes away a particular, ethereal kind of joy. There is a way of getting into the joy of creating, and the magic of romantic love, which can take you away from the extremes of suffering – but one must be willing to let the ecstatic moment pass, and enter ordinary life.

Audience: I also have a Saturn-Neptune aspect, a sextile, and I often experience depression after I have finished a painting. I am an artist. I lose the confidence to create, sometimes for a long time, because I always feel that what I have created is not good enough. It never seems anything like what I first envisioned.

Liz: This encapsulates the dilemma of Saturn-Neptune. I doubt that it will ever be "cured". It is the inevitable consequence of the realm of the transient and physical meeting the realm of the eternal and noncorporeal. It also encapsulates one of the characteristic experiences of Saturn in transit. As we move on to Uranus, I think it is worth remembering the image of Saturn castrating Uranus. Saturn is a castrator, although psychologically this event is not always the horror it is in physical terms. The moment one puts something in form, one has not only separated oneself from the ideal realm. One has also destroyed that thing's capacity to have endless possibilities. One has to accept something limited.

So there is always a sense of heaviness around Saturn's transits. No matter how successful one is at producing something on a material level, or how psychologically successful one is at making peace with oneself, there is always that sense of, "Is this all there is?" because once we define something, it ceases to be fluid and boundless. It ceases to have potentials; they have been curtailed. This is Saturn's castration. It can only be what it is, from now on. In terms of creative work, that often results in depression, because one has struggled and struggled, and there is the painting or the book or the piece of music staring one in the face, and one says to oneself, "It isn't perfect yet!" And it won't be even after thirty rewrites, and then one has to accept the fact that it never will be perfect, because there is no way that the vehicle can contain the entirety of the initial vision or idea. It is not possible. Form is limited in what it can convey of the ineffable. If one makes peace with this, it means one has to give up something of immortality – one has to separate from the divine.

On a psychological level, when we make peace with something in ourselves, we are, in fact, saying, "I accept myself as I am," which means we have curtailed the fantasy that we can become anything if only we work at it or wait long enough. All psychotherapeutic approaches, in the end, depend upon an individual making peace with what he or she is in order for any healing to take place. In doing so, the person may enter a time of depression. This was the process which Melanie Klein placed such emphasis on – the movement from the "paranoid–schizoid" world of the infant (which is full of idealised images and inevitable disillusionment and rage) to the "depressive position" which heralds an acceptance of the mixed and limited nature of life and of oneself. In this barren and stony place, we acknowledge that we cannot be all things, nor can other people be all things to us. We can only live the maximum of what we are, and what we are is limited, one way or another. So depression, or melancholy, is a common, perhaps even an inevitable, accompaniment to Saturn's cycle, no matter how successful the product. It is the price we pay for granite.

Too much Saturn?

Audience: I have several planets in Capricorn and a strong Saturn in my chart, and I sometimes feel I need less separateness, not more. I tend to be very self-sufficient and reluctant to experiment with life.

Liz: You feel you are overly Saturnian?

Audience: Yes.

Liz: Then you'll have to wait for a Uranus transit to liven things up.

Audience: I feel I ought to be trying to be different, more spontaneous, less earthbound.

Liz: I think you must take what you are, appreciate it, and make the most of it. Any "improvements" we try to make on ourselves need to be made from a place of self-acceptance and self-appreciation. Otherwise they may represent a compulsive attempt to fulfill others' expectations or an idealised image of perfection, and are therefore inauthentic and ultimately useless. Being strongly Saturnian is as much an asset as any other chart emphasis. If you feel too constricted and self-contained at times, there may be issues which you could look at, perhaps connected with early inhibitions or feelings of rejection or mistrust, which make it hard for you to express joy and spontaneity. But it is a question of degree, and of the strength of your defences, rather than an issue of becoming somebody else.

There is no cosmic rule book which says that we should all have nicely balanced charts with a little something in each element, or that it is preferable to be Jupiterian or Uranian rather than Saturnian. Whatever we are given, that is our unique gift, and I believe that if we live our lives creatively and honestly, we will be able to say to ourselves, "I may have areas I need to work on, but I don't wish I were someone else." I cannot think of a better way to greet the eternal than with the deep knowledge that one made the best of what one was with as much integrity as one could find, and did not leave this world wishing one had been somebody else. But I doubt that many people can do this, because they have other ideas about why they are alive, usually acquired from family or social milieu or conventional religious background.

Being strongly Saturnian is a bit like having one special talent, a skill which one does exceedingly well. Let's say you are an

---

extremely good carpenter, absolutely wonderful with wood-carving, furniture-making and so on. You would have liked to have been a great artist, and you might also have had fun being a composer, and you dream of writing a few novels, but really, you have got this one thing, this one talent which makes you special. Now, either you are pleased that you have got it, and you do the absolute best you can with it, and make as creative a life as you can based on it, or you waste your life whingeing about all the things you don't have that other people seem to have, and then you spoil the thing that is your special gift.

It is the same with a psychological quality. As individuals, we are all good at some things and rotten at others. The scale of measurement which says one quality is "better" than another is a highly subjective one, and like beauty, it is generally in the eyes of the beholder. A gift at relating to others may be subtle and will not earn a mention in the *Times Literary Supplement,* but it is just as valuable, and perhaps more so in many ways. A gift at dealing with reality may also be subtle and attract no prizes, and you might not get an OBE for staying out of debt and discharging your daily tasks honourably and well, but it is just as valuable as the showier acts of public service which win gongs. Although you may have to work to create a better balance within yourself, and find out whether some of your constraints are due to fear or old hurts, you might do well to remember that there is no such thing as a perfectly balanced human being. The limits of the personality have to be accepted, and if you have got a great overdose of a certain planet, it means you have got all the gifts of that planet as well as its failings.

Whatever our imbalances in the natal horoscope, of course we would be better off developing some flexibility, and greater adaptability in those areas where we do not possess natural ease of adaptation. But we also need to learn to make the best of something very precious, because the more concentrated something is, the deeper it is. To have a chart which is heavily weighted in one direction, whether Saturnian or otherwise, is not a "bad" thing, and it may be a very "good" thing, because it means that one has access to a much greater range of the archetypal level of that planet.

When we are motivated by the compulsion to live up to others' expectations of what we are "supposed" to be, I don't think deliberate, calculated compensation for imbalances ever works. When we try to compensate for the feelings of failure and inadequacy associated with Saturn, this can be very productive, because we develop certain skills and strengths in the process. But it is a rather different matter when one is attempting to compensate for who one truly is. Compensation based on self-dislike is hardly a way through.

You may need to cultivate the ability to laugh at yourself and at life, which is one of the things the Saturn nature does least well. Life can be so bloody serious for Saturnian people, partly because they sense the profound importance of time, and partly because of innate pride. Saturn can always benefit from the occasional good belly-laugh; it sometimes needs a bit of loosening up. But that doesn't mean you should try to be something you are not. And the seriousness and reflectiveness of Saturn are a major part of what you are. This is what deserves to be valued and developed, not "replaced" by efforts to produce a fake Jupiter.

If Saturn is very powerful in a chart, the Saturn cycle may be just as fraught as for those who are more aligned with other planets. But there may also be a sense of "coming home", which allows one to carry the crisis points with greater containment. The lessons that transiting Saturn brings to the person dominated by Saturn are lessons which are generally recognised straight away as lessons. It is an instinctive sense of, "Oh, yes, I recognise this, and however restricting it is, it's also where I need to be." One can get a great deal more out of such an attitude than people who are kicking and screaming every inch of the way, and feeling resentment and bitterness afterward.

Saturn's defence systems

Saturn tends more than any other planet to try to fake it when anxiety is felt. There is a tendency to hide behind external appearances, hoping that if the thing "looks" right, maybe the inner problem will go away. But the essence of Saturnian strength is not external, it's internal. Repairing the façade of the house while the inner structure is falling apart does not generate the kind of strength and serenity which reflects the best side of Saturn. The essence of Saturnian solidity does not lie in being able to control other people; it lies in being able to sustain oneself, from within as well as without. But that kind of Saturnian resource only comes slowly, over the course of the Saturn cycle.

We tend to begin with a kind of "fake" Saturn. I think we all do this when we are younger – we try to compensate for our feelings of inadequacy by appearing to be strong and impermeable in the outer world. We may do this on intellectual, emotional, material, physical, or spiritual levels. But the strength is false, because it exists in relation to the outer world, in order to make an impression. It isn't coming from within. It is hollow and brittle. It may be expressed as a domineering, controlling quality, although this can be subtle and not the "Do it because I say so!" variety of domination. But the inner authority is lacking, and instead there may be a need to have authority over other people in order to feel safe, important and effective. We can see this happening around us all the time, and yet fail to recognise what we are seeing. And we may be doing it ourselves.

For example, we may encounter a person at work who seems to be very strong and capable, who appears very Saturnian (and may be, astrologically), but who has a Neptunian partner. If we get to know the person, we may hear all about his whining, hysterical wife, or her dependent, alcoholic husband. But why has this tough, self-sufficient individual got a Neptunian partner who is irritating him or her all the time? What has happened to Saturn's famous realism and sound judgement? Saturn doesn't like Neptune much; there is an innate antipathy between these basic types. So why hasn't our Saturnian colleague found a Venusian partner, where they are different enough to make sparks but have some shared values through a mutual appreciation of quality and security; or a Mercurial partner, who is fluid and interesting, but still rational enough to dialogue intelligently and shrewdly with Saturn? Why a Neptunian?

When I see this kind of situation, I know that I am going to find a strong Neptune in the chart, hiding behind that apparently strong Saturn and projected onto the partner. Or I will be looking at someone who hasn't learned how to work with Saturn in an authentic way. The strength is not for real, and deep inside, the person is probably floundering around in a Neptunian soup. He or she hasn't grown into Saturn yet. The only way such people can convince themselves that they are really strong and Saturnian is to find somebody who is such a mess that it makes them look better. Are you laughing because it's funny, or because it's familiar?

Audience: It's familiar. It's also funny, although I don't know why I'm laughing. I usually get to be the somebody who is a mess. I'm a Pisces with the Moon in Libra conjunct Neptune. You've just described my relationship.

Liz: It wasn't meant personally. But never mind. It reminds me of a quiz show which used to run on television when I was a child, called "To Tell the Truth." Will the real hysteric please stand up?

The world is full of people who haven't really taken Saturn on board, and I suspect every one of us has done this at one time or another, if not on a regular basis. This kind of defence is like a Saturn costume, a Saturn disguise, rather than a strength and self-sufficiency which exist inside and have been built up over time through self-knowledge and hard experience. During the first part of life, before the first Saturn return, we usually get a mixture of genuine and fake Saturn, and hopefully the genuine begins to outweigh the fake as the Saturn cycle progresses. If we persist in asking others to provide us with strength, and fail to develop it inside, our underlying weakness will invariably begin to show itself in relationships that mirror us back to ourselves. Then we may find ourselves having to keep somebody else helpless, in order to continue feeling strong. And sooner or later our prisoners will rebel and break out, and then there is hell to pay.

Audience: I think this is where the black humour comes in. If I can laugh at myself when I am trying to prove how strong I am, and laugh at the irony of everything secretly being the reverse of what it seems, then I can bring the sand-castle into reality. Then I don't mind making a fool of myself while I am learning how to be strong. I think the secret lies in Saturn's fantastic black humour.

Liz: Yes, I am inclined to agree. But Saturn's humour depends on time and experience to give it its cutting edge. We don't know how absurd life is until we take it, and ourselves, too seriously, and wind up with egg on our faces. I will tell you a terrible joke which I heard, which somehow conveys this sentiment. There was a man who died and found himself in hell. He was taken by the guards to choose which punishment cell he was going to spend eternity in. First he was shown a cell in which everyone was standing up to the neck in shit. He said, "No, that one isn't for me." Then he was shown a cell in which everyone was standing up to the waist in shit. He turned that one down as well. Finally he was shown a cell in which everyone was standing up to the knees in shit. He thought to himself, "That one's not so bad," and told the guards he would take it. He went in and stood for a while up to the knees in shit, and thought, "I can cope with this," and then suddenly a bell rang, and a voice snapped out, "All right, everyone, tea break's over, now stand on your heads."

Time, experience and a well-developed sense of irony can help us to shift from the superficial, defensive level of Saturn to a sense of solid inner ground, where we know we can survive and cope alone if necessary. Over the course of the Saturn cycle, it is our struggling attempts to try to do something that we don't really know how to do, which gradually builds that inner ground. I can't really think of a better parallel than the sexual act. The first time we try it, we usually make a ghastly mess of it, because we are trying to remember what we saw in the X-rated film, and what our friends told us we are supposed to do. We are paralysed with shyness, fear, and the expectation of failure, so we consider it a miracle if anything happens at all. Then we say, "Was it good for you?" which is a really dumb question, since if it has been a disaster, it isn't likely we will be told the truth. Compare that with what we develop and experience over many years when we are really relating to the person with whom we are making love. It is not unlike where we start with Saturn, and where, with some insight, hard work, and humility, we actually wind up.

Each stage of the Saturn cycle throws up what is fake, and lets us know what we have not properly built within. If we have been paying Old Cheesefoot his due, we will be able to appreciate what we have done well, knowing that it is truly ours and cannot be taken away again, no matter what life does to us. One way or another, this is what the Saturn cycle reveals. So our hypothetical strong Saturnian stuck in a Neptunian relationship will be told, "You haven't really dealt with Saturn's deeper issues yet, and that's why you are in this involvement. Your Neptunian partner's problem is actually your problem. Real strength would allow you to recognise it, contain it, live with it, and stop projecting it on somebody else." We can see this process of transition and transformation from fake to authentic most vividly if we review the stages of our own Saturn cycle. Perhaps "fake" is the wrong word, because it implies something negative. Unformed Saturn is more a kind of try-on. It is an initial fumbling attempt to develop something which we first think is "out there", and then gradually realise isn't out there after all. It was inside all along. Then we can afford to have humour, because we have become truly separate.

Saturn transits to other planets

When we consider Saturn's transits to other planets, we are dealing with exactly the same kind of cycle as when we examine Saturn's transiting aspects to itself. If we really wish to learn how this works, we need to track our own Saturn transits to other natal planets, in the same way we look at the Saturn cycle to its own place. Take, for example, an approaching transit of Saturn coming up to conjunct one's natal Sun. To really make sense of this transit, we need to look at the first conjunction Saturn made to the natal Sun, which would have occurred some time in the first twenty-nine and a half years of life, perhaps when one was quite young. This "kick-off" conjunction is the beginning of the Saturn-Sun cycle.

If the two planets are conjunct at birth in a separating conjunction – in other words, if the Sun has already passed Saturn – then Saturn by transit will catch up with the Sun in the first few years of life. We might see this as a time when the inner meaning of the natal Sun-Saturn conjunction is expressed outwardly, through some sense of restriction or unhappiness in the environment, or in relation to the parents. For example, it is not uncommon for such an early transit of Saturn over the Sun to reflect a separation from the father, through the parents' divorcing, or a time when family financial difficulties made the early home atmosphere tense and unwelcoming.

If Saturn and the Sun are conjunct at birth in an applying conjunction – in other words, the Sun has not yet reached Saturn at the moment of birth – then Saturn will not actually make its first exact conjunction until the person is around twenty-nine and a half or thirty, and experiencing the Saturn return. The internal feeling of restriction and lack of self-esteem, combined with the determination to "become" somebody real and effective, is likely to externalise at just the time when the individual is in the best position to make the choices which ensure real effectiveness in the world. Equally, he or she may make exactly the wrong choices, thereby apparently justifying the underlying insecurity which the natal aspect reflects.

If Saturn and the Sun form another aspect, the first conjunction of transiting Saturn to the Sun might occur any time during the first twenty-nine years of life. Whenever this takes place, it marks the beginning of the Saturn-Sun cycle. If the Sun is further along than Saturn in the zodiac and forms a square back to Saturn (say, from Sagittarius to Saturn in Virgo), then the first conjunction would take place at around age seven. If the Sun is in square to Saturn while moving toward the conjunction with it (say, from Sagittarius to Saturn in Pisces), then the first conjunction would occur at around age twenty-one or twenty-two. If the Sun and Saturn are not in aspect, the first conjunction could occur at any time before twenty-nine. But it will not have quite the same vital importance as if the two planets are in aspect in the natal chart, because then one of the major life-themes will always involve Saturnian issues. This should be obvious because, whenever transiting Saturn touches the Sun by major aspect, it will touch its own place at the same time.

The process of separation which Saturn's cycle represents on the inner level will occur in relation to the formation of individuality every time it forms a major aspect to the Sun. We can therefore expect issues around father, authority, standing in the world, self-expression, and faith in oneself to be constellated in a challenging way. Although the events may differ, the inner core of meaning will not. In getting a sense of this inner core, we make valuable connections between different experiences at different times of life, and may recognise a profound and intelligent pattern at work. If we take Saturn's cycle in relation to the natal Moon, Saturn's separative, crystallising effect will constellate issues of emotional self-sufficiency and aloneness whenever Saturn makes an aspect to the Moon. The challenges of the squares, the confrontations and realisations of the opposition, and the enforced acceptance and transformative potential of the conjunction apply to any planet when we consider Saturn's transits in relation to it. We need to track these times back in our own lives, and see if we can discover the thread of meaning – and feeling – which connects the various episodes that relate to these important stages of Saturn's involvement with other planets. Although the events may seem unrelated, they are likely to be deeply connected on the inner level, and involve the same themes, depending on the house in which the natal Sun, Moon, and so on, are placed.

Even more importantly, we need to consider the natal planet being aspected by transiting Saturn in context of its own aspect patterns in the birth chart. Unless the planet is unaspected (and then it will still have a dispositor and be placed in a house ruled by another planet, unless it is an unaspected Saturn in Capricorn), it will form relationships with certain other planets, and any transit of Saturn will trigger the entire configuration. Because of Saturn's crystallising nature, it tends to anchor such configurations in reality through direct confrontations – often involving relationships, money, work, health, or other "concrete" situations which we encounter in outer life.

So the whole configuration becomes "incarnated", and we have a chance to make it our own – in other words, we separate it out from the collective unconscious level and begin to live it in a highly individual and defined way. Very often the effect transiting Saturn has on natal configurations is like that of a midwife, bringing something to birth which previously only existed in the realm of unconscious potential. And in bringing it to birth, the potentials are limited, "castrated", and we then have a specific set of experiences which we cannot undo. They become our past, and are ineradicable. And each time transiting Saturn makes another aspect to the configuration, we "remember" what happened to us, and bring an already formed set of responses and attitudes to all the future stages of the cycle.

Transiting Saturn conjunct Venus

Audience: I have transiting Saturn approaching a conjunction to my Venus in the next couple of years, and it's been worrying me terribly. My Venus is in Aries, and it's opposite Saturn conjunct Neptune in Libra. I am afraid my marriage will break up. I don't know why, because I think my husband and I have a good relationship, but I am filled with fear. I suppose it's a bad idea for someone like me to study astrology! I have been thinking about the past while you have been talking, and I just realised that when Saturn made its first conjunction to Venus, I was fifteen, and my parents divorced. I blamed my father, and we have hardly seen each other since. Is this what you mean by a connection between events?

Liz: Yes, although so far, it seems to be a connection on the emotional level. Whether your marriage really does break up remains to be seen. But your feelings toward your father, and therefore toward men in general (including your husband), are likely to be very complex, and probably need to be explored. If you don't work with the connection, you might unconsciously provoke what you fear. Blaming one parent for a marriage breakup is never very helpful, since it usually takes two to dance. But most people tend to do this when they are young, because divided loyalties are very hard for a child or teenager to sustain, and

---

usually there will be pressure coming from the parent one lives with (generally the mother) to abandon all feelings of love for the other parent.

Sadly, it sounds like typical marital crossfire in which yet another child has been caught. Beware of identifying too much with your mother, lest you wind up acting out her life-pattern rather than your own. I suspect your feelings for your father may be much more complicated than you have recognised, and they are coming out in relation to your husband, who may be an innocent hook for unconscious projections. Or he might not be so innocent, and you might have chosen him unconsciously because these issues need to be worked through and he's the ideal person to work them through with.

Natal Venus opposite Saturn-Neptune suggests a deep conflict between the search for an ideal, perfect love and the recognition that all love is limited and flawed. We looked at Saturn-Neptune earlier, with its battle between ideal and reality, and here it impinges on your values and perceptions in relationship. You may have idealised your father to an exalted degree, and when your parents parted your response was probably deep disillusionment and cynicism. You may have been a little too quick to cast blame. You may also have idealised your husband, as a kind of "opposite" of your father, and now may have to face the reality of his limits as an ordinary human being. I think you could turn this approaching transit into something deeply healing, if you can work on these issues in the time preceding it. I don't mean that this will guarantee the safety of your marriage. No astrologer is in a position to judge that. But if it were to break up under this Saturn transit, then insight would help you to make sense of such an event. And whether it breaks up or not, you may be able to finally heal some of your fears, which I suspect have been plaguing you all your life.

Audience: That's true. I'm always jealous and suspicious. I always think that people whom I love will leave me.

Liz: Do I need to point out the obvious? One did, once. Apparently you haven't come to terms yet with why. I will actually risk giving you a piece of concrete advice – not as an astrologer, but simply based on psychological common sense. Is your father still alive?

Audience: Yes.

Liz: But you hardly ever see him.

Audience: No.

Liz: Go and see him – *before* the Saturn transit. Try to find out who he really is. Ask him why what happened happened, and try to listen, rather than judge. If you didn't love him, you wouldn't be suffering the consequences now. Stifling love can be as destructive as stifling anything else which belongs to our souls. If he rejects you, go back and try again, and apologise. Maybe you owe him one. After all, you have been rejecting him for nearly thirty years. And he isn't a young man. It will be a lot harder if you don't deal with this while he's still in incarnation. Even if your attempt fails, at least you will know you have tried, and have finally been loyal to your own heart.
Audience: I wouldn't dare let my mother know I tried to contact him.

Liz: No, I expect you wouldn't, not at the moment. And if you ever do, maybe that will mean that you have healed some of this very ancient wound.

The meaning of the Uranus cycle

Shall we move on to Uranus? Saturn and Uranus are intimately linked, and myth tells us this very clearly. The processes which these two planets reflect through their cycles depend on each other, balance each other, oppose each other, and build on each other. The mythic Cronos-Saturn is the son of Ouranus, and as most of you know, he castrates and overthrows his father and becomes ruler of the gods. This revolution occurs because Ouranus has rejected his Titan children and condemned them to the underworld. Culpability lies on both sides;

each commits a "wrong" against the other. These two are not only father and son in myth, and therefore of the same stock, but they are also mortal enemies. They are linked in astrology by being co-rulers of Aquarius. They are antithetical, yet of the same substance. In some ways they deal with the same issues, but from opposite perspectives, from a different viewpoint and world-view, and on different levels. Their cycles are interwoven, not only in terms of timing and meaning, but also in terms of events and emotional responses. Each one's transits trigger the other.

Because both mythic figures are rulers of the gods, divine kings, we are looking at images of authority and power. What function does a king serve? He governs, and sets the laws by which those whom he governs must live. I am, of course, speaking of mythic kings, not today's "bicycle monarchies", which do not govern. The battle between Saturn and Uranus pivots on the issue of authority and government. Where does authority ultimately lie? What truth is the final truth by which we must live? Does it lie in heaven, or does it lie on earth? Where do power and control ultimately rest? In reality, or in ideas? With the individual, or with the group? Does reality shape our thinking, or does our thinking shape reality? And are we ultimately responsible for our own fate, or are we, in the final analysis, part of a larger system – social or cosmic – whose laws and movements define the course of our individual lives?

I know you will all wish to say, "Both!" because, on the rational level, that is the obvious, albeit paradoxical, solution. It is also a philosophically elegant solution. But in terms of how we experience this polarity, we are generally cornered into choosing, at various points in life. Sometimes our allegiance must be given to the ideal, and sometimes to the real; sometimes to the future, and sometimes to the past; sometimes to ourselves and our own survival, and sometimes to the whole of which we are a part. And sometimes we are torn apart through indecision and an inability to know where the truth, the final authority, lies in a particular situation.

The cycle of Uranus shadows Saturn's cycle, although only approximately, and there are certain critical junctures where one experiences both of them aspecting their own birth places within a period of a few years. They do not do this exactly on the same date, but if you can remember what I was saying earlier about orbs, you will see that one may be within orb of one of its cyclical critical points when the other is also within orb of one of its own cyclical critical points. Within the framework of a couple of years, they may gang up on each other. The mythic images can prove very helpful in getting a sense of just what kind of ganging up this is. Uranus condemns Saturn to the underworld; Saturn castrates Uranus. The Saturn part of us is threatened with repudiation and suppression by Uranus; the Uranian part of us is threatened with castration by Saturn.

Uranus has an eighty-four-year cycle. It makes its first square to its own place between twenty and twenty-two years of age. This happens to coincide with the second Saturn square, which also occurs at around twenty-two years of age. These squares do not arrive at exact aspect on the same afternoon at tea-time. Because of the variability of their direct and retrograde motions, they may overlap for some time, although Saturn invariably follows Uranus. These transits bracket the extremely turbulent and vulnerable period of the early twenties. I am sure all of you can remember important things that have taken place at that time, related to the Saturn cycle. But we are not only looking at Saturn's second square to its own place. This is also the time of the first Uranus square. Now, what does that mean? What is Uranus' cycle really about?

Because Uranus is not a personal planet, it does not deal with the building of the ego as Saturn does. Saturn serves the individual, and provides the container for the expression of the Sun. What the Sun symbolises on the inner level – destiny, sense of purpose and meaning, vessel for that which is eternal – Saturn builds on the outer level, through the process of separation. It gives shape and containment to all the personal planets, especially those which it aspects directly.

But Uranus does not serve the personal ego. Its collective, Promethean, visionary process shakes and shatters those inner and outer structures which confine life and prevent the individual from experiencing the larger unity of which he or she is a part. Uranus reveals the workings of the cosmos, which transforms our perspective and irrevocably alters our definitions of reality. Saturn and Uranus are

---

inimical, just as the gods are in myth. But mythic enemies are always secretly part of the same unity, and in some way the conflict serves a greater end. The same may be said in astrological symbolism, which describes the same processes as myth, in a different and more individualised way.

The teleology of the Saturn cycle concerns our capacity to form as independent incarnate entities, living within mortal limits. The cycle of Uranus is concerned with the potential perfection of the whole. While Saturn is busily putting bits of cement into the cracks and underpinning the foundations of the ego's walls, Uranus comes along and says, "There is no window in that wall. You can't see out. How are you going to know there is a whole cosmos out there? That wall interferes with the progress of the group, and stands as a barrier to collective evolution. Sorry, but it has to come down. I might let you have a wall, but you will have to make it more flexible. Put in a couple of extra doors. Put in some windows. Use wood instead of brick. Better yet, use lightweight prefabricated panels, and then it can be dismantled and moved when necessary."

Uranus serves the collective. Like Prometheus the Titan, it does not bring its inspirations, its divine fire, to one special, deserving person. It offers a vision of progress and evolution to everyone, for good or ill. It serves the human family, through the evolution of ideas and concepts; it serves the larger entity of which the individual is part. Any person who has become too locked into his or her own little ego-world may suffer from Uranus transits, because Uranus shatters all of the bastions that we create in order to make ourselves safe and affirm our stability in the world.

Thus these two planets are always opposed to each other on the level of meaning and inner experience. Of course they aren't always in astrological opposition, 180° apart, although they sometimes are in the birth chart, or one may transit opposite the other. They are antithetical in terms of their functions.

Sometimes the events connected with their transits may appear the same on the superficial level. We tend to assume that, because the concrete form of an event is identical, the meaning and response will also be identical. But they are not. Separation and loss may accompany an important Uranus transit, just as with an important Saturn transit, and upheaval on the material level can be common to both. So can "good fortune", on both material and emotional levels. Both planets can also be connected with inner, spiritual revelations, and both planets can coincide with a period of depression. Yet the inner logic and meaning are very different. When a transit of Saturn coincides with the severing of a relationship, we may need to learn greater self-sufficiency. When a transit of Uranus coincides with the same experience, we may need to let go of our attachments in order to open ourselves to new ideas and a new perception of life.

Individual and collective

Here is another simplistic diagram, although this one looks a bit like a guide to growing puffball mushrooms, or where to place your golf ball. It is meant to demonstrate the relationship between the individual and the collective, which we need to understand as best we can in order to make sense of the Uranus cycle. The three larger circles represent three people. Each has been shaped as an individual by the Saturn cycle, and each thinks he or she is separate. Beneath the threshold of the ego's awareness lies the personal unconscious, which is fluid and constantly interacting with consciousness. And beneath that, and permeating it, lies the sphere of the collective unconscious, which contradicts the experience of separateness on which the ego depends. For the sake of brevity, I have put the three outer planets in this sphere, each symbolising a dimension of this vast collective psychic life – collective mind, collective feeling, and collective instinct.

Although it was Jung who coined the term "collective unconscious", the concept goes back to the ancient Greek idea of *cosmos*, the unified and orderly living system of which all life is a part. The emotional experience of oneness which reflects this unity may be linked with Neptune, but Uranus and Pluto too can bring an experience of oneness, although without the poignant, sacrificial flavour that Neptune reflects. We humans all share certain ideals, dreams, needs, visions, and survival instincts. At this level, we are the same creature – one enormous body with a lot of little heads.

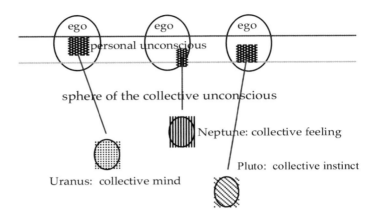

When we experience the collective movements represented by the outer planets, they tend to intrude first into the sphere of the personal unconscious, inflaming our personal complexes and stirring up thoughts, feelings and sensations which are new and disturbing. We don't quite know what has hit us. Eventually we may succeed in bringing some of this into consciousness, and shaping it according to the ego's direction and values. That is the job of the Sun and Saturn in particular, although hopefully we recognise that we are sharing in something much larger. But we may also be buffeted, compulsively driven, or even torn apart by these collective currents.

Uranus in the early twenties

In the early twenties, there is a terrific impulse to become a defined individual and move out into the world – to leave mother and family behind, and build a life as a self-sufficient personality with independent ideas and goals. This is reflected by Saturn's challenging second square to its own place, which is not complete until around twenty-three. In order to achieve such separateness, we must close doors and create boundaries. We say, "I am going to do a post-graduate degree, I am going to become a teacher, I want to train as a nurse." We might have made such decisions earlier, but at the time of the second Saturn square, we feel compelled to put our choices into practice, or, to use the more down-market expression, to put our money where our mouth is. This is what we do in the early twenties – at least, what we try to do, or think we ought to do, or are pressured to do. Even if we are pressured from outside, there is something within us that is in accord. We may refuse the call, but we know, deep down, that it is time to leave home. We are starting to limit our possibilities. We have to, because if we don't make these kinds of choices, we wind up swimming around in maternal soup, and fail to form as individuals.

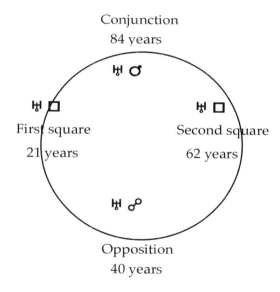

But at the same time that we are making these Saturnian choices, there is something else going on as well. We may experience a disturbing sense that we are incarcerating ourselves at the same time that we are choosing. We run the risk of closing off potentials, abilities, talents, and facets of the personality which matter to us, and which we intuitively know are going to be needed later in life as part of the whole person we eventually become. So there is a terrific conflict which occurs in the early twenties.

The Uranian spirit, which makes itself felt a year or so earlier than Saturn, says, "Leave the doors open! Don't commit yourself! There are so many potentials waiting to be developed! The world needs changing, and only you can do it! You're too young to nail yourself into a coffin. Don't promise anything, don't sign anything – travel with a light suitcase, and be prepared to shop around. Life is bigger than you thought. Stay true to your ideals!" Of course, this voice may not be conscious. It may even be acted out by one's friends, partner, or employer, or even one's body. It may be projected, and comes back at us as an unexpected event which forces us to leave the past behind. But it is a very insistent, even irresistible voice.

But in the aftermath of all this excitement and sense of life opening up, the wet-blanket, realistic voice of Old Cheesefoot can be heard, saying, "Stop behaving like an adolescent. Learn to look after yourself. You have to get a job, train at something, prepare for the future. You can't rely on your parents any more. If you make stupid decisions and waste your time flitting from one thing to another because of wild ideals, you'll regret it later. You may believe in cosmic unity and equal rights for all, but the world out there isn't like that. Get out and do something practical."

There is enormous tension generated by both these planets making critical transits to their natal places. It is potentially a creative tension, propelling us out into life. Whether these inner voices are conscious or not, nevertheless they do battle within, and we are buffeted between them. When we look back at this age, and consider these transits, we may well wonder how we have survived it. For many people the conflict is not that painful; rather, it is stimulating and action-provoking. It depends on how able one is to contain the conflict, and do something useful with it. This depends on the condition of both Saturn and Uranus in the birth chart, and other transits and progressed aspects occurring at the time, and the horoscope as a whole. It also depends on whether we have successfully managed to steer through earlier Saturn transits, and have enough inner solidity to see, more or less, where we are going.

A couple of years before the Saturn return, Uranus is trine its own place, and as the Saturn return begins to bite, Uranus makes a sesquiquadrate to its own place. The same conflict and tension occur, but the balance is different. Saturn, because it forms a conjunction to its natal placement, will usually dominate the scene, and the restlessness of the Uranian spirit forms a low-key backdrop as the solidification of the ego takes centre stage for a while.

The energy, inspiration and enthusiasm of the twenty-seven-year-old give way to the inward-looking reflection and sobriety of the twenty-nine-year-old, which in turn give way to renewed restlessness at thirty as the Uranus sesquiquadrate begins to raise doubts about the decisions made. As we are considering the minor aspects of the Uranus cycle, we might also think about Saturn's first opposition to its own place at around fifteen, which follows Uranus' semisquare to its own place at around eleven or twelve. The coincidence of both aspects with the process of puberty, bracketing its beginning and its end, tell us a great deal about the psychological tensions involved.

Uranus in mid-life

Uranus keeps ticking away like a time bomb, and between about thirty-nine and forty-two it makes the opposition to its own place. This opposition well precedes Saturn coming opposite its own place in the mid-forties, although due to the way orbs work in transit, there are usually lingering echoes of Uranus as Saturn comes within orb of its opposition. By mid-life, the two have begun to become more and more loosely knit in their cycles, because Uranus follows fairly tight seven-year multiples, while Saturn's multiples are slightly more than seven years. So the older we get, the more discrepancy we get between the two. In the early twenties, the cycles are closer together. At mid-life, Saturn comes well after Uranus, and the nature of the relationship is less a conflict than a cleaning up of rubble, a narrowing and focusing of vision, and a compromising of ideals.

After the often shattering impact of Uranus opposite Uranus, Saturn comes along to clean up the mess. This entire period – late thirties to mid-forties – is now euphemistically known as mid-life crisis. This term is currently used as a justification for all sorts of messes into which people land themselves. It straddles a period of up to six years, and is a long and complex process, not a three-week instant enlightenment job. This notorious mid-life crisis really reflects two different, although interlinked, processes at work, one of which is Uranian and the other Saturnian.

Uranus is the enemy of anything which has become too fixed into a rigid shape, because stasis is the enemy of evolution and therefore makes ultimate perfection impossible. By the time we arrive at mid-life, many of us have crystallised too much. We have got ourselves too rooted in security structures, or have overdeveloped certain dimensions of the personality at the expense of other, unlived possibilities and potentials. Family structures, work structures, social identifications, sexual roles and models – all these can start as support systems and, by the late thirties, have become prisons in which we are incarcerated. We have become so preoccupied with our own survival that we have forgot the whole of which we are a part.

Our relationships may have fulfilled the people we were when we were younger, but might not be able to accomodate the people we are becoming. The image we have of ourselves may be comfortable and familiar, but may be stifling us within. We become bored. We say, "Is this all there is?" We sense that our possibilities are becoming more and more limited, and soon there won't be any left at all. The Saturn square which occurs in the mid-thirties has reminded us that soon the body will be middle-aged, and the experience of growing old can't be put off for much longer. But rather than settling comfortably into this Saturn process, something lights a fire under us, and we erupt, claiming the right to be youthful once again, to be free of confines, to reach for the starry heavens.

Uranus says, "Look, you don't have to identify with all these structures. Your body may be growing older, but you are only as old as you feel. You aren't limited to what you have built so far. Don't give up. Don't sell out to time, tradition, and timidity. You are only halfway through your life. You haven't really lived yet. What about the ideals you had when you were twenty-one? Where have they gone? What about your belief in human potential? Where did your vision go? You have become boring and straight. What about the wider world out there? What about the talents and potentials you glimpsed when you were young, that have got closed off gradually, year after year, as you sought to survive and build security? And are you really going to wake up, morning after morning for the rest of your life, and look at the same face on the pillow next to you?"

To many people, this is the voice of the devil. It represents a terrible temptation and a terrible threat, and they begin to fix padlocks on all the doors as soon as the planet gets within a 10° orb of opposing its place. By the time the aspect gets close, they are in a frenzy of anxiety, behaving in compulsively Saturnian ways, terrified that something will happen to upset their nice, orderly little world. They cage themselves, their partners, their children, and their bodies, in the hope that they will be protected. They dream disturbing dreams, of houses falling down, avalanches, explosions, and spaceships landing. They become "neurotic" because life seems so full of danger. This apparently devilish onslaught is, of course, coming from within, but often it seems as though it is outside.

Sometimes Uranus transits are accompanied by sudden events over which we clearly have no control, and which cannot be construed as our own creation or personal respnsibility. But we have a choice as to how we respond to such events. And sometimes we unconsciously provoke disruption outside, frequently through our partners, who get fed up with our Saturnian padlocks, and have a little or a big fling to get some breathing space; or our employers, who want a bit more risk and experimentation, and look for someone younger, with more enthusiasm and energy. Then Uranus is "done" to us, rather than reflecting a spirit of growth and movement with which we voluntarily cooperate.

Whether we are the initiators or the recipients, the Uranus opposition is often a severe shock to people. They may say to themselves, "I am trapped. I don't want to spend the rest of my life like this. I am suffocating." And they either erupt and blow up long-existing structures, or find somebody else to do it for them. Or they say nothing to themselves, but somehow find their way into a situation in which the structure collapses on them, through no one's evident fault.

With some people this shattering of redundant structures is very dramatic; with others it is quiet and low-key, although no less powerful and transformative. Uranus opposing Uranus may not

---

necessarily shake us loose from a marriage or career or world-view, but something has to give, and depending on how rigid one has become, the disruptive impact of Uranus opposite Uranus will be that much greater. Some people go haywire, and do some very funny things. They try to reclaim youth in ways that sometimes work, but equally may leave them looking like absolute asses. They may succeed in opening life up in immensely creative ways, but sometimes they must also cope with looking and feeling very foolish. And a few people – although I have not met many – manage to put so many padlocks on the doors that Uranus cannot get through at all. It merely rumbles for a while, goes away, and comes back later, at the next semisquare which occurs at around fifty-one (just before the next Saturn square), with bigger explosives.

Mid-life is a time of great tension and stress. There is sometimes a feeling that the clock is ticking on, time is running out, and there are so many things one hasn't done. A sense of desperation may pervade one's choices and actions. Because the desperation is not always conscious, it can be suppressed. There are people who just don't want to acknowledge the advent of Uranus. They do not want to hear the knock on the door, and they push all awareness of it into the unconscious. Then anxiety begins to rise to the surface. This anxiety is often very intense, and accompanied by a sense that, any minute, something is going to blow up. One can become quite phobic in the face of such anxiety. The electrical sockets have to be checked every time one goes out, as well as all the locks on the windows. Every street seems to be peopled with muggers and rapists, and danger lurks at every corner.

Sometimes people experience nothing for a while, other than depression and loss of meaning, and that awful anxiety that they don't understand and can't find an explanation for. This is, of course, when many people turn to their doctors for help, to get anti-depressants to control the anxiety and depression, rather than looking at the mine-field they are walking through. Everything that is stagnant in one's life is under threat, and long-suppressed emotions will also demand to be recognised. It is really much better to try to live honestly with

Uranus. Prometheus didn't go to all that trouble stealing fire, just to have it ignored by recalcitrant humans.

At the time of the square, in the early twenties, such honesty isn't easy. Getting a perspective, and containing the difficult feelings rather than reacting impulsively, depends on Saturn's function, and as we have already seen, this is not fully developed until the time of the Saturn return. It is easier to get perspective in your forties than your early twenties. That doesn't mean it can't be done. But sadly, those on whom young people depend for advice are often in the dark about what is happening, and it is a case of the blind leading the blind – especially if one is having one's Uranus square Uranus at twenty-one and one's parent is having Uranus opposite Uranus at forty, which will happen if one marries young and has children immediately.

Uranus in later life

The second Uranus square to its own place occurs at around sixty-one or sixty-two. This is after the second Saturn return and before Saturn's first square to its own place on the next round of the cycle. This sandwiching of Uranus between two junctures of the Saturn cycle could, in an ideal world, provide a time of inspiration, following the re-evaluation and coming to terms of the late fifties, when retirement is approaching and the recognition of incipient old age tends to make people reflective and inward-looking. The world is not, unfortunately, ideal, and so the restlessness and craving for new horizons, which echoes a similar feeling at twenty-one, is often treated with fear and suppression.

This, like the early twenties, is a critical period, although the gap between the Saturn and Uranus squares is longer than it is in the early twenties. It is a difficult age, as every pensioner knows. When people retire, statistics show that a large proportion of them die soon afterwards, which is why private pension and annuity companies make such huge amounts of money. What keeps these companies in business is not the pensioners who live to a ripe old age, but rather, the ones who make their exit before they have had a

_____

chance to enjoy the benefits of their accrued savings. One has been saving up a large amount of pension money hoping that one will live for another thirty years, anticipating all kinds of nice things which one never had time to do during one's working life. And if one dies prematurely, the insurance company gets the lot, except for a little portion which may be paid in monthly installments, for a finite period, to one's spouse.

That is why insurance companies try to sell us pension and annuity schemes which swallow up our savings, rather than encouraging us to invest our money, live on the interest in retirement, and keep the lump for ourselves or our families. This age is when the majority of people are preparing to finish their work. For those who are wholly identified with that work, it also means losing their place in society, and then suddenly they have lost all point in being alive. In addition, work can conceal a multitude of sins, not least a bad marriage, which one can escape by rushing to the office early each morning and coming home late each night, with the odd working weekend thrown in. Suddenly one is at home all the time with someone who became a stranger years ago; and the prospect may be horrifying. And there are also many people who simply do not possess the inner resources to find any meaning in life beyond who they are at work. They think about playing golf, or travelling, but when it really comes down to it, they are no one without the job and the social position that goes with it.

For all these reasons, many people in their early to mid-sixties go into a dreadful depression, which may sometimes manifest as illness, because they don't cope well with the change which is upon them. Uranus square its own place in maturity seems to promise all kinds of golden opportunities. Interestingly, I recently came across some statistics which indicate that the divorce rate rises sharply at around sixty, just as it does around forty. The belief that one still has another chance to find happiness and meaning does not necessarily decrease with age. But then, as usual, Saturn comes along, saying, "The doors are closing, Sunshine, not opening. Your options are pretty limited. You are now an OAP. In society's terms, you are no one any more. You may have a free bus pass, but you are old and useless. You might have a pension. But what have you managed to save in the inner world?" This is a harsh voice, and if we have no answers, it may even be a fatal voice. But as usual, we are given no education about the psychological ramifications of retirement, just as we are given no education on this level about any of the critical stages of life.

If one is self-employed, one is better off, because one can go on working. But the body may not allow the same kind of commitment of energy and time as it once did. So once again, Saturn may remind us of our limits through our bodies. Uranus has just finished squaring its own place not so long ago, saying, "You haven't finished yet. There are still things you haven't done, things you haven't become, potentials you haven't lived. Get out there and do it. Your life isn't over. What are you doing trapped on a Saga coach tour with all these wrinklies?" The sense of letdown when Saturn castrates Uranus can be enormous, and it is not surprising that people pop off with heart attacks on the golf course or the Mediterranean cruise, and one's friendly insurance company gets another £100,000 to pop into the kitty.

In an ideal world, Saturn can give shape and permanence to the new ideas which burst forth at around sixty, at the time of the Uranus square. Retirement could be a new beginning, concretely as well as spiritually, and certainly it is for some people – but too few. Compromise will naturally be necessary; but depression and loss of hope are not. The late fifties and early sixties are a make-or-break time in terms of making sense of what one has done with one's life, because it is difficult to begin again at this age without enormous effort. Uranus, because it reflects a Promethean spirit of reform and renewal, tends to make us want to try again, to remodel or redeem the old, to stretch beyond our personal boundaries. Despite the increasing limitations of age, some people really do manage to overturn the habits and structures of a lifetime, sailing off into the unknown with the intellectual and spiritual vigour of youth – despite the antagonism which the collective tends to show toward those who do things considered "inappropriate" for an older person.

Because Uranus is a collective planet, we feel in touch with important movements and currents in the world around us, and the status quo – both personal and collective – seems like anathema. It takes courage to expand one's horizons at this time, rather than settling drearily into an old age which consists mainly of looking back at what one hasn't done. This is the opportunity provided by the second Uranus square. If it is not taken, deep resentments may rise to the surface, creating bitterness over what has been wasted, and sometimes also taking their toll on the body, which can no longer bounce back as it once might have done.

The Uranus return

The Uranus return, which occurs at eighty-four, is not guaranteed for us all. Although statistics keep changing and we are living longer now than we did a decade ago, we still cannot assume that we will reach this ripe age. Because our opportunities for any external expression of Uranian rebellion are greatly reduced because of the frailty of the body, the eruption is more likely to occur on the inner level, if it does not coincide with actual death itself, and this is often a time of intense spiritual awakening. Religious conversions are not uncommon, and repudiation of an earlier, narrower religious approach in favour of a more holistic one is, in the examples I have seen, one frequent expression. There may also be surprising insights and revelations in terms of one's relationships with family and community. A healing detachment is often one of Uranus' gifts.

One appropriate task at the end of life is to recognise life and death as a unity. One's own life may be seen in a greater context, and patterns which escape our notice earlier now become vividly apparent. The return of Uranus to its own natal position can offer us a sense of a larger cosmos, which provides a new perspective on death and a new sense of one's role as part of that greater unity.

The combined cycles of Saturn and Uranus

12-14 years: Uranus semiquare and Saturn opposition
20-22 years: Uranus square and Saturn square

28-30 years: Uranus sesquiquadrate and Saturn return
38-42 years: Uranus opposition and Saturn square
56-60 years: Uranus square and Saturn return
84-89 years: Uranus return and Saturn return

When we begin to look more closely at the interplay of these two planetary cycles in relation to well-known critical stages of life, we can begin to realise how many lives are dominated by the repeating Saturn-castrating-Uranus, Uranus-obliterating-Saturn sequence, without any real understanding of what is happening. Through astrology, we have a remarkable opportunity available to us, of making some sort of sense of what these cycles are about, and working more creatively and consciously with them. So many people are merely victims of the inevitable life processes which these planets describe. I do not think we should consider our interpretation of the cycle of either planet without keeping the cycle of the other in mind, because one opens up what the other closes down. They are dependent on each other to fulfill their meaning, and we need to recognise their mutual interaction so that we can make the most of the critical times, rather than feeling like victims of life.

Mid-life is, arguably, the most fraught of all the critical times, because we have the additional pleasure of Neptune square Neptune to confuse matters further. We seem to handle Uranus better at mid-life if we have been able to make sense of the Saturn return. But even then, with all the insight in the world, we still cannot predict or control the Promethean spirit, which has its own impersonal logic and laws. And perhaps it is not a bad thing to blunder about under the Uranus-Uranus opposition. It is our mistakes as well as our inspirations which open us up, and if we lunge at the future and make a mess, at least we will have tried. We may not know what on earth is going on, or what we should be doing with ourselves, and every decision we make might get changed a day later. The Uranus opposition can be exhilarating and exciting, but usually there is a price to pay if we smash apart existing structures. And the bill comes due when Saturn approaches the opposition to its own place.

A deep and very important re-evaluation seems to be required at the time of the second Saturn opposition, which will raise echoes of the first opposition at fifteen. Disillusionment and regret are not uncommon, and a recognition that there are some potentials which will never be fulfilled in one lifetime. Saturn says, "All right, you have had your Uranian fling, and you may think you have got free at last. But the limitations which are part of you haven't gone away. Nor have the people who have been in your life for a long time, and to whom you owe certain responsibilities. You will still have to deal with these, and you aren't getting any younger. Now you must define and justify what you have done, who you are, and what you are going to do next."

So Saturn comes back again, demanding definition, separation, and crystallisation – just at the moment when one thought one had got rid of all of that restriction and depressing sense of mortality. This time is a sort of psychological motorway junction, and it requires a very alert driver, because the sense of breaking free with Uranus leads very rapidly to the sense of, "Oh God, I have made a mess." If one has begun something entirely new – a new relationship, a new career, a new environment – it is likely to be challenged when Saturn opposes Saturn.

Saturn's opposition coming on the heels of Uranus opposite its own place is a hard follow-up, because Saturn, as is its wont, attempts to castrate Uranus. All the new possibilities that opened up under the Uranus opposition now come under some very hard scrutiny, and one is challenged to make one's dreams real, or give them up as a bad job. There is often a lot of leftover rubble to clean up from the Uranus opposition, which might not have seemed like a problem at first, but which is now likely to clutter everything up. Mistakes become evident, whereas in the grip of the Uranian vision, there is no such thing as a mistake – only an experiment that didn't work out.

In the days when social and relationship structures were more rigid than they are now, Uranus tended to explode more covertly, because it was not so easy to leap out of marriages, leave children, emigrate, or alter one's work or social position. The explosion tended to be confined, and more often it imploded. I have no statistical proof, but

I suspect that the frequency of what used to be known as "conversion hysteria" in Freud's time is linked to the inability to express Uranian energy at this critical time of life. I do not know, but I suspect, that the "sudden event" school of Uranian experience may also be more in evidence when there are no other levels through which the planet can be expressed. Today we have much greater mobility, and new ideas are instantly accessible to everyone because of media and communications technology. So Uranian eruptions have more scope of a creative kind. Uranian behaviour is no longer viewed in the same invariably pathological light that it once was. Our grandparents, for example, couldn't really get away with being Uranian, in terms of their personal lives, without suffering considerable public censure. Uranus has more freedom now. In fact it has so much scope that, on a collective level, Saturn is becoming more and more defended. There will be consequences and a price to pay on the reality level for this increased openness to Uranus. We may already be seeing it in the kind of Saturnian backlash which is presently occurring in America. Fundamentalism is one of Saturn's responses to too much Uranus.

Audience: You have said that Saturn castrates Uranus – after the Uranus opposition, the Saturn opposition comes along and curtails all the new possibilities. Could you say the reverse as well? Does Uranus dethrone Saturn, when the opposition comes along after the Saturn square in the thirties?

Liz: Yes; but dethronement might not be the best image. If we think in mythic terms, Uranus does not overthrow Saturn. Uranus is the ruler of creation, and Saturn is his child. He banishes Saturn to the underworld, which is another way of saying that the Saturnian sense of mortality and limitation is banished to the unconscious in the face of the eternal vision which Uranus brings. This is really what the Uranus opposition does. It banishes the encroaching sense of age, limitation, and mortality which occurs in the mid-thirties, and raises our eyes to the heavens. This is one of the reasons why people can always rationalise what they do under the Uranus opposition. They can behave in extraordinary ways, sometimes very brutal and hurtful

---

to others, but somehow it makes sense in the context of the larger picture.

Audience: I was just thinking of something that happens in relationships. Very often it happens that you get married, and very often the man is two or three years older, so he starts getting the Uranian restlessness while the wife is going through Saturn square Saturn, and he may overdo it. Afterward, the structure may still be there, but he has broken things. Then he wants to nail down the carpets because his Saturn is opposing Saturn, and then the wife is having Uranus opposition Uranus.

Liz: You are clearly speaking from experience. Yes, it is one possible scenario. The chap goes haywire for a bit, and then he comes back and says, "It didn't really mean anything, it's you I really love, and I don't want to lose you and the family and the home," just as her Uranus opposition is coming up. And with admirable Uranian spirit she says, "Sorry, but you're too late." But it isn't really because of what happened in the past – it is because she is ready to try her wings, and he has given her the perfect excuse. I don't know how statistically frequent a two- or three-year age gap is. Age differences between partners can vary enormously. Sometimes people of the same age group get together, and have the Uranus opposition at the same time.

Audience: My parents were around the same age, and they separated and both decided to remarry at the time of the Uranus opposition.

Liz: Examples like this are not uncommon in the same age group. You may also get the interplay of cycles between parents and children. The child is experiencing Uranus square Uranus at twenty-one, for example, while the parent is having fun with Saturn opposite Saturn in the mid-forties. Both planets deal with issues of authority and structure, but from different perspectives. While Saturn is concerned with the formation of the separate ego (personal authority), Uranus is concerned with the ego's expansion and transformation through exposure to the larger whole (collective or cosmic authority). One crystallises while the other shatters. But identical outer experiences can be reflected by both.

Sometimes one person's Uranian need to break out of a structure is mirrored in his or her partner's having to accept the limits of reality, including the limits of the relationship, or the limits of the other person. The Uranus person is experiencing being catapulted out of an existing structure, either voluntarily or involuntarily, while the Saturn person is having to face issues of aloneness and the necessity of inner structure. Often, when the two planets' transiting aspects coincide between two people, one can get a separation as the external manifestation. Sometimes marriages take place. Then the deeper motives and feelings behind the marriage will be very different for each partner, although the event is the same for both.

Sometimes there are more serious repercussions with Uranus transits – the sudden onset of an illness, for example, or serious financial difficulties, or accidents, or parental deaths. One may encounter some of the more jarring elements of life's array of goodies. Uranus can be extremely difficult for the predictive astrologer, because it is so unpredictable on the level of events. Saturn is easier to predict, because the underlying causes which have led to the present consequences are understandable, with a little reflection. But whatever one thinks of an impending Uranus transit, it will invariably reflect the one thing one didn't think of, because the planet's meaning and process seem to depend on the element of surprise.

The transformative impact of Uranus depends on the ego's unpreparedness. That is its teleology – it stretches the ego through exposure to greater, more impersonal laws, and shatters the ego's identification with existing structures and attitudes. It can't do this if it is merely presenting us with something we already thought of and have time to prepare for. It can only achieve its revelation by presenting us with something the ego cannot conceive of, because this "something" is larger than the ego – "trans-personal". Uranus' gift of Promethean fire is a new and unknown gift, stolen from the gods. Prometheus didn't go to all that trouble just to recycle something human beings already had.

This is why it is pointless to try to anticipate in any specific concrete way what will happen under Uranus transits. We will unconsciously overlook, avoid, or not deal with the one area where Uranus is going to make its appearance, because it is what we do not yet know that changes us. If we can think of it, then we know it already. We can, of course, make a general assessment. If natal Uranus is sitting in the 7th house, for example, and transiting Uranus is making an opposition to its own place while moving through the 1st house, then fine – no prizes awarded for a good educated guess. Something in the area of relationships – personal or professional – is going to blow.

But we must never get too confident about what we think is going to blow, or in what way and with what result, because it will usually surprise us. Uranus makes us realise that we are very narrow in our perceptions. We see only a little bit of life, and then we are woken up out of sleep and realise how little we see and know. Uranus' effect is to wake us up with a short, sharp shock. The shock may be happy, unhappy, or a mixture of the two, but it invariably depends on surprise, because what the ego anticipates, it interferes with, and then there is no surprise any more. Uranian awakenings have enormous power because we cannot tell Prometheus what to do with his fire.

The nature of events

Audience: But Uranus transits take a long time, and you said earlier that we have to consider the orbs. Something that takes so long is no surprise!

Liz: No, but Uranus transits also involve the acquisition of hindsight, and I think it is, in part, the process of assimilating the ramifications of the shock which takes so long. Events that occur under Uranus transits, whether inner or outer, are usually very sharp and quick. Unwittingly setting the stage, and cleaning up afterward, can take considerably longer.

Let's say transiting Uranus is approaching the opposition to its own place, and you leave this seminar and go home, and your partner is waiting for you and says, "I have something to tell you. A few months ago, I met someone." That takes him only thirty seconds. But it took him a lot longer to get to breaking point. And for you to fully process what it means may take years. First of all, there is going to be an emotional reaction, and that is likely to be complex. Anxiety is likely to pervade any Uranian event, whether it is this kind of short, sharp, nasty shock, or an event of a more benign kind. Sometimes Uranus isn't predisposed to such dramatic occurrences. Sometimes it reflects happy events, because Uranus oppositions are not inherently nasty by nature. A great deal depends on what the planet is doing in the natal chart, and also on the receptivity of the individual to being woken up in the Uranian way.

A specific event will usually be very quick. But the implications – getting out from under outworn structures, undoing ties that are too tight, extricating oneself from suffocating situations, discovering ideas that transform one's world-view, or learning to recognise that the freedom one has unwillingly received from someone else is in fact the freedom that one most desperately needs oneself – may linger on and on. That is what takes the time. The ego must stretch beyond its confines and look at the world differently, and less self-centredly.

Uranian events can occur at any point during the course of the transit, including the period when it comes within a 10° orb and the period when it has passed exactness and is still within a 10° orb. Events don't necessarily take place during the first stage of the transit, when the planet is direct and moving into aspect, or when it is retrograde, and moving away from the aspect or back toward it. Sometimes there are two or three apparently unconnected events which are linked by a shared meaning, because Uranian awakenings may illuminate several situations which may look as if they don't have anything to do with each other. Of course they do, because they have all taken place under the same transit, and they will all be concerned, on one level or another, with freeing energy, expanding vision, and breaking down outworn structures.

With important transits, events are not necessarily singular. This should be obvious if we think of the different levels of a transit, and recognise that the inherent meaning, and the emotional responses, may be triggered by or embodied in a whole series of external occurrences. Not only are Uranian events not necessarily singular, or even predictably good or bad; they may not be concrete in the physical sense, but may occur on the emotional, intellectual, or spiritual level. A sudden revelation of the unity of the cosmos, or the validity of astrology, or the interconnectedness of human beings, is a real event, but it is not concrete in the material sense. There is nothing that can be held in one's hand, or weighed and measured.

Also, the nature of the transiting aspect won't always tell us how we will feel about what happens, because squares and oppositions do not necessarily produce "bad" results. They are challenging aspects, but for some people challenges are the elixir of life. Uranus squares and oppositions to other planets can produce very creative, positive and exhilarating results, and trines can sometimes produce unpleasant situations in which one feels trapped but too passive to find a way through.

Audience: An important relationship broke up when Uranus opposed my Uranus, and oddly, other members of my family also went through a rough time. It was very strange. Around the same time, my mother fell ill, my sister's marriage went through a very bad patch, and my partner's father died. It was as if we were all having my Uranus transit!

Liz: Yes, it often happens like that, especially with families which are "enmeshed", or strongly linked on the unconscious level. If one person – especially one of the parents – is suppressing Uranus, it tends to be acted out by everybody around him or her, especially by children, and sometimes even without the relevant Uranus transits in the other charts. One gets the feeling that all the family members are being shoved into Uranian roles against their wishes, because of the urgent necessity of the person who won't acknowledge what is within. Or perhaps we might say that a family complex, rather than an individual, is having a Uranus transit.

Uranus tends to favour such expressions, because it is a collective planet. If we don't give the planet room to breathe, others will open the door for us and give us the room anyway, because everyone needs it. Then we have to be wise enough not to be tempted by the great luxury of blame, and I think it takes a fairly big person to do this. It is one of the most difficult issues in working with clients having Uranus transits. Often we can see Uranus hitting its own place, or hitting another planet (particularly the Sun, Moon, or Venus, or the Ascendant or Descendant), and somebody else has elected to say, "I am leaving." To encourage the client to understand that this transit is happening in his or her own chart, and therefore in his or her own psyche, may require a good deal of tact and persistence. There is something in the client that needs this experience. It isn't just the other person; it is mutual. But pride and the desire to take revenge can sometimes be so great that recognition is resisted. When this kind of thing happens under someone's Uranus-Uranus opposition, and the Saturn-Saturn opposition follows a couple of years later, the recognition may finally arrive, painfully and long overdue.

Audience: How can we live out other people's charts?

Liz: Easily. All it takes is unconsciousness. Usually there needs to be a hook for the projection, however small, but since we all have every planet in our charts, including Uranus, the hooks are always there. When something powerful is projected on us, we may find ourselves becoming that thing, even if we know perfectly well it is out of character. It is especially common for children to act out what their parents cannot or will not live. This is why we become different people when in the presence of different people. Each relationship invokes special areas of our own characters, and some relationships invoke these areas out of proportion to what we know of ourselves, because we are being asked to carry something of the other person's psyche.

When powerful transits occur in our charts, we experience them in a unique way, according to our own individual natures and level of consciousness. But if we are close to another person, then we may experience their important transits as well, and the more blurred our ego-boundaries are, the more we may fail to distinguish between our own psychic experiences and those of our loved ones. If we can recognise when we are being unconsciously asked to act something out, we may be in a position to help both the other person and ourselves. In psychotherapy, the understanding of what is known as transference and countertransference is a major part of therapeutic work. Jung explored this issue of unconscious identification very deeply in "The Psychology of the Transference". It is sometimes very difficult to refuse the invitation to act something out for another person when it coincides with a transit of our own. It is virtually irresistible.

Audience: You said Neptune transits also figure during the mid-life time. Doesn't Pluto as well?

Liz: Sometimes, but not for every age group. Transiting Neptune is plugged into the seven-year multiple (it takes fourteen years to move through a sign), so its transits tend to coincide with the Uranus cycle at certain junctures. I haven't mentioned this in any detail because it really merits another seminar. Neptune's orbit takes a hundred and sixty-eight years, while Uranus' orbit takes eighty-four, which is just half. At the mid-life period, when Uranus is opposite Uranus, Neptune will square its own place. So we must also contend with disillusionment and the relinquishing of fantasies of perfect love. One may also get Pluto square Pluto thrown in for good measure, depending on which part of the zodiac Pluto was in when one was born. This may mean becoming aware of the struggle for survival on a collective level, and dealing with powerful primal emotions. Pluto's orbit is elliptical. Those with Pluto in Leo and Virgo are getting this square at mid-life.

That is bad luck. Not everyone gets a Pluto-Pluto square at this age; because it moves so rapidly through Scorpio and Sagittarius, it will pick up the square to natal Pluto in Leo and Virgo earlier in life than when it transits through Taurus and Gemini. It gets these people when they are much older. A person with Pluto in mid-Gemini, born around 1905 or 1906, would have had Pluto square Pluto around the mid-1960's, when he or she was already fifty-five or so. By that time Uranus had long finished opposing its own place, although the second Saturn return would have been looming. So it is bad luck for people with Pluto in Leo and Virgo, because the planet is moving so quickly right now that it is squaring its natal place while they are right in the middle of Uranus opposite Uranus and Neptune square Neptune.

Audience: Why is it bad luck?

Liz: Because it is one more thing to deal with. In theory, we can talk of wonderful challenges and opportunities for growth. This looks great on paper, and the teleology may be eminently positive. But getting all these transits at once is not always a lot of fun on the emotional or material level.

Audience: At least you have got it all out of the way.

Liz: Yes, you have got it all out of the way, always assuming you survive it, and in that sense it may be construed as good luck. It depends on whether you like all the bills arriving on one day, or whether you like them spread out during the course of the month. Perhaps, if you are a double Aries with Scorpio rising and Mars conjunct Pluto trine the Sun, it's really a laugh a minute.

Transits of Uranus to other planets

When we look at transiting Uranus aspecting any natal planet, it will form a cycle to that planet, just as Saturn does with its transits to natal planets. But of course the cycle is much longer. It takes around twenty-one years to move from a conjunction with a natal planet to a square to the same planet, and the conjunction may have taken place before one was born, suggesting that the issues really began in the family background and come to fruition in one's own life later. If you are new to this kind of tracking of transits, I would suggest that you begin with the big cycles of Saturn to its own place and Uranus to its own place, and think about what was going on in your life at the time. Try to get a sense of how these critical cycles work. We all get them at around the same age, so in this area we are not individual. We all experience Saturn and Uranus as a human collective. We go through the same kinds of experiences and the same sorts of processes, although the arena of life will vary according to the sign, house placement and aspects of natal Saturn and Uranus.

The transits of Uranus to individual planets in the birth chart can occur at any age. They reflect the impingement of the collective mind on the life of the individual, and the individual is changed as a result. Rather than talking about these transits in cookbook fashion, I will start with an example. Later we will look at some charts offered by members of the group. Now we can use the chart of a "famous person" to track the cycles of Saturn and Uranus and try to ground some of the things we have been exploring.

Example Chart 1

I thought this one would be particularly interesting because of the natal Saturn-Uranus opposition, which means that any transit of either planet to its own place will automatically trigger the other one. This is, of course, the chart of C. G. Jung.[14] Many of you will be familiar with it. We know quite a bit about his personal life – despite efforts on the part of the family to suppress information over the years – and I will try to link one or two important periods, events, and creative developments with corresponding points in the transit cycles. We can begin by looking at natal Saturn and Uranus and getting a sense of what they might describe. Any initial observations?

Audience: Well, Uranus is in the 7th, and he had a pretty colourful personal life.

Liz: That is a polite way of putting it. Although he was married to one woman all his life, and maintained the veneer of a normal family

---

[14]Birth data furnished by Jung's daughter, Gret Baumann.

life, he had a number of major and minor love affairs, including involvements with patients. In the second half of his life he maintained a *ménage à trois* with his wife and Toni Wolff, which caused both women considerable pain.[15]

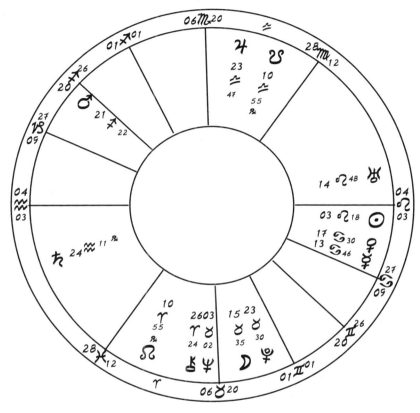

C. G. Jung
26 July 1875, 7.32 pm LMT, Kesswil, Switzerland

---

[15]Relevant information on Jung's personal life is from Frank McLynn, *Carl Gustav Jung: A Biography*, Bantam Press, London, 1996. This biography is unashamedly hostile, which might be acceptable if the author had a better understanding of Jung's concepts and greater experience of the analytic process, and had showed some capacity to distinguish Jung's private behaviour from the viability of his psychological theories. However, despite this failing, it is a useful book for the details of Jung's personal life.

Uranus is closely square the Moon, and Jung's relationships with women in general, and his mother in particular, were erratic and difficult. He seems to have believed, from the evidence of various letters and comments he made to others, that he had a kind of God-given right to conduct himself in this fashion, and despite the richness and depth of his theories about animus and anima, his personal opinions about the respective roles of the sexes were, to say the least, rather dogmatic. Yet he had an intuitive genius in assessing the potential and unconscious dynamics of other people, and the core of his work is about relationship as a dynamic "system" – between ego and unconscious, and between individual and collective. So we have a very vivid enactment of a 7th house Uranus.

Audience: He also had a falling out with Freud. That was a kind of divorce.

Liz: Yes, Freud was his "partner" in the most profound sense, a kind of father-figure as well as a close working colleague, and there was great acrimony between them once they had split. Jung seems to have had a problem with many of his male colleagues. He found it hard to tolerate anyone who didn't agree with him, and as these colleagues had minds of their own, conflict was inevitable. He also suffered at the hands of the public, and his reputation still does, for that matter, since he has been seen at various times and by various critics as a Nazi sympathiser, a con-artist, a sinister cult leader, or a schizophrenic. But Uranus is also trine Mars in Sagittarius in the 11th, and Jung's self-willed and autocratic nature also contained great courage, inventiveness, and physical and mental stamina. Uranus in the 7th often comes across to the public as alien, abstracted, and disturbing, because it embodies a collective vision which the individual may not articulate tactfully to the outside world. Now, what about Saturn?

Audience: Saturn in the 1st would make him very defensive and tough.

Liz: This has often been said about him. Jung does not come across well in biographies, because he struck many people as a hard, domineering man. I don't doubt that he was very difficult to relate to on the personal level. He seems to have preferred disciples and acolytes to friendships between equals. Saturn's controlling tendencies are very much in evidence. Saturn is also square Pluto, which is often a defensive, suspicious aspect, incredibly tough and resilient, and ferociously resistant to any dependency on others. But Saturn in Aquarius opposite Uranus in Leo suggests more than just defensiveness.

Audience: Saturn is trine Jupiter in Libra in the 9th.

Liz: And?

Audience: This makes him a serious thinker, a philosopher.

Liz: Yes, the rising Saturn in Aquarius gives great depth of thought, and a preoccupation with universal issues. Not always a nice man, and certainly not a kind one with regard to women, but with a profound and innately religious mind and outlook, and a strong need to serve the collective in some way. What about Saturn opposite Uranus?

Audience: A rebel.

Liz: I think it reflects a conflict between a rebellious, autocratic, visionary side and a deeply conservative, traditional side. This Saturn seems to reflect the repressive late 19th century Swiss background. The opposition between Saturn and Uranus suggests enormous tension, a kind of living-on-the-edge feeling, as though he was constantly torn between wanting to be acceptable in the eyes of the collective, and wanting to usher in a Brave New World all by himself. He wrote a good deal about the mythic figure of Prometheus, as well as the figure of Faust, and both of these seem to have embodied his dilemma – the *hubris,* the theft of fire, and the terrible consequences. Saturn in Aquarius fears being different; Uranus in Leo will fight to the death in order to pursue an individual vision. In defining a philosophical and psychological model in which individual and collective are constantly moving in an ongoing dance, he attempted to resolve this conflict on the theoretical level. But in personal terms, I doubt that he ever did.

Now let's look at one or two critical Saturn and Uranus junctures. We can't do the whole thing or we will be here for three days. It is worth examining first what was going on when Jung began to part ways with Freud. This was a gradual process. The first signs became apparent in 1910. In May of that year Saturn entered Taurus and conjuncted Jung's Neptune and squared the Ascendant and Sun. This suggests disillusionment with a father-figure, and an urgent need to establish his own identity.

But the real rift showed itself following the publication of *Symbols of Transformation*. This book was published in parts, from late 1911 to early 1913, and reflected a decisive break with Freud's theories. At the end of 1911, overt animosity between the two began to be displayed in their correspondence. You will also all be amused to know that it was during this time that Jung began studying astrology. And his lifelong affair with Toni Wolff seems to have begun, or at least accelerated to something serious, toward the end of 1911, leading to violent rows between him and his wife.

In mid-1911 Saturn had moved to mid-Taurus, forming a conjunction to Jung's Moon and a square to natal Uranus in June. During the latter part of the year Saturn was retrograde, again square the natal Moon-Uranus square. In January 1912 it made a station direct in 13° Taurus, close to the natal square. Amongst other things, Jung must have felt deeply trapped in his marriage. As Saturn moved direct and aspected the Moon-Uranus for the third and last time in February 1912, Uranus entered Aquarius, approaching Jung's Ascendant and natal Sun-Neptune square. In May 1912 Uranus made a station exactly opposition the Sun and square natal Neptune. Saturn by this time had reached 24° Taurus and was square natal Saturn in the same month. Various incidents occurred during this month which effectively made the relationship between Freud and Jung permanently untenable, although it took the remainder of the year for this to become apparent to everyone else. Personal relations between the two men were entirely severed by the beginning of 1913, when Uranus, having retrograded back into late Capricorn, moved into Aquarius again to make a final opposition to Jung's Sun.

I don't think I need to elaborate on the way these important transits – Saturn square Uranus, conjunct the Moon, and square its own place, and Uranus opposition the Sun and square Neptune – were expressed in Jung's life. The Saturn-Saturn square was the outgoing square of the second Saturn cycle, heralding a separation from "father" Freud and the establishing of what would later become Jung's particular individual contribution to depth psychology. Interestingly, at the time of the outgoing Saturn square during the first Saturn cycle – when Jung was just over seven years old – he suffered from croup and choking fits, and had nightmares about suffocation. He developed strongly negative feelings toward Jesus and hated going to church. Although there was no overt rift with his father at this time, his father was, after all, a pastor, a representative of the very church which Jung was repudiating. This first Saturn square seems to have reflected a profound separation from his parental background, echoed in the later separation from Freud as a parent-figure.

Transiting Uranus opposition the Sun was literally enacted, not only by his "divorce" from Freud, but also through his personal life. By the time Uranus moved into opposition with its own place for the first time, in early 1915, he was well into that phase which is generally interpreted by biographers as a psychotic episode. He spent three full years in the darkness, virtually the entire time that Uranus was within orb of opposition to its own place. During this period his interest in Gnosticism and alchemy were born, influencing all the work which followed later. This time of confusion is seen by most Jungians as the seeding-ground for the most creative and original work he produced. It would certainly accord with what we know of Uranus. Promethean fire, with its vision and access to the larger cosmic system, scorched him, but left him with a far deeper and broader understanding.

By the latter part of 1918, when Uranus had moved into the third decanate of Aquarius and conjuncted natal Saturn, completing its long transit across the natal Saturn-Uranus opposition, Jung had emerged from his crisis. He had also succeeded in establishing his *ménage à trois* on a permanent basis. In October 1918, Saturn reached 24° Leo and opposed its own place, as well as opposing transiting Uranus in the heavens. Coincidentally with Jung's psychologically arriving safely in port, World War I ended. This sequence suggests that the heavy-duty expressions involved with such transits are evident from the time the transiting planet comes within orb. The break with Freud took many years to ripen, although it seemed to be abrupt – one minute Jung was the "crown prince" of the psychoanalytic movement, and the next minute the two were vilifying each other. By the time the transit is complete, the real psychological work is finished. What remains is the job of clearing away the rubble, and anchoring the changes in actual life.

Group charts and discussion

Here is a chart given to me by someone in the group. Can you tell us what you are concerned with, Judith? You seem to be having a double whammy at the moment – Saturn over the Sun, and Uranus opposite Uranus. I expect we can find something to talk about.

Judith: I have worked for a number of years at a museum, mainly administrative work in the textile department. For some time I've been feeling very frustrated at this job, and lately I began to put out feelers as an independent consultant, with the idea that I could build up a clientele and eventually leave the museum and set up on my own. There is a lot of scope for this kind of consultancy work, in areas like costume design in films, for example. But I am feeling very unsure of myself. Sometimes I think I can't stand my job one minute more, but then I start wondering what my chances are of working independently. There isn't a lot of money around at the moment. People aren't so prepared to pay high consultant's fees like they were during the late 1980's, and maybe I'm being too ambitious and blind about striking out on my own. I am feeling a lot of confusion and indecision.

Liz: So you are trying to keep one hand on the idea of independent consultancy work, which is mobile and self-expressive, and the other hand on the security of the established structure of the museum, and you are discovering that you can't have your cake and eat it.

Example Chart 2

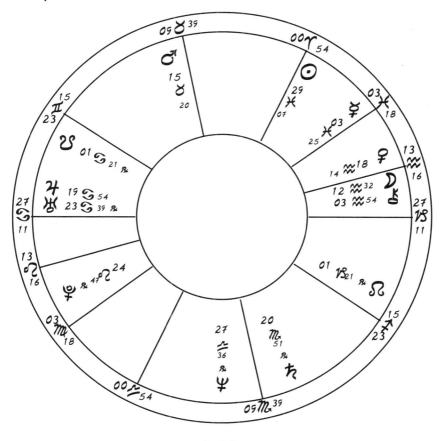

Judith
[Chart data withheld for reasons of confidentiality]

Judith: Yes, that's it, but I can't seem to make a decision.

Liz: I know a bit about the museum world, from clients and friends who have worked in it. Please correct me if I'm wrong, but I believe it is a highly institutionalised world, and very much a parental container. Certain educational credentials are required, and a certain social background is advisable. Once you get set on a track, you go up a particular ladder to a foreordained "top", with no real leeway to develop independently. It is a very Saturnian, hierarchical world, and it doesn't encourage originality. If a discovery is made, or a new idea turns out to be successful, it is the museum director who gets the credit for it, not the individual staff member who came up with it. This is ostensibly "team work" – at least, that is how such an approach is rationalised – but it is hard on the individual.

Judith: That is it exactly.

Transiting Saturn conjunct the Sun

Liz: Let's look first at the transit of Saturn to the Sun. In order to make sense of this, we need to consider the aspects that the Sun makes to other planets, as well as its sign and house. The Sun is just behind the MC, trine Saturn in Scorpio, and also trine the Jupiter-Uranus conjunction just behind the Ascendant in the 12th house. So there is a grand water trine here. Saturn transiting conjunct the Sun will trigger this grand trine.

The museum world might suit Sun trine Saturn. But you also have Sun trine Jupiter-Uranus, which suggests that there is something freer and more flexible within you, not necessarily unconventional in the rebellious sense, but intuitive and inspired. With the Sun in the 9th, which is Jupiter's house, emphasising the Sun-Jupiter trine, something that gives you independence, a chance to travel, and a chance to open up 9th house areas and meet 9th house people, might be very fulfilling. Also, the Sun is so close to the MC that it could also be read as a 10th house Sun, which suggests that you need to have authority in your own right. Your strong Saturn, which is part of the grand trine, gives you shrewdness and common sense, and allows you to work within conventional structures. But you don't have a conventional outlook toward life. You are an imaginative person who thinks in universal terms, and climbing the museum ladder must seem devoid of joy.

The transit of Saturn over the Sun is a time of self-confrontation, when you are called upon to define who you are and what you value. Questioning your work and your future is appropriate right now. Saturn will arrive at the MC immediately after the Sun, and that emphasises the need to re-evaluate your direction, and make decisions which shape the next thirty-year cycle. Because the Sun is involved with such benign aspects, it may also be a time when you can find new ways of synthesising the diverse needs of the planets involved in the grand trine. Saturn wants security, but Jupiter-Uranus wants inspiration and challenge. Also, although you are a Pisces, Jupiter is, after all, king of the gods, and enjoys a little limelight. This adds fuel to the ambitions of the Sun at the MC. Being merely one of the staff, unknown to the public, with all your creative ideas going to feed your museum director's prospects of an eventual gong, may not please you much.

The 10th is also concerned with the image of mother and the nature of the maternal inheritance. So we need to consider this deeper level of the transit to the Sun at the MC. There may be issues around trying to live the life your mother hoped you would live, or the life she wished she could have lived herself. There may also be guilt about being "selfish", which generally means being oneself, and pleasing oneself rather than others. Often, with a 10th house Sun, one is closely identified with the mother, who may have had far more creativity and ambition than life allowed her to express, and who may have hoped for a great deal from her child. There is often great love between mother and child, but it can be full of redemptive fantasies and narcissistic dreams.

This kind of identification may have impelled you to make work choices which are not entirely based on your own values and identity. A transit of Saturn will challenge these choices, and a feeling of deep discontent and frustration can emerge. Inevitably you would start asking whether you really want to be the person you have become. The weight of unconscious parental expectations starts feeling very heavy, and you may want to get free of them. But to do what?

Your anxiety and indecision may be related to the fear of forming as an individual – the fear of becoming yourself, which is, on the most profound level, a separation from the parental matrix.

Transiting Saturn at the MC

When transiting Saturn crosses the MC, issues that have to do with family and family expectations tend to rise to the surface, even though it may look as if you are dealing with a worldly situation. But usually the roots go much deeper than that. It isn't as simple as a job decision. It's also a decision about who you are, and in the past, separation anxieties involving the mother may have clouded your ability to live who you are. So whatever it is you are struggling with in your effort to come to a decision, the source of your dilemma was probably established a very long time ago.

Learning to stand alone in the present situation – striking off on your own, relying solely on your own talents – means separating yourself from what may have been a fairly enmeshed early family environment. Because the Sun is so well aspected, you may not have experienced this as a conflict earlier in your life. That is why trines are so ambiguous. They are lovely aspects which reflect innate talents and abilities. But we also tend to be lax and unconscious in our trines, and if the family has been too demanding or claustrophobic, we don't even recognise it. It's so comfortable that we don't realise we haven't been born yet.

It would be interesting to track earlier Saturn aspects to your Sun, to see whether the connecting thread is discernible. You are not finished with this transit yet. Saturn is still in Pisces, and still hanging about the Sun, and the meaning of the transit will still be relevant even after it moves into Aries. It will not get to 9° Aries, and out of orb of the Sun, until 1997. It will make a station in 7° Aries, within range of the MC, in the middle of 1996. So the dilemma is likely to continue, in one form or another, for quite some time. Perhaps your initial enthusiasm for starting a consultancy was an intuitive Jupiter-Uranus flash of foresight, but then you panicked. This would be understandable, because Jupiter's intuitions have to be backed by hard Saturnian common sense, and very sensibly, with the trine between Saturn and Jupiter, you have chosen to reflect further. Also, you are very watery, and other people's acceptance means a lot to you. But you may have to forgo it, at least in the sense that you had it – being embedded in the establishment.

Audience: Wouldn't transiting Saturn at the MC make Judith want to be part of the establishment?

Liz: Not necessarily. We reap the rewards of what we have built when Saturn crosses the angles, but if we have been building somebody else's edifice, then the rewards may be deep discontent and disillusionment with the establishment. Saturn doesn't make us what we are not. This transit is triggering a grand trine, and that bodes well, in the sense that definite material opportunities may be available to anchor the grand trine in external reality. But look at what the grand trine is made of. Jupiter and Uranus are in the 12th, behind the Ascendant, although they are "rising" because they conjunct it. They are in Cancer, and they midwife images and inspirations from the collective psyche. This is a wonderfully imaginative placement, full of artistic feeling and a deep love and understanding of the past. One would think the museum world would be perfect. But it is so highly structured, and so hard on individual creative talent. Transiting Saturn at the MC often reflects a time when one reaches a height professionally, because it crystallises the identity that one is trying to build in the world. Equally, it can represent a time when one fails, or feels one has failed, because the identity that one is crystallising is not a true reflection of one's innermost heart. Do you have a sense of failure?

Judith: Yes. It's absurd, but I do feel that. No one else seems to feel it about me. But I feel I ought to be producing more.

Liz: Is there a quota? Set by whom?

Judith: As you say, the museum world is institutionalised. We are expected to produce a certain number of reports, publications, whatever, and we are judged by that. The quality isn't as important as the right number of productions. I'm very tired of it. I don't want to have to force myself to wait too much longer.

Liz: The feeling that you should be producing more, no matter how well you have done, may be an echo of childhood feelings. This makes me suspect that the museum is a kind of surrogate parent for you, and no matter what you do, you can't please it, and you are getting angry because you keep feeling you have to please it, which means betraying something in yourself. But it isn't a question of forcing yourself to wait. You yourself have said that you are still uncertain and undecided. It might be wise to avoid forcing yourself to make decisions before you are ready. No one is standing over you demanding an answer, except yourself. Something is not fully "cooked" yet. The process, like the transit which reflects it, isn't finished.

Judith: I tend to resist pressure from other people.

Liz: I am sure that you resist it wildly. But you might be pressuring yourself, if you are fixing a time limit within which you have to choose. There is a grand fixed cross in this chart as well as a grand trine, and the cross involves Venus in Aquarius opposite Pluto in Leo and square Saturn and Mars. The Moon is not technically part of this, but it conjuncts Chiron in Aquarius, and also squares both Saturn and Mars. When you are forced to bow to someone else's requirements, I think it provokes very deep resistance. Something in you closes down and simmers. If you have been trying to fulfill other people's expectations – your mother's, the collective's – then you may be extremely angry right now, whether you are aware of it or not.

Judith: I have such a strong need to please other people.

Liz: How interesting. A moment ago you just said you resist pressure from other people. Actually, there isn't all that much in this chart that describes such a powerful need to please. I find it curious how powerful this desire to please seems to be, without any clear astrological representation of it. This kind of discrepancy always intrigues me. When the desire to please is represented in the chart in an obvious way, such as a rising Neptune in Libra, or the Moon in Pisces trine a rising Venus in Cancer, it is a natural and healthy dimension of the personality, and is usually linked to a gift of relating fluently and easily to others. We could assume that here was someone deeply and quite rightly dependent on the approval of others – at least to some extent – in order to feel happy, real, and of value.

But in your case, I wonder what is really going on, because your temperament, as described by your chart, is not really a fluid one. The Sun in Pisces is fluid and adaptable, and there is a lot of water, which suggests that you want to be close to others and need their acceptance. But there is so much which contradicts this. The Sun is at the MC, and this brings out solar qualities. And it aspects powerful and uncompromising planets: Saturn, Jupiter and Uranus. Moreover, the grand cross is anything but willing to please. An appearance of excessive fluidity and adaptability may mask something underneath, which isn't very happy about being so accomodating. The desire to please may arise from deep insecurity and fear, rather than from genuine joy in sharing and merging with others.

A grand fixed cross can be stubborn, passionate, tenacious, loyal, proud, intractable, self-willed, self-sufficient, and even downright bloody-minded, but it does not suffer from the burden of too much flexibility. But the Venus-Saturn square, the Moon-Chiron conjunction, and the Moon-Saturn square, all of which can carry a pervasive feeling of childhood loneliness and isolation, may lie behind this constant effort to be what you believe others want you to be. You may be deeply afraid you will be rejected if you define yourself too clearly. Perhaps this was the case in childhood. I suspect there is a deep hurt at work here, and you may keep hoping that somehow you will get healed if the Saturnian world "out there" accepts you and deems you worthy. Fear of failure if you work independently may be only the surface of the problem, and fear of emotional isolation may be the real fear underneath.

The decisions we make under Saturn transits – especially the conjunction to the Sun – are very binding. If we are honest with ourselves, these decisions come from the heart, because so much is stripped away, and we are no longer hiding from ourselves. The choices we make at these times set the course for the next thirty years. Once we have made that statement of individual definition, we can't unmake it. It sounds as though you need to put more faith in what this transit can offer you. The unease and confusion you have been feeling is understandable and natural; there is more at stake than a salary. Try not to let your anxiety get in the way of a deeper understanding.

Audience: Natal Saturn is in this lady's 5th house. So the issue of personal expression is very important, but there is a difficulty. I think she likes playing with ideas and creative images. But maybe with Saturn there, it's hard to play. The spark is there, ready to be ignited.

Judith: I think it's more than just a spark.

Liz: Are you the oldest child?

Judith: Yes.

Liz: Did you have to look after younger siblings? This is common with Moon-Saturn. One doesn't get to have a real childhood.

Judith: Actually, yes. I was expected to look after my younger sister and brother when my mother was ill, which was often.

Liz: As you say, this spark is more than just a spark, it is a volcano. But somebody keeps putting a giant cork in it. I think we are all getting a sense of a very repressive background. The image of the mother is very powerful, but very heavy, very trapped, very frustrated. And with the Sun in Pisces trine Jupiter-Uranus, I have an image of a father who is noticeable by his ability to remain out of the line of fire. He must have been a charming and ingenious man, but elusive. Perhaps your mother tried to carry it all, and found she couldn't do it.

Judith: That's true. My father was delightful, and very intelligent, but when there were problems, he just wasn't around.

Liz: This may sound odd to you, but I wonder whether you are trying to be your father, rather than your own spontaneous self. I don't mean you want to be your actual father. But perhaps you are trying to be what your father wasn't – strong and reliable. The role you have been playing in your working life is so Saturnian, it is almost as though you were unconsciously echoing your childhood, and trying to offer your mother a stability her husband couldn't give. You had to be Saturnian in childhood, looking after the family. In that sense, you were a surrogate husband for your mother. Then you found yourself playing the same role at work. This may injure not only your creative expression, but your sense of being a woman as well. It must be difficult for you to use your very fine instinct and feeling in your work, because it is not very acceptable to use such functions in a world where everything has to be documented and measured. You can't go by hunches, or get too poetic in describing something.

Judith: This is something I feel constantly frustrated with. There isn't any place for my imagination.

Liz: I think I can understand what attracted you to this work to begin with. There seems to be a great love of beauty in you, and love of the implications of an old object – especially textiles, which human beings have worn, and which preserve a sense of continuity with human beings in the past. Your fantasies can play about with such things. It is not just bits of cloth for you. The people were alive who used these fabrics, and they all had personal stories. But that isn't really what a museum director wants to hear.

Judith: I suppose, deep down, I have already made my decision.

Liz: Yes, it sounds that way. It's just that, at the moment, you may be panicking, because, as I have said, there are deeper issues involved, which go back to your childhood and your family relationships.

Transiting Uranus over a grand fixed cross

Now, what about Uranus? What do all of you make of its transits? It's on the Descendant now, and once it enters Aquarius it will begin to move onto the grand fixed cross.

Audience: Uranus opposing a Cancer Ascendant seems to me to say she is leaving home, leaving mother.

Audience: It's the beginning of a whole new life.

Audience: Upheaval in personal relationships.

Liz: There you are – the prognosis is to fasten your safety belt and prepare for takeoff.

Judith: It's not the takeoff I'm worried about. It's where I'm going to land!

Liz: The pilot is not likely to tell you. The opposition of Uranus to its own place over the last year or two has probably contributed to your feelings of anxiety, since it is triggering the 12th house and all the unlived imaginal and spiritual life which is implied by the Jupiter-Uranus conjunction placed there. But it seems to have woken you up. Now it will begin its conjunction with Chiron and then the Moon in a year or two, and gradually it will move on to square Mars, conjunct Venus, square Saturn, and eventually oppose Pluto. We can't look at these configurations separately. We need to look at the fixed cross as a whole, and think about what transiting Uranus will do to it. Uranus' transit over the cross will take five or six years.

Audience: Relationship issues are going to be triggered.

Judith: I'm not actually in a relationship.

Liz: I expect you have had a difficult pattern in relationships, with a lot of disappointments.

Judith: Yes.

Liz: Saturn or Chiron aspecting Moon or Venus, or Saturn or Chiron in the 7th – and you have virtually the lot – tend to reflect a lot of distrust and expectation of rejection. The mistrust is often based on valid reasons, because usually there have been extremely hurtful experiences quite early in life. These aspects describe deep self-doubt, feelings of being wounded or damaged, and a tendency to unconsciously set up a repeating pattern of hurt and disappointment.

Also, relationships are terribly serious when Saturn and Chiron touch Venus and the Moon. Shallow relationships tend to be boring. One is attracted to complex people who have their own wounds. There is a need to experience love in great depth, so that both people can be transformed or healed. Obviously the healing is not guaranteed, and further suffering can sometimes be the result of involvements of this kind. After a while, one might begin to feel it isn't worth the pain.

Judith: I have been feeling that way lately.

Audience: Maybe Uranus will open up the Moon-Chiron, and give it a chance to heal.

Liz: Yes, that is how I would see it too. There is the possibility that the old wounds may be opened up, and the insight you gain – Uranian insight into the larger patterns at work – might release a lot of old poison, and break an old chain. You may need to understand why you have been attracted by the people you have. Your own defences, rooted in a fear of rejection and abandonment, may be dictating a certain type of relationship. Some of these issues may have arisen under the Uranus-Uranus opposition and the Uranus-Descendant conjunction, because by its nature Uranus tends to release dimensions of the personality which have been unlived. And with these powerful

Saturn and Chiron aspects to the relationship planets, much of your emotional and passional life has probably been curtailed, hemmed in, or spoiled by fear.

Uranus transiting over the fixed cross, which is bound up with the way you relate to others, is likely to be a continuation of the Uranus opposition. When Uranus hit natal Uranus, you probably made some surprising discoveries about yourself and the person that you thought you were. Your image of yourself has been in a process of radical change, exacerbated by Uranus crossing the Descendant.

All this is like Chapter One of a story. Chapter Two will probably get you into much deeper water, because the first planet of the grand cross to be transited is your 7th house Chiron. That seems to encapsulate so many feelings of mistrust, betrayal, personal inadequacy, damage, and unfair treatment at the hands of others. It is likely to be very interesting. You may be surprised by what happens. Uranus is going to spend a long time on the grand cross. It goes stationary at 4° Aquarius, retrogrades back to 0°, and then stations right on Chiron in May 1997. That is only the beginning.

Judith: The last relationship I was in ended in December 1994, when the Uranus-Neptune conjunction was opposition my Uranus. I did have some revelations then. I realised that there were power issues going on, and that underneath I was terribly insecure.

Liz: Can you tell us what you mean by "power issues"?

Judith: Manipulation, I suppose. I realised I was deliberately holding back my feelings, or making things very difficult for my partner, whenever I felt insecure. I kept sort of testing him. I wanted him to get through it all and see what was underneath. But he never did.

Liz: In the chart, both Saturn in Scorpio and Venus opposition Pluto may be connected with this kind of behaviour. You are unusually honest with yourself about this, and it may help a lot in avoiding a future repetition of the scenario. Saturn in Scorpio often utilises withdrawal, heavy emotional atmospheres, and manipulation of others' feelings as a defence against rejection and humiliation. It attaches itself with great intensity to one person, and has a tremendous capacity for loyalty. So does Venus opposition Pluto, which may see loss of power in relationship as a life-and-death issue. And Saturn in the 5th also tends to offer absolute dedication and devotion to one person, with little flexibility. With all this, the quality of your love is very intense and binding. That can leave you feeling terribly vulnerable, and your pride is very great. So the defences you describe are not surprising.

You have been deeply hurt, and haven't forgot or forgiven it. There may be a lot of hard, congealed bitterness and cynicism in you, which contradicts the gentler qualities of the Pisces Sun quincunx Neptune, and the idealism of Venus in Aquarius trine Neptune. There may also have been a similar kind of bitterness in your mother. The aspects of Chiron and Saturn to the Moon suggest this. If she was badly hurt and disappointed by life, she may have felt unconscious jealousy of you. This is not an uncommon situation. One can feel some sympathy for a mother who has spent the best years of her life being miserable, and sees her daughter growing up healthy, attractive, free, and with the potential for a happiness that she herself will never achieve.

Because of the Sun at the MC combined with the Moon-Chiron conjunction and Moon square Saturn in Scorpio, I wonder whether, when you began to develop as a young woman, any sign of sexual attractiveness and vitality was met with unconscious animosity by your mother, because she had so little fulfillment in her own life. The underlying theme is, "I didn't have it, so why should you have it?"

There may have been a lot of hurt in both your parents, who in turn managed to hurt you, without consciously meaning to. So you have no reason to trust anybody's love, because it either disappears or comes with strings attached – obligations which are burdensome rather than fulfilling. Your parents' marriage probably didn't give you a very happy model of relationship. So it isn't "abnormal" that you try to maintain control in a relationship. It's just terribly human. Uranus' transit over these planets may loosen everything up, just enough for you to try out ways of relating which are not so heavily defended. I couldn't promise that you will learn these things without pain. I suspect you may have to go through something difficult, before you get to the other side. But I think it will be worth it.

There is a huge part of you which is still unlived, and the Uranus transit probably won't allow you to remain defended in the way you have been. Uranus breaks down old defences and structures which are blocking the flow of life, and you may open up in ways which initially provoke a great deal of anxiety because you feel so vulnerable. Yet it is time for all that unlived life to get free.

Audience: I have noticed that Uranus can bring a necessary experience of relationship which may change your life, but which might not stay in your life. Suddenly there is a relationship which brings you to life.

Liz: Yes, Uranus does go in for trial runs. Relationships which form under Uranus transits sometimes work out very well in the long term, but equally often they don't stick. But they are catalysts. They are transformative. They break an old pattern, and then one is ready for a different quality of love. What goes on under the transit is like an experiment; it doesn't remain in one's life, but it kicks open the door and provides a glimpse of the larger cosmos. Even though the person might go, the door remains open.

The dark side of love

Audience: Can you say more about this business of being attracted to complicated people?

Liz: Well, think about it. If we have been badly hurt by life, we see life in deeper and darker dimensions. If our early experiences of loving have been complex and full of unconscious undercurrents, this is what we know of love. So we are robbed of innocence, and cannot blunder along actually believing in the white wedding gown and the happily-ever-after story. No matter how romantic we are, there is that insistent awareness, deep down, that love is not so simple. We see through things. So we have to have a very special kind of partner who has lost his or her innocence too – hopefully not a victim or a victimiser, although usually one has to try one or both of those at least once, but someone who has been through it and come out the other side. Then there is a very deep place of meeting, which may start with falling in love, but which has much greater compassion and duration. That is the potential of Venus-Chiron, Venus-Saturn, and also Venus-Pluto.

These aspects do not do well in superficial relationships. One gets very bored with relationships which, for other people, may be perfectly acceptable and rewarding. After one has done all the billing and cooing, what does one talk about? The weather? If we don't understand what these aspects need for fulfillment, then we create nasty messes and crises, always seeking the healing and transformation which we know is out there somewhere, which vindicates life's depth.

Audience: So you are saying that these aspects create their own unhappiness. It isn't "fated".

Liz: In the early part of life, these aspects do not create unhappiness. They experience unhappiness, and usually there is a real reason, although selective perception may make us remember only the bad bits. Later, I think they can reflect unconscious patterns which trap the person into repeating the early hurts. This is not "fate". I think you are touching on something very important. There is a conundrum here. We can look at it one way – the causal way, which is usual in conventional psychology – and say that, because of childhood experiences, there is a compulsion to seek crises which carry the potential for transformation and healing. This doesn't always work, and a repeated pattern of suffering may result.

But we can also look at it the other way. One is born with a Venus-Chiron or Moon-Chiron conjunction, or a Venus-Saturn square, or a Venus-Pluto opposition. One's childhood experiences did not create these aspects in the birth chart. The aspects are synchronous with a moment in time when the environment and family background, as well as the newborn child, partook of the qualities of the time. So we could say that the person is born with an instinctive sense that human relationships are deeply complex, encompassing a spectrum from very light to very dark, with all the shades in between. This person knows that love can contain poison as well as ecstasy, and can wound as well as heal; and he or she also knows that life can be very unfair. This knowledge is inherent at birth, in nascent form.

There seems to be a mysterious synchronicity at work with these things. The parental background usually reflects the child's perceptions; the parents do wound or are wounded, and the early home life may be fraught with difficulties that other children do not have to face. But there is also selective perception at work, and we must never forget this. Whatever the parents do, and however hard they try, a child with these complex aspects will always remember the wounding, and always "sniff out" the undercurrents. And such a child will want a quality of love which may be quite beyond what either parent is capable of giving. These aspects want an honesty and maturity which very few parents can offer.

Most, if not all people have family problems in one form or another. But here we have a Moon-Chiron conjunction, a Venus-Pluto opposition, a Venus-Saturn square, and a Moon-Saturn square. And Chiron is in Venus' natural house. All these aspects are acutely attuned to the ways in which love can go wrong as well as right, because their needs and values are so complex. No matter what your parents did, they could not have got it right. No matter what your partner does, you are likely to be left with a sense of disappointment and rejection, because you are always looking for something more. In youth, it isn't likely that you will find it, and even in maturity you will still be seeking something that no human being can provide – a solution to life's unfairness and limitations. But if you know what this pattern is about – and transiting Uranus might give you that knowledge – you can begin to see other people as people, and not expect them to redeem all the childhood wounds.

In the end, fate is soul, which is what the poet Novalis said. Rather than viewing the painful repetitive patterns of these aspects as the fault of the parents, you might go further by understanding that the aspects describe something about you and your values, expectations, fears, and defences in relationship. The good news about these aspects is that, like a good wine, they improve with age. As you get older, you are likely to meet more people who can respond to your particular level of relating. In your early twenties, your peer group would probably have seemed very uninteresting from the romantic point of view, or threatening. As you get older, your confidence will increase, because your experiences have caught up with your perceptions. When you were a child, your perceptions were too old for your experiences. That is another way of looking at it.

Look at all we have got into, by probing these Saturn and Uranus transits more deeply. We can't really understand transits without doing this kind of work. And if we had another week to do it all properly, we should also go back through every past aspect transiting Saturn has made to the Sun, and every past aspect Uranus has made to the grand cross, in order to get a better picture of how the cycles work. Obviously we cannot do all this with every client. But we can do it with our own charts, and this gives us a background and a perspective from which to ask relevant questions of the client.

Venus in Aquarius

Audience: I thought Venus in Aquarius had a problem with commitment.

Liz: I haven't found this to be so, and I think we need to be more precise about the terms we use, especially when describing personal situations through astrological symbolism. Aquarius is a fixed sign, and it is capable of immense loyalty. It is emotional suffocation that Venus in Aquarius fears, rather than commitment. One may be totally devoted and uninterested in looking elsewhere for love and affection, but one may still fear being swamped by too many emotional demands, whether one's own or one's partner's. Venus in Aquarius has a horror of choking to death on uncontrolled emotion. These people need breathing space in a relationship. Some things need to be left unsaid, and attempts at emotional manipulation may provoke a distinctly hostile response. Venus in Aquarius perceives the partner as a friend, and the requirements of friendship involve respect for each other's privacy, as well as tolerance and a sense of fair play. Venus in Aquarius may back off from a relationship in which boundaries are not respected.

A more emotional nature, observing the retreating back of the Venus in Aquarius partner walking out the door, may well feel there is a commitment problem. Venus in Aquarius may seem distinctly chilly to those with the Moon or Venus in Cancer, Scorpio or Pisces. But fear of suffocation and fear of commitment are not the same thing. Not everyone expresses love in the same way. Being co-ruled by Saturn as well as Uranus, Venus in Aquarius needs security in relationship, and a willingness to build strong structures – on the level of shared ideals, if not materially – but not when there is emotional hysteria going on.

Example Chart 3

Let's look at another chart from the group. Is it the approaching Uranus transit or the approaching Saturn transit that you wanted to explore, Gwen?

Gwen: I particularly wanted to look at the Saturn transit.

Saturn transiting over a new Moon

Liz: All right, we can begin there, but I think we should try to have a look at both. It's not a good idea to ignore Uranus, especially since it is forming a sextile with the Sun-Moon conjunction and an opposition to the Saturn-Pluto conjunction. You have had Saturn over your Mercury-Mars conjunction already, a while back, and as it moves into Aries it will go over the Sun and then over the Moon, and then it will oppose Neptune. This opposition between transiting Saturn and natal Neptune in Libra may prove quite surprising. It will take some time before it is exact; Saturn goes back and forth over the Moon in Aries throughout this year and into the beginning of 1997. Could we first hear something about what was going on when Saturn went over the Mercury-Mars conjunction and squared natal Uranus? This would have been throughout the last year. Saturn stationed square to Uranus in the 6th house last summer.

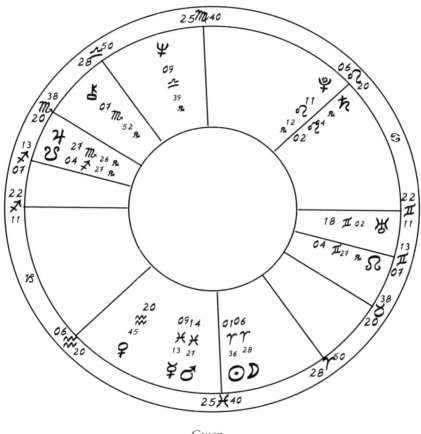

Gwen
[Chart data withheld for reasons of confidentiality]

Gwen: I am a programmer for the BBC World Service. I am often in a position where I have to make choices about programmes which can turn out to be terrible mistakes, although sometimes they also turn out to be exactly right. I have a number of people working under me, but the final decisions are mine, and if there is a blunder, then I have to take the blame.

Liz: So you are in a job which, in a sense, serves the collective. Thousands of listeners all over the world have learned to speak English from listening to the BBC World Service, as well as expatriots for whom it is the only link with home. But your job also requires you to take gambles, and sometimes make public mistakes.

Gwen: Yes. But I actually enjoy the feeling of gambling. When I get it right, and there is positive feedback, I feel I have done something really useful. If I get it wrong, I can usually learn from it. I don't mind looking foolish in public. You win some and you lose some.

Liz: You are very Saturnian, despite the emphasis in Aries. You have Saturn in trine to the Sun-Moon conjunction, and it is also your chart ruler, so tough challenges probably appeal to you. Even if you get knocked down, you will keep going. The conjunction of Saturn and Pluto trine Sun and Moon in fire reflects enormous determination and tenacity, and the ability to channel new creative ideas into practical, workable forms. So I don't really associate the difficulties of your job with this transit coming up. You live with those difficulties all the time, and seem to be able to deal with them and even feel invigorated by them. This transit has a different feeling to me, a more personal feeling. The approach of transiting Saturn to the natal Sun-Moon conjunction, and opposing natal Neptune in the 8th, at the same time that transiting Uranus is coming into opposition with the natal conjunction of Saturn and Pluto in the 7th, seems to be more involved with deeply personal emotional and perhaps sexual issues.

The 2nd house, like all the houses in the chart, has several levels of meaning. As a *templum* used for "secular purposes", it is associated with how you earn your living, and how you manage in the material world. But on a deeper level, the 2nd house is concerned with self-worth and self-value – how worthwhile you are as a person. Being born under a new Moon in Aries in the 2nd, there is a powerful emphasis on this house, so your capacity to make your way in the world will form the basis of your sense of self-worth. That is partly why you like challenges so much – every time you win, you redefine your value in your own eyes and in the eyes of those around you. You can't just achieve success and sit on it. You have to keep renewing it, and each time has to be as though it were the first time.

Gwen: I have been thinking about whether or not to change my work. Maybe I've run out of challenges.

Liz: It's possible that this might be part of the enactment of the transit. But I think it is more complex than that. In terms of material manifestation, the end product might be a shift in direction. But the meaning, the teleology, has deeper roots, and the psychological repercussions and ramifications also need to be considered.
Gwen: Such as?

Liz: Such as starting to question certain basic values which you have taken for granted in the past. You might begin to ask yourself some rather heavy, serious questions. Who are you, and what do you really want? Now that you have proven yourself in the outer world, what is your worth as a person, and as a woman? You are successful, but are you emotionally contented? What do you really value, and what do you have to give? And what has your work helped you to avoid on the personal level?

I think this transit may reflect a long period of soul-searching, but it may not be linked with events so much as with seriously re-evaluating the way you have structured your life and defined your identity. You may come to some uncomfortable conclusions about what you have done with your inner needs in order to achieve standing in the world. Your life may be too constricting or too earthbound, and you may feel you have outgrown many things which previously you wanted very much. By the end of the transit, perhaps you may wish to change your job because you yourself have changed so much.

Gwen: I have a vague inkling that there is more to this than just job issues.

Liz: Yes, I expect you do. Fire signs are usually quite intuitive in sensing the deeper meaning of the time. Think of Saturn coming along and saying, "All right, everything that is fake here has to go. What is genuine is your own, and you can keep it. But don't be too sure you know right now which is which." With Saturn transiting over the Sun, this challenge generally raises the question, "What is my purpose in life?" For many people, work and direction are usually bound up with this question. So work issues will often come up when Saturn transits over the Sun. Underneath are some profound questions: "What am I here for? What am I meant to be giving? What is my special gift, and how can I develop it?" All solar issues are concerned with a sense of destiny, even if we call it by other names. "What is my purpose as an individual, based on what I value most highly?"

The Moon, in contrast, is not concerned with destiny; it is concerned with emotional and instinctual needs. The Moon reaches out for immediate experience, and through relationship – with others and with life – informs us of what we need to feel safe, secure, and emotionally fulfilled. The Moon connects us with others through our shared emotional experiences. When Saturn transits over the Moon, instead of saying, "Why am I here?" the Moon says, "Why am I so lonely? Why is there no one around on whom I can depend? Why is no one here to look after me?" Saturn's effect on the Moon is one of emotional crystallising. It reflects a maturing process which allows us to become aware of what we instinctively need to feel safe and happy. In order to discover this, we have to first recognise what is making us unsafe and unhappy, through feeling separate and alone. Saturn may require the Moon to let go of dependencies which are keeping us infantile, always seeking mother's milk in someone or something "out there".

One of the special qualities of a new Moon is that, very often, the Moon's needs are occluded by the power and expressiveness of the Sun. So one doesn't always see them, just as, in the heavens, a new Moon is a dark Moon. We don't see it in the sky. At a full Moon, the earth is between the Moon and the Sun, which are astrologically in opposition, and so the Moon reflects the Sun's light. At the new Moon, the Sun obscures the Moon, and this can be taken psychologically as well as literally, especially in the sign of the Sun's exaltation in Aries, where the solar drive is particularly energetic. The ego's goals and aspirations dominate the instinctual needs, which are in shadow.

So everything has probably been focused on work for you, and important emotional needs – the need to belong or be part of a group, or the need for a certain kind of response from other people – may not register as being important. But they *are* important, and the Moon may be "uncovered" when Saturn transits across it. You may initially only feel discontented, lonely, neglected, and resentful. At first, it may not be clear just why you feel so low. Saturn has a way of making us aware of what we are by discovering what we are not, and you may discover that you are not as emotionally independent as you have thought.

New Moon people often don't know what they are feeling, because the Sun is so powerful. Or they don't think their feelings are important, even when the conjunction is in a water sign. Then some powerful transit hits the conjunction, and the Moon is triggered, and suddenly there is a revelation – "Good God, my feelings really do matter!" There are also parental implications with a new Moon. The Sun and Moon tell us a lot about the archetypal patterns at work in the parental marriage, which is the model we "inherit" of what relationships are all about. When the Moon is occluded by the Sun, the implication is that the mother is "in the shadow", obscured by the more powerful energy of the father. I have seen this configuration in the charts of many people whose mothers appeared to be more or less mirrors of what the father wanted, and sacrificed their own identity and needs for the sake of unity in the marriage. The Moon, as well as the Sun, may be bound up with other planets, so the mother's reality may be much more complex. And the occluded mother may be seething underneath. When a new Moon occurs in a woman's chart, and other factors suggest great strength of will – as they do in your chart – then she may unconsciously seek to be "anything but" the passive mother, by competing with men in a man's world, and making a mark which defines her potency and rejects the mother's passivity.

I am not suggesting that such a course is "wrong", but sometimes trying to be the opposite of something is as enslaving as identifying with it. And paradoxically, you may be sacrificing just as much as your

mother did, even though, in the world's eyes, you are no one's doormat
or victim. You might also be more dependent on the people you work
with, and more eager to please them, than you have admitted. This
may be part of the "uncovering" of the Moon. It is the Moon-Neptune
opposition which makes me suspect this. Or you may choose partners
who take a great deal from you, and you may wind up being their
sacrificial "victim" without realising it. There may be some very
surprising personal realisations coming up under this transit, and they
may have to do with discovering your deep need of other people. You
may be unconsciously using them to give you a feeling of security. This
is a 2nd house Moon.

Audience: There isn't any earth in the chart.

Liz: Earth is indeed a missing element, except for the Ascendant, but
nevertheless the Ascendant seems to be very powerful. It is a kind of
singleton in earth, and the trines from the chart ruler, Saturn, to the
Sun and Moon seem to emphasise the Saturn-Capricorn qualities.
Although a rigid "count" of planets in elements would, in theory, show
up earth as weak, in fact it seems to be water which has the hardest
time being expressed. I suspect this is partly because the realm of
water is one in which there has been a great deal of hurt in the early
part of life. This is suggested, in part, by Chiron in Scorpio square the
Saturn-Pluto conjunction. We don't always automatically exhibit a
strongly tenanted element. If we have been badly injured or
disappointed through the sphere of life it represents, then we may
avoid it as we grow up, distorting the natural balance of the chart.
Although it is strongly represented in the chart, water may seem
dangerous to you, and is therefore suppressed a good deal of the time.
The Moon-Neptune opposition is watery in nature, and it also seems to
have a hard time being expressed.

Gwen: I think my Moon-Neptune comes out through lying in bed for
three weeks.

Liz: Do you actually lie in bed for three weeks? Or do you get involved with people who lie in bed for three weeks?

Gwen: Both.

Liz: But not at the same time.

Gwen: Unfortunately, no.

Liz: Ah, well, Neptune always wants what it can't have. This Moon-Neptune opposition strikes me as extremely important. It is both hidden and prominent, because it is the only opposition in the chart. It is very powerful, and cuts right across the Sun-Moon conjunction. It is like the secret half of you. Underneath the strong and capable Aries-Capricorn nature is a fragile, intuitive, mystical, vulnerable side which probably feels helpless a lot of the time. When you do your three-week oblivion act, you are expressing it. When you choose partners who do it, you are projecting it. There is a very strong emphasis on Neptunian qualities in the chart, yet there is such a ferocious resistance against such qualities. Saturn-Pluto is deeply suspicious by nature, and perceives everything as a fight for survival. That enhances the Aries-Capricorn drive. If this Neptunian side could be integrated in your work, that would be best of all – if you could involve yourself with projects which allow you to function imaginatively rather than confined within a tight Saturnian structure.

Have you thought of writing? You are well placed to write scripts, rather than restricting yourself to the administration side of the media. That could help to bring Neptune in. It would also make excellent use of your Mercury-Mars conjunction in Pisces, which is such a highly imaginative and expressive configuration, full of ideas. At the moment, the only way Neptune seems to come out is to spend three weeks in bed. Because you have Sun trine Saturn, you can do Saturnian jobs well. You have proven you can do them, but you must be very exhausted. This is often the problem with people who have a strong Saturn. They are so good at being responsible. Their colleagues and friends and family say, "Oh, you're so capable. We'll load this one on you." And the Saturnian person discovers at a pretty early age that he or she can earn points by being responsible. But you may not realise the price that you are paying. Your responsibilities are protecting you from being vulnerable, and helping you to hide from yourself.

Gwen: I don't like feeling dependent on people. I would rather be the one in charge.

Liz: I think that is apparent to all of us. You have great strength, and the ability to handle responsibilities in a thorough and conscientious manner. But I am sure you can see how effective a defence this strength is. No person is just one thing, and there is a "weakness" in you as well (although this is not a term I would use – it is one I believe *you* would use) – a longing to dissolve and merge with others. In a sense, those for whom you take responsibility – the weak ones, the vulnerable ones, the needy ones – are also within you.

There is an enormous dichotomy in this chart, reflected in part by the Sun-Moon in Aries trine Saturn-Pluto on the one hand, and Moon opposite Neptune on the other. You are genuinely strong, and, not surprisingly, prefer the position of strength. But there seems to be a deep fear of the position of "weakness", as if, in your mind, it is equated with humiliation and powerlessness. It may also be linked with having to mother your mother, at far too young an age. Yet the Moon-Neptune is also the key to your imaginative and emotional life, and your ability to feel with and for others. By stifling it, and projecting it, you amputate something fragile, delicate, sensitive, and extremely important to the life of your soul.

These Saturn transits really revolve around the challenge of becoming who you are – not just on the solar level, which is one you have already developed well, but also on emotional and imaginative levels. I think we must also look at the transits of Uranus, which are occurring at the same time, to get a more rounded picture. While Saturn is conjuncting your Sun-Moon in Aries, Uranus will be sextile them. It will also be opposing natal Saturn in the 7th, and square natal Chiron, and will eventually square natal Pluto, setting off the entire Saturn-

----

Pluto-Chiron configuration over a long period of time. It has already begun this process, so you probably have some inkling of what it might be about. Would anyone like to comment on the transit of Uranus opposite natal Saturn?

Audience: Some kind of breakthrough in relationships. Or the breakup of a relationship.

Audience: A breaking down of defences.

Audience: Paranoia!

Liz: Yes, any of these, or all of them. The area where your defences are likely to be strongest is in the sphere of relationships, and this period might see the end of an old pattern of setting up relationships in which power battles and control issues make it difficult for real emotional intimacy to take place. This could involve leaving an old relationship in which hidden themes of dominance and dependency have created restrictions. Or it could involve an opening up, and a willingness to let other people get closer to you. The former may be the event level, and the latter the eventual inner result. Paranoia – in the colloquial rather than the clinical sense – is characteristic of Saturn-Pluto, which is often deeply suspicious of other people's motives and extremely reluctant to be in a situation of vulnerability where others might take control.

Gwen: I think that's how I feel a good deal of the time. People are guilty until proven innocent.

Liz: This attitude may change over the period of the transit. At the least, you may become more conscious of your defensiveness, and more aware of the degree and nature of the bitterness and suspicion you have toward others. Chiron in Scorpio in the 9th seems to suggest a deep mistrust of life, perhaps even of God, or whatever you understand as God. There may be issues in the family religious background which are relevant here. There is a wound in the area of faith, hope in the future, and belief in life's essential goodness. This is a very mistrustful and defensive configuration, and I would expect it to show itself as a deep need to control any situation in which you are at risk emotionally. The transit of Uranus may loosen this up a bit, and help to bring greater flexibility. Some painful experiences may be necessary before that happens. One can't predict what kinds of circumstances are likely to occur, although Saturn-Pluto in an angular house certainly suggests changes in your relationship life.

Transiting Uranus sextile a new Moon

At the same time, transiting Uranus is forming sextiles to both the Sun and Moon. This suggests an awakening of a gentle, inspirational kind – perhaps an increased consciousness of the greater whole of which you are a part, which might help you to gain a happier perspective on people and life. It may also have repercussions on the work level, of course, and correspond with new creative opportunities, but I would see this as a possible by-product, rather than the actual meaning of the transit.

Close encounters of the Uranian kind, especially by trine or sextile, often coincide with a realisation of the connections between experiences, and an awareness of the "system" as a whole. One sees one's life in perspective. This kind of perspective, although it is not in itself an emotional healing, can alter your attitudes toward yourself and others, thereby allowing new kinds of relationships and greater emotional openness. Because natal Uranus is in the 6th, it will carry themes of work with it by transit, so a more creative approach to work, or new and exciting ideas and projects, are certainly suggested. But I don't think we can separate a person's emotional nature from the capacity to express creatively. Both spring from the same person, and both reflect the heart and the degree of its openness to life.

Example chart 4

Perhaps we could look at another chart from the group. What did you want us to explore, Sarah?

Sarah: Transiting Saturn is square my Saturn, and also square Pluto. I'm feeling very lonely right now, as if I have no parents, no home, nothing. I wanted to know what was really going on, what this means.

Transiting Saturn square Saturn

Liz: Yes, I can understand that you aren't feeling very good at the moment. There is a cardinal T-cross in the chart, with Saturn in 2° Cancer square Pluto in 1° Libra, and Venus in 11° Aries widely opposite Pluto and square Saturn. The transit of Saturn is setting off the whole T-cross. Uranus has just finished the first square to its own place in 24° Libra. We can look at that in due course, because the Saturn transit will challenge and curtail what the Uranus transit invoked. But let's begin with transiting Saturn triggering the cardinal T-cross, and forming the second square to its own place. That seems to reflect the feelings you are describing.

Natal Saturn in the 10th house suggests a great deal of importance placed on being "somebody" in the eyes of the world. This may relate to parental expectations, but it is also your own ambition which is reflected. I was talking earlier about "fake" Saturn and "authentic" Saturn. At this point in your life, Saturn's strength, which in the 10th might be expressed through a sense of having something solid and practical to contribute to others, would most likely show itself through depending on others to validate you. The challenge of transiting Saturn square Saturn will inevitably involve a lot of self-questioning about where you are going, what you are supposed to be doing, what your parents expect you to become, and whether or not you have the ability to really make it in the world.

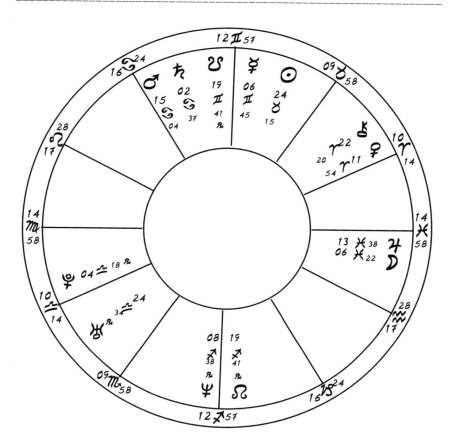

Sarah
[Chart data withheld for reasons of confidentiality]

Transiting Saturn conjunct Venus

But that isn't all, since natal Saturn squares Venus, which is in the 7th house. Transiting Saturn will therefore conjunct Venus, although this won't happen until 1997. But it is within orb now. This suggests that personal doubts and insecurities are likely to be activated, and old hurts going back to childhood will be triggered – feelings of being unlovable and unacceptable, and expectations of rejection or abandonment. A lot of what you are feeling, especially the loneliness and sense of being unparented and unsupported, may be a

----

kind of emotional memory of the very early part of your life, when perhaps you felt that you had to be acceptable in order to be loved.

If we look at the natal Saturn-Venus square more carefully, we can see that Saturn, transiting on from where it was at birth, would have completed the exact square within the first two years of life. At around seven, it would have opposed Venus, just after it conjuncted Pluto. When it opposed its own place between fourteen and fifteen, it would have squared Venus just afterward. So you have already had three important periods of life when this sense of loneliness and rejection would probably have been very strong.

Venus-Saturn is an aspect which often reflects "conditional love" in childhood. This doesn't mean that your parents didn't love you, but they may have used your need of their love as a means of getting good behaviour out of you. And their love might have been limited by, or mixed up with, their circumstances, aspirations, and social position. I think you know the sort of thing I mean – "If you don't do well at school, I'll be very hurt, and I'll behave coldly to you for three weeks." One is made to feel that one must perform in order to earn love. It isn't shown freely and unconditionally. Saturn in Cancer is particularly sensitive to the withholding of affection, and as a child you would probably have noticed every subtle shift of feeling and interpreted it as a rejection. You probably do the same now.

Sarah: That's true. But no one knows it. Everyone thinks I'm very confident and self-contained.

Liz: No doubt you do everything you can to encourage this false impression, since your pride is involved. Showing need and uncertainty would have made you vulnerable to hurt in childhood, and I expect something in you is determined not to be put in the same position again. By the way, who is "everyone"?

Sarah: People I don't know well. Acquaintances. People I work with.

Liz: 10th house people. Yes, they will assume you are on top of everything and will expect you to stay there, because you are showing them a "fake" Saturn. No doubt people who are close to you know very well how sensitive you are, and see the Moon in Pisces square Neptune, and Venus opposite Pluto and trine Neptune. They know you're really a dreamer and a romantic, cleverly disguised as a pragmatist. You have described your Saturn in what you have just said. Everyone expects you to be somebody, confident and successful. But I think this "everyone" is really yourself, and perhaps also your mother, who may have instilled these expectations in you because she wanted to be somebody herself. Saturn is in the 10th, which is one of the parental houses.

Sarah: I was born under my mother's Saturn return. We have Saturn conjunct across our charts. She did manage to let me know what a burden I was to her. She would have liked to have had a university education and a proper career.

Liz: So in your early years you felt you were a burden, who somehow spoiled your mother's chances. In order to expiate this crime, you have to become what she would have liked to be. You can't be an ordinary person with ordinary needs, flaws, and feelings. That must be how you interpreted your mother's messages. How serious and true these messages really were is open to question. Sadly, parents often say many hurtful things, never realising how long the effects will last, because they don't feel too good at the time. Whether your mother truly felt this way is debatable. I can't really judge. But she was clearly pretty clumsy in the way she expressed herself to a Saturn in Cancer child who, with Saturn in the 10th, perceived her as the essence of all worldly authority. This tells us a great deal about what Venus-Saturn contacts often reflect. I wonder whether the desire to prove yourself in the outer world is a way of saying to your mother, "You may not want me around, but I cannot live without your love, so I will make you love me by doing something important." There is the earthy Sun and Ascendant, taking up the hurt and finding a practical way to deal with it.

When earth signs feel insecure, they tend to try to do things for others, to make themselves indispensable, so that they can earn love and esteem. Fire just throws tantrums and says, "Look at me! Pay attention to me! I'm special!" But earth says, "I can't throw myself around like an hysteric, that's completely out of control, and I'll be rejected even more. But if I work very hard and achieve something everyone values, then people will acknowledge me." Saturn in Cancer in the 10th is trying to earn Cancerian love and affection – family love, mother's love – through achieving things in the worldly arena. But every time transiting Saturn hits its natal place, the gap between the effort to earn love and the reality of how you feel rises up to hit you.

Sarah: Everyone thinks I have it easy, that I haven't had to struggle to get where I am. But it isn't the case.

Liz: You know a great deal about what "everyone" thinks, don't you? Unless you are a cosmic telepath, I wonder if you believe that everyone thinks these things because you think them yourself. If I were to translate what you are saying out of Saturn-ese, I would hear something quite different. I would hear you saying, "My mother had to struggle, and things were even harder because I was born. I have it too easy in comparison. I should be struggling and suffering like her. She thinks I have it easy, because my life is easier than hers was." I wonder whether you try to give the impression to people that you are seamlessly competent because you don't like sounding as if you are complaining. So you give the impression that it is all a piece of cake, even if you have struggled very hard. Then people take you at your word, and you are angry with them because of it. They should know better. They should know how you feel without your having to tell them. Your mother should have known too. This defensiveness is also Saturn in the 10th. It stifles Venus in the 7th. It is saying, "See, I am in control. I am competent and strong. I don't have any problems." To actually say, "I'm really struggling and I need some help!" seems very difficult. You don't ask for help. Why is it so terrible to ask for help?

Sarah: I feel I have to do everything myself.

Liz: What is the merit in doing everything yourself?

Sarah: If I rely on other people, they could cut off their support.

Liz: And then?

Sarah: And then...I suppose I wouldn't cope.

Liz: But you already know you can cope, since you won't let anyone help you. Or is it the rejection you are afraid you couldn't cope with?

Sarah: Yes.

Liz: All this is very painful stuff. It is right at the core of what the transit is bringing up. It has always been there underneath, but Saturn square Saturn is bringing it to the surface, which seems to me to be a very good thing, since you have a chance to heal it if it is conscious. When it is unconscious, you are in the grip of the complex. That Venus-Saturn square from the 10th to the 7th is a place of great hurt. But I am also mindful of the fact that, in asking us to look at your chart, you are asking us to understand how you really feel, and help you if we can. That is a big step in itself.

Audience: What about her Jupiter at the Descendant? Wouldn't that help her feelings of isolation?

Liz: A lot of the time, it probably does – when transiting Saturn isn't squaring its own place and setting off the Venus-Saturn. Jupiter is conjunct the Moon in Pisces, which conjuncts the Descendant from the 6th house. This is a highly emotional, theatrical, generous, gregarious placement which suggests that your work and relationships need to be interrelated, and that you would be happiest working with others in some creative or artistic field, if not the actual helping professions. Some of your appearance of outgoing confidence is genuine, and you probably have no difficulty in attracting people. It's just that, once you have attracted them, you become convinced they won't want you if they get to know you. Mars in Cancer trine Jupiter-Moon in Pisces is a highly inspired and energetic configuration. It is not especially suited to working in an office, doing routine things. There is a great need for emotional and imaginative expression, which can be given form by the earthy Sun and Ascendant. It's a positive, optimistic and courageous combination, not inclined to gnaw away at itself with self-doubt.

What is concerning me is that something appears to be driving you that comes from deep personal insecurity. The feeling of being unlovable and a burden makes you feel you have to do something that other people define as worthwhile. What you feel is worthwhile doesn't really get a look-in. Until you break the grip of that complex, you won't get much pleasure from what you do, even if you are very successful, because you are not doing it for yourself. You are doing it in order to earn a response which you are constantly terrified will be taken away if you lapse, for even a minute. What was happening earlier, when Uranus squared its own place from Capricorn? Was this a happier, more confident time?

Sarah: Yes. That was when things began to really open up. I came to London, and all the doors seemed to start opening. I felt I could accomplish anything. But I don't feel that any more. I am wondering now whether I am following the right direction. I was thinking of working as a professional astrologer, studying and getting a qualification and doing charts. But now I don't really think I would be any use to people at all.

Liz: Questioning your direction may be the wrong question at the moment. Whatever answer you give yourself, it's going to come from your complex, not from you. During the course of the transit it may be better not to make any practical decisions, until you have looked at the extent to which your decisions are governed by the insecurity of the Venus-Saturn square, and also by the compulsiveness of Saturn square Pluto. This aspect pits ego-control against instinctual needs, and turns everything into a life-and-death struggle. With Saturn-Pluto, one feels one must struggle to survive. Sometimes this is linked with actual danger in infancy, but often there is no concrete "reason" – one

---

simply feels under threat. The sense of threat may be linked with undercurrents of great anger and frustration in your early environment. When you put this together with the insecurity of Venus-Saturn, rejection is more than just hurt; it is annihilation. Are you working in therapy with anyone?

Sarah: Yes.

Liz: Then stick with that. Don't rush too quickly into deciding what to do with the rest of your life. You are at one of the critical stages, between Uranus square Uranus and Saturn square Saturn. Take your time; something will get freed with these transits. This stage of the Saturn cycle could help you to get free of the desperation that seems to be driving you underneath. This is a very personal hurt, which is coming out through the medium of the 10th house, but direction is not really the core of what it is about. Your acceptability in the eyes of the world is, at this stage of your life, dominated by your fear of being unacceptable and unloved in any close relationship. You may need to be on your own for a while, as Saturn transits through the 7th and conjuncts Venus. Are you in a relationship?

Sarah: No. That's part of the loneliness.

Liz: I understand. But it may be better if you don't rush about desperately hunting for a relationship because you feel so lonely. Anyone you found in such a state of desperation would probably not make you very happy, because you would attract someone who wanted a desperate partner, and what kind of person would that be? Also, the loneliness is part of a parental complex which is coming to the surface, and you may need to deal with this independent of a partner or lover. Perhaps your therapy is the best place to explore it. Otherwise you may turn a partner into a surrogate parent. Saturn's transits often bring the challenge of loneliness, and if one can bear it, and explore what one feels and what lies underneath, one may be much freer afterward to choose a person one wants, rather than choosing someone because one feels that is all one can get.

In a way, you have been digging your own grave, because you are competent and talented, and also too proud to admit that you are struggling. So consequently some people may be impressed by this, and think, "Oh, you have it really easy." But you are helping them to think that, and it might be better if you were more honest. We haven't yet looked at the transits of Uranus coming up. Uranus will gradually move into some very nice aspects as it goes through the first decanate of Aquarius. It is trining Mercury and Pluto at the moment, making a grand air trine. This could trigger many deep insights and revelations. It will then come into sextile with both Neptune and Venus, setting off the natal Venus-Neptune trine. Before you begin placing ads in the Lonely Hearts columns, it might be of value to remember this approaching transit, which will undoubtedly be worth waiting for.

I am going to have to stop here. I would love to go on, but we have run out of time. Thank you all for contributing to the day.

Bibliography

Jung, C. G., "The Psychology of the Transference" in *The Practice of Psychotherapy,* Vol. 16, *Collected Works,* Routledge & Kegan Paul, London 1976.

Jung, C. G., *Symbols of Transformation,* Vol. 5, *Collected Works,* Princeton University Press, 1976.

McLynn, Frank, *Carl Gustav Jung: A Biography,* Bantam Press, London, 1996.

Taeger, Hans Hinrich, *Internationales Horoskope Lexikon,* Verlag Hermann Bauer, Freiburg, 1992.

About the CPA

Director: Liz Greene, Ph. D., D. F. Astrol. S., Dip. Analyt. Psych.

The Centre for Psychological Astrology provides a unique workshop and professional training programme, designed to foster the cross fertilisation of the fields of astrology and depth, humanistic, and transpersonal psychology. The main aims and objectives of the CPA professional training course are:

- To provide students with a solid and broad base of knowledge within the realms of both traditional astrological symbolism and psychological theory and technique, so that the astrological chart can be sensitively understood and interpreted in the light of modern psychological thought.
- To make available to students psychologically qualified case supervision, along with background seminars in counselling skills and techniques which would raise the standard and effectiveness of astrological consultation. It should be noted that no formal training as a counsellor or therapist is provided by the course.
- To encourage investigation and research into the links between astrology, psychological models, and therapeutic techniques, thereby contributing to and advancing the existing body of astrological and psychological knowledge.

History

The CPA began unofficially in 1980 as a sporadic series of courses and seminars offered by Liz Greene and Howard Sasportas, covering all aspects of astrology from beginners' courses to more advanced one-day seminars. In 1981 additional courses and seminars by other tutors were interspersed with those of Liz and Howard to increase the variety of material offered to students, and Juliet Sharman-Burke and Warren Kenton began contributing their expertise in Tarot and Kabbalah. It then seemed appropriate to take what was previously a random collection of astrology courses and put them under a single umbrella, so in 1982 the "prototype" of the CPA – the Centre for Transpersonal Astrology – was born.

In 1983 the name was changed to the Centre for Psychological Astrology, because a wide variety of psychological approaches was incorporated into the seminars, ranging from transpersonal psychology to the work of Jung, Freud and Klein. In response to repeated requests from students, the Diploma Course was eventually created, with additional tutors joining the staff. The CPA continued to develop and consolidate its programme despite the unfortunate death of Howard in 1992, when Charles Harvey became co-director with Liz Greene. In February 2000, Charles tragically died of cancer, leaving Liz Greene as sole director. In the new Millennium, with Juliet Sharman-Burke capably handling the administration, the CPA continues to develop along both familiar and innovative lines, always maintaining the high standards reflected in the fine work of its former co-directors.

Qualifications

Fulfilment of the seminar and supervision requirements of the In-Depth Professional Training Course entitles the student to a Certificate in Psychological Astrology. Upon successfully presenting a reading-in paper, the student is entitled to the CPA's Diploma in Psychological Astrology, with permission to use the letters, D. Psych. Astrol. The successful graduate will be able to apply the principles and techniques learned during the course to his or her professional activities, either as a consultant astrologer or as a useful adjunct to other forms of counselling or healing. Career prospects are good, as there is an ever-increasing demand for the services of capable psychologically orientated astrologers. The CPA's Diploma is not offered as a replacement for the Diploma of the Faculty of Astrological Studies or any other basic astrological training course. Students are encouraged to learn their basic astrology as thoroughly as possible, through the Faculty or some other reputable source, before undertaking the In-Depth Professional Training Course. The CPA offers introductory and intermediate courses in psychological astrology, which run on weekday evenings.

THE CPA DIPLOMA DOES NOT CONSTITUTE A FORMAL COUNSELLING OR PSYCHOTHERAPEUTIC TRAINING. Students wishing to work as counsellors or therapists should complete a further training course focusing on these skills. There are many excellent courses and schools of various persuasions available in the United Kingdom and abroad.

Individual Therapy

In order to complete the In-Depth Professional Training, the CPA asks that all students, for a minimum of one year of study, be involved in a recognised form of depth psychotherapy with a qualified therapist or analyst of his or her choice. The fee for the CPA training does not include the cost of this therapy, which must be borne by the student himself or herself. The basis for this requirement is that we believe no responsible counsellor of any persuasion can hope to deal sensitively and wisely with another person's psyche, without some experience of his or her own. Although it is the student's responsibility to arrange for this therapy, the CPA can refer students to various psychotherapeutic organisations if required.

Criteria for Admission

The following guidelines for admission to the In-Depth Professional Training Programme are applied:

- A sound basic knowledge of the meaning of the signs, planets, houses, aspects, transits and progressions, equal to Certificate Level of the Faculty of Astrological Studies Course. The CPA's own introductory and intermediate courses will also take the student to the required level of knowledge.
- Being able and willing to work on one's own individual development, as reflected by the requirement of individual therapy during the programme. Although a minimum of one year is required, it is hoped that the student will fully recognise the purpose and value of such inner work, and choose to continue for a longer period.
- Adequate educational background and communication skills will be looked for in applicants, as well as empathy, integrity, and a sense of responsibility.

Enrolment Procedure

Please write to the Centre for Psychological Astrology, BCM Box 1815, London WC1N 3XX, for fees, further information, and an application form. Please include an SAE and International Postage Coupon if writing from abroad. The CPA may also be contacted on Tel/Fax +44 20 8749 2330, or at www.cpalondon.com.

PLEASE NOTE:
- The CPA does not offer a correspondence course.
- The course does not qualify overseas students for a student visa.
- The course is for EU and Swiss residents only, although exceptions may sometimes be made.

About the CPA Press

The seminars in this volume are two of a series of seminars transcribed and edited for publication by the CPA Press. Although some material has been altered, for purposes of clarity or the protection of the privacy of students who offered personal information during the seminars, the transcriptions are meant to faithfully reproduce not only the astrological and psychological material discussed at the seminars, but also the atmosphere of the group setting.

Since the CPA's inception, many people, including astrology students living abroad, have repeatedly requested transcriptions of the seminars. In the autumn of 1995, Liz Greene, Charles Harvey and Juliet Sharma-Burke decided to launch the CPA Press, in order to make available to the astrological community material which would otherwise be limited solely to seminar participants, and might never be included by the individual tutors in their own future written works. Because of the structure of the CPA programme, most seminars are "one-off" presentations which are not likely to be repeated, and much careful research and important astrological investigation would otherwise be lost. The volumes in the CPA Seminar Series are meant for serious astrological students who wish to develop a greater knowledge of the links between astrology and psychology, in order to understand both the horoscope and the human being at a deeper and more insightful level.

The hardback volumes in the series are not available in most bookshops, but can be ordered directly from the CPA or purchased from Midheaven Bookshop, 396 Caledonian Road, London N1, Tel. +44 20 7607 4133, Fax +44 20 7700 6717, www.midheavenbooks.com. Paperback volumes may be ordered from Midheaven Bookshop or from The Wessex Astrologer, PO Box 2751, Bournemouth BH6 3ZJ, Tel/Fax +44 1202 424695, www.wessexastrologer.com.

Hardback volumes available in the CPA Seminar Series:

The Astrologer, the Counsellor and the Priest by Liz Greene and Juliet Sharman-Burke

The Family Inheritance by Juliet Sharman-Burke

Venus and Jupiter: Bridging the Ideal and the Real by Erin Sullivan

Water and Fire by Darby Costello

Where In the World? Astro*Carto*Graphy and Relocation Charts by Erin Sullivan

Planetary Threads: Patterns of Relating Among Family and Friends by Lynn Bell

Earth and Air by Darby Costello

Astrology, History and Apocalypse by Nicholas Campion

Paperback volumes available in the CPA Seminar Series:

The Horoscope in Manifestation: Psychology and Prediction by Liz Greene

---

Apollo's Chariot: The Meaning of the Astrological Sun by Liz Greene

The Mars Quartet: Four Seminars on the Astrology of the Red Planet by Lynn Bell, Darby Costello, Liz Greene and Melanie Reinhart

Saturn, Chiron and the Centaurs: To the Edge and Beyond by Melanie Reinhart

Anima Mundi: The Astrology of the Individual and the Collective by Charles Harvey

Barriers and Boundaries: The Horoscope and the Defences of the Personality by Liz Greene

Direction and Destiny in the Horoscope by Howard Sasportas

The Astrological Moon by Darby Costello

The Dark of the Soul: Psychopathology in the Horoscope by Liz Greene

Incarnation: The Four Angles and the Moon's Nodes by Melanie Reinhart

Relationships and How to Survive Them by Liz Greene

The Art of Stealing Fire: Uranus in the Horoscope by Liz Greene